Requirements for Certification

Requirements for Certification

of Teachers, Counselors, Librarians, Administrators

for Elementary and Secondary Schools

Sixty-fourth Edition, 1999–2000

Edited by
John Tryneski

The University of Chicago Press
Chicago and London

The University of Chicago Press, Chicago 60637
©1935, 1936, 1938, 1939, 1940, 1941, 1942, 1943, 1944, 1945, 1946, 1947, 1948,
1949, 1950, 1951, 1952, 1953, 1954, 1955, 1956, 1957, 1958, 1959, 1960, 1961, 1962,
1963, 1964, 1965, 1966, 1967, 1968, 1969, 1970, 1971, 1972, 1973, 1974, 1975, 1976,
1977, 1978, 1979, 1980, 1981, 1982, 1983, 1984, 1985, 1986, 1987, 1988, 1989, 1990,
1991, 1992, 1993, 1994, 1995, 1996, 1997, 1998, and 1999 by The University of
Chicago
All Rights Reserved
Sixty-fourth edition 1999
International Standard Book Number: 0-226-81321-5
International Standard Series Number: 1047-7071
Library of Congress Catalog Card Number: A43-1905

Contents

Introduction to the Sixty-fourth Edition
1999–2000

In this era of educational reform, the certification requirements of many states have been undergoing significant revisions. Changes—some minor, others substantial and extensive—have occurred in the requirements of thirty-three states this past year. This publication updates in clear and concise form the pertinent information for teachers, administrators, librarians, counselors, and other school personnel. Starting with this year's edition, we will no longer be carrying the recommendations of the regional associations of schools and colleges. Although important to state departments of certification, these recommendations were of little use to the individuals consulting this volume. At the same time, we have added a section on reciprocity listing the states that participate in the Interstate Contract.

Requirements for Certification had its inception in the Board of Vocational Guidance and Placement (now Career Counseling and Placement) at the University of Chicago. The original study was made by Robert C. Woellner, professor of education and head of the Board, and M. Aurilla Wood, placement counselor. The digest continued under the direction of Elizabeth H. Woellner until her retirement in 1983. Produced only in mimeograph form its first year, the digest was published and made available for sale by the University of Chicago Press in 1935 and has appeared in annual editions since that time.

Every year the academic and professional requirements for each state are submitted to the proper authorities for updating and correction. The growing number and diversity of the special fields have precluded listing their detailed requirements in every instance. Nonetheless, the information in each volume increases from year to year. We suggest that those wishing more detailed information on particular fields write to the office of certification of the appropriate state. For addresses, please consult appendixes 1 and 2.

We again thank the state certification officers for their interest and cooperation. With their help, this volume is the most thorough and up-to-date of its kind, and we trust that it will continue to be of value to educators throughout the United States and its possessions and territories.

Alabama

In addition to the requirements listed below, applicants must demonstrate abilities and knowledge specific to the certification being sought. Please write the State Department of Education (address in Appendix 1) for further information.

The basic program of teacher education includes three components: general studies, teaching fields, and professional studies. Successful completion of the basic program qualifies the student for certification at the Class B (baccalaureate) level. Advanced programs are extensions of basic preparation and are required for certification at the Class A (fifth year) or Class AA (sixth year) levels. Persons who did not prepare as teachers at the Class B level may enroll in an Alternative Fifth Year program.

Early Childhood Education (P–3)
Elementary Education (K–6)

I. General Studies (Class B)
   A. To include courses and/or experiences in the humanities, social science, mathematics, and science
      1. Programs in early childhood education or elementary education shall include at least 3 mathematics and 4 science courses.
II. Teaching Fields and Professional Studies (Class B)
   A. The teaching field shall include at least one-third upper division course work and provide the student with abilities and knowledge specific to the grade levels in which certification is being sought.
   B. Professional studies will consist of a coordinated and integrated program of courses and/or experiences which includes methodology, curriculum, evaluation, reading, technology, and direct observation and participation in a variety of school settings.
      1. A full-time internship for at least 12 weeks which should not be limited to one classroom or grade level, with experiences of the intern progressing to the full responsibilities of the teacher for at least 20 days including at least 10 consecutive days
         a. For early childhood programs, the internship shall include a pre-school or kindergarten placement unless substantial field experiences were completed at those levels.
         b. For elementary education programs, the internship shall include upper and lower elementary placements unless substantial field experiences were completed at both levels.

III. Fifth Year Program (Class A)
   A. The intent of the fifth year program shall be to help the teacher develop higher levels of competence than is possible in the Class B program; admission to the program requires baccalaureate level certification in the teaching field(s) in which Class A certification is being sought.
   B. Curriculum: Completion of either of two types of programs (survey of special education course work must be part of all programs, unless previously completed)
      1. Traditional teacher education program in which at least one-third of the program shall consist of teaching field courses
      2. Alternative fifth year program
   C. Evaluation for Fifth Year Certification
      1. Grade point average of 3.0 (on a 4.0 scale) in all courses in the approved teacher education program
      2. Initial subject area certification programs at the Class A level require the successful completion of an internship or practicum.
      3. Passing score on a comprehensive written examination covering the content of the curriculum

IV. Sixth Year Program (Class AA)
   A. The intent of the sixth year program shall be to extend further the level of competence of the teacher; admission to the program requires master's level certification in the same teaching field(s) in which the Class AA certificate is being sought.
   B. Curriculum: Completion of an approved program (survey of special education course work must be part of all programs, unless previously completed); the curriculum shall be in work approved by the graduate school of division of the institution.
      1. Traditional teacher education program in which at least one-third of the program shall consist of teaching field courses
   C. Evaluation for Sixth Year Certification
      1. Grade point average of 3.25 (on a 4.0 scale) in all courses in the approved teacher education program
      2. Same as III, C, 3

Middle Level (4–8), High School (6–12), and All Grades (P–12)

I. General Studies (Class B)
   A. See Early Childhood /Elementary Education, I, A.
II. Teaching Fields and Professional Studies (Class B)
   A. The teaching field shall include at least one-third upper-division course work and provide the student with abilities and knowledge specific to the gradelevels in which certification is being sought.
      1. To include two teaching fields, *or* a comprehensive teaching field, *or* a single teaching field in a middle school (or high school) subject, *or* a single career/technical teaching field
   B. Professional studies will consist of a coordinated and integrated program of courses and/or experiences which includes methodology, curriculum, evaluation, reading, technology, and direct observation and participation in a variety of school settings.

      1.   A full-time internship for at least 12 weeks which should not be limited to one classroom or grade level, with experiences of the intern progressing to the full responsibilities of the teacher for at least 20 days including at least 10 consecutive days

         a.   For middle level and secondary programs, the internship shall be divided between two teaching fields, if applicable.

         b.   For P–12 programs, the internship shall be divided between early childhood/elementary and secondary grades.

III. Fifth Year Program (Class A)

    A. See Early Childhood/Elementary, III, A.

    B. Curriculum: Completion of either of two types of programs (survey of special education course work must be part of all programs, unless previously completed)

      1.   Traditional teacher education program in which at least one-third of the program shall consist of teaching field courses.

         a.   Language arts, general science, and social science programs require at least one course in two areas

      2.   Alternative fifth year program

    C. See Early Childhood/Elementary, III, C.

IV. Sixth Year Program (Class AA)

    A. See Early Childhood/Elementary, IV

Special Education Teaching Fields

I. Endorsements may be earned in each of the following areas: early childhood special education (birth through age 8), collaborative teacher (K–6 and 6–12), gifted, hearing impaired, speech and language impaired, and visually impaired.

Instructional Support Personnel

I. Fifth Year (Initial) Program for Educational Administrators (Class A)

    A. There are two options for eligibility for admission to a program in educational administration.

      1.   Option 1: Endorsement in Educational Administration in which the applicant must have earned master's level certification in a teaching field or instructional support area

      2.   Option 2: Master's Degree Program in which the applicant must have earned baccalaureate level certification in a teaching field

         a.   To enter either option, the applicant must have completed three years of educational experience, including at least one year of classroom teaching.

    B. The fifth year curriculum shall provide the prospective administrator with abilities and knowledge as specified by the Alabama State Board of Education.

    C. Evaluation for Certification

      1.   Completion of specific option requirements with a grade point average of at least 3.25 (on a 4.0 scale) in all courses in the approved educational administration program

2. Completion of a 300 hour, supervised internship (with specific distributions)
3. Passing score on a comprehensive written examination covering the content of the curriculum

II. Fifth Year (Initial) Program for Library-Media (Class A)
    A. To be eligible for certification in library-media, the applicant must have at least baccalaureate level certification in a teaching field.
    B. The fifth year curriculum shall provide the prospective library-media specialist with abilities and knowledge as specified by the Alabama State Board of Education.
    C. Evaluation for Certification
        1. Grade point average of at least 3.00 (on a 4.0 scale) in all courses in the approved library-media program
        2. Performance as a library-media specialist in clinical experiences which total 300 hours, with at least half the time in a P–12 school library
        3. Passing score on a comprehensive written examination covering the content of the curriculum

III. Fifth Year (Initial) Program for School Counseling (Class A)
    A. Same as II, A and B above, except for school counselor
    B. Evaluation for Certification
        1. Grade point average of at least 3.00 (on a 4.0 scale) in all courses in the approved school counseling program
        2. Practicum which includes at least 30 hours of supervised, direct service work in individual and group counseling with early childhood/ elementary and secondary school students
        3. Supervised, P–12 school-based internship of at least 300 hours, begun subsequent to the completion of the practicum in which the prospective counselor performs all the activities expected from a school counselor
        4. Passing score on a comprehensive written examination covering the content of the curriculum

IV. Sixth Year Program for Instructional Support Personnel (Class AA)
    A. The intent of the sixth year program shall be to extend the depth and quality of competence of the candidate; admission to the program requires master's level certification in the instructional support field in which the Class AA certificate is being sought.
        1. Those seeking sixth year certification as an educational administrator must have master's level certification as a superintendent/principal, superintendent, principal, supervisor, vocational administrator, or educational administrator.
    B. The curriculum shall be in work approved by the graduate school or graduate division of the institution for study in the sixth year (survey of special education course work must be part of all programs, unless previously completed).
        1. The curricular program in educational administration shall require mentor training and a problem analysis project, thesis, or dissertation.
    C. Evaluation for Certification
        1. Grade point average of at least 3.25 (on a 4.0 scale) in all courses in the approved program
        2. Passing score on a comprehensive written examination covering the content of the curriculum

Alaska

Initial Certification

I. Two completed fingerprint cards and a $66.00 processing fee are required from all applicants for initial certification.

II. The completion of 3 semester hours in Alaska studies and of 3 semester hours in multicultural education or cross-cultural communication is required for initial certification under a Type A, Type B, or Type C Certificate.

    A. Applicants lacking these courses but meeting all other requirements will be issued a two-year nonrenewable provisional certificate.

Elementary and Secondary Schools

I. Regular Certificate (Type A. Valid 5 years. $165.00 application fee.)

    A. Requirements

        1. Bachelor's degree from a regionally accredited institution.

        2. Completion of an approved teacher education program (based on National Council for Accreditation of Teacher Education standards), plus institutional recommendation.

        3. Completion of 6 semester hours within the 5-year period immediately preceding the date of application.

    B. Renewal Requirements

        1. May be renewed not more than six months before expiration date upon application and upon submission of official transcripts showing 6 semester hours of credit earned during the life of the certificate.

        2. Three of the 6 semester hours may be earned by completing workshops or institutes, or by travel for which nonacademic credit has been approved by the Commissioner of Education prior to the activity. The remaining 3 semester hours must be course work on the upper division or graduate level.

    C. Additional endorsements

        1. Endorsements will be granted as recommended by the preparing institution (program must be based on NCATE standards or, in a content area, upon completion of a doctoral degree, master's degree, major, or posted minor in that area). Application and $165.00 fee required.

        2. An endorsement may be deleted if the individual is not under contract in the endorsed area.

Administration

I. Administrative Certificate (Type B. Valid 5 years. $165.00 application fee.)

    A. Requirements

1. At least 3 years of satisfactory public school teaching experience.
   a. For a superintendent endorsement, 5 years of satisfactory employment as a teacher or administrator, with at least 3 years of experience as a teacher and at least 1 year of experience as an administrator with an administrative certificate.
2. Master's degree from a regionally accredited institution, and completion of approved program based on NCATE standards in administrative specialty plus institutional recommendation.
3. Six semester hours must have been earned in the 5-year period immediately preceding the date of application.

B. Renewal—same as for Type A.
C. Additional endorsements.
1. Endorsements will be granted as recommended by the preparing institution (program must be based on NCATE standards). Application and $165.00 fee required.

Special Services

I. Special Services Certificate (Type C. Valid 5 years. $165.00 application fee.)
A. Requirements
1. Completion of a program through the bachelor's or higher degree with specialization in a supportive area which can be utilized by a school district.
2. Verification from the college that the applicant has completed a program in specific specialization.
3. See Administration A, 2, 3.

B. Renewal—same as for Type A.
C. Endorsement—same as for Type A.
D. School psychologists and speech and hearing specialists require a master's degree.
1. School psychologists also must complete an approved NCATE or APA program.
2. Speech pathologists also must be recommended by an institution which has an approved NCATE or American Speech-Language-Hearing Association.

Limited Certificate

I. Limited Certificate (Valid 5 years. $165.00 application fee. Nontransferable to other school districts.)
A. Requirements for the Vocational Trade Endorsement
1. Completion of at least 4 years of full-time work experience in a trade or vocational pursuit, of which not more than 2 years of formal training (trade school or technical institute) are acceptable. Letters of reference from former employers must be submitted.
2. Proof of employment in the trade or vocational area by an Alaskan school district having an approved vocational education program.

B. Requirements for the Alaska Native Language or Culture Specialty Endorsement
1. Submit a résumé demonstrating competency in an Alaskan native language or at

least four years experience involving an Alaskan native culture as verified by the school district.

C. Requirements for the Junior Reserve Officer Training Corps (JROTC)
1. Meet the criteria of the U.S. Department of Defense to be a Junior Reserve Officer as verified by the school district.
2. Submit a résumé demonstrating competency in a military sciences specialty.

D. Renewal Requirements
1. Three semester hours of professional courses related to applicant's field of employment, or additional training and/or work experience acceptable to the Commissioner, all of which must have been completed within the 5 years immediately preceding the expiration date of the current certificate.
2. Proof of employment in the trade or vocational area by a school district in Alaska.
3. Application and $165.00 fee required.

Temporary

I. Temporary certificate (Type A, B, or C. Valid 1 year. $165.00 application fee).
A. Requirements
1. Meet all application requirements except the six semester hours of recency.
2. Proof of satisfactory teaching service for at least three years.
3. Never possessed an Alaska teacher certificate.
B. Nonrenewable

Provisional

I. Provisional certificate (Type A, B, or C. Valid 2 years. $165.00 application fee)
A. Requirements
1. Meet all application requirements except completion of 3 semester hours in Alaska studies and 3 semester hours in multicultural or cross-cultural communication (course work must be approved).
2. This certificate is nonrenewable.

Arizona

A professional knowledge test and a subject knowledge test, both parts of the Arizona Teacher Proficiency Assessment, are required for most certificates. These tests are under development now. If an applicant meets all other requirements, a certificate will be issued.

Elementary Education Certificate (K–8)

I. Provisional Elementary Certificate (Valid for two years, not renewable)
   A. Bachelor's degree from an accredited institution
   B. Passing score on the professional knowledge portion of the Arizona Teacher Proficiency Assessment
   C. Passing score on the elementary education subject knowledge portion of the Arizona Teacher Proficiency Assessment
   D. Completion of a teacher preparation program in elementary education from an accredited institution or completion of a State Board-approved teacher preparation program,
   or
   Forty-five semester hours of education courses from an accredited institution to include at least 8 semester hours of practicum in grades K–8 (Two years of verified teaching experience in grades PreK–8 may substitute for the 8 semester hours of practicum),
   or
   Valid elementary certificate from another state
   E. Applicants meeting the above requirements will have one year to meet the following requirements:
      1. Arizona Constitution (a college course or the appropriate examination)
      2. U.S. Constitution (a college course or the appropriate examination)
      3. Passing score on the basic skills portion of the Arizona Teacher Proficiency Assessment
   F. Upon receiving the Provisional Elementary Certificate, the candidate must meet the requirements for the Standard Certificate within two years.
II. Standard Elementary Certificate (Valid for six years, renewable)
   A. Qualify for the Provisional Elementary Certificate
   B. Passing score on the performance portion of the Arizona Teacher Proficiency Assessment

Secondary Education Certificate (7–12)

I. Provisional Secondary Certificate (Valid for two years, not renewable)
   A. Bachelor's degree from an accredited institution

B. Passing score on the professional knowledge portion of the Arizona Teacher Proficiency Assessment

C. Passing score on one or more subject knowledge portions of the Arizona Teacher Proficiency Assessment

   1. If a proficiency assessment is not offered in a subject area, an approved area shall consist of a minimum of 24 semester hours of courses from an accredited institution in the subject.

D. Completion of a teacher preparation program in secondary education from an accredited institution or completion of a State Board-approved teacher preparation program,

or

Thirty semester hours of education courses from an accredited institution to include at least 8 semester hours of practicum in grades 7–12 (Two years of verified teaching experience in grades 7–postsecondary may substitute for the 8 semester hours of practicum.),

or

Valid secondary certificate from another state

E. Applicants meeting the above requirements will have one year to meet the following requirements:

   1. Arizona Constitution (a college course or the appropriate examination)

   2. U.S. Constitution (a college course or the appropriate examination)

   3. Passing score on the basic skills portion of the Arizona Teacher Proficiency Assessment

F. Upon receiving the Provisional Elementary Certificate, the candidate must meet the requirements for the Standard Certificate within two years.

II. Standard Secondary Certificate (Valid for six years, renewable)

A. Qualify for the Provisional Secondary Certificate

B. Passing score on the performance portion of the Arizona Teacher Proficiency Assessment

Special Education Certificates (K–12)

Special Education certificates are issued in the following areas: cross-categorical, mental retardation, emotional disability, learning disability, orthopedic/health impairment, hearing impaired, visually impaired, speech and language impaired, severely and profoundly disabled, and early childhood special education (birth to age 5).

I. Provisional Certificates (Valid for two years; not renewable)

A. Bachelor's degree from an accredited institution

B. Passing score on the professional knowledge portion of the Arizona Teacher Proficiency Assessment

C. Passing score for the specified disability on the special education portion of the Arizona Teacher Proficiency Assessment

D. Completion of a teacher preparation program in the specified disability area from an accredited institution or completion of a State Board-approved teacher preparation program,

or

Forty-five semester hours of education courses from an accredited institution, which will include courses and a practicum specific to the disability area of the certificate (contact the Arizona Department of Education for details; address in Appendix 1)
or
Valid certificate in the specified disability area from another state
  E. See Secondary Education, I, E and F
 II. Standard Special Education Certificates (Valid for six years; renewable)
  A. Qualify for the Provisional Special Education Certificate in the specified disability area
  B. Passing score on the performance portion of the Arizona Teacher Proficiency Assessment

Vocational Education Certificates (K–12)

  I. Provisional and Standard Vocational Education certificates requirements are issued in the following areas:
  A. Agriculture, Business, Family and Consumer Sciences, Health Occupations, Industrial Technology, and Marketing.
  B. Contact the Arizona Department of Education (address in Appendix 1) for specific requirements for each area.

Endorsements

  I. Endorsements are attachments to teaching certificates and indicate areas of specialization. Once issued, they are automatically renewed with the teaching certificate. Local governing boards may require optional endorsements. Endorsements are issued in the following areas:
  A. Art; Bilingual Education; Computer Science; Cooperative Education; Dance; Dramatic Arts; Driver's Education; Elementary Foreign Language (K–8); English as a Second Language; Gifted; Library Media Specialist; Mathematics Specialist (K–8); Middle Grade (5–9); Music; Physical Education; and Reading Specialist.
  B. Contact the Arizona Department of Education (address in Appendix 1) for specific requirements for each area.

Administrative Certificates (PreK–12)

  I. Supervisor Certificate (This certificate may be renewed with a concurrently held teaching certificate; the expiration date shall be the same as the expiration date of the teaching certificate.)
  A. Standard Elementary, Secondary, or Special Education Certificate
  B. Master's or more advanced degree from an accredited institution
  C. 3 years of verified teaching experience in grades PreK–12)
  D. Completion of a program in educational administration from an accredited institution, which shall consist of a minimum of 18 graduate semester hours of educational administration, courses

E. Practicum in educational administration from an accredited institution or 2 years of verified educational administrative experience in grades PreK–12

F. Passing score on the professional knowledge portion of the Arizona Administrator Proficiency Assessment

G. Passing score on the performance portion of the Arizona Administrator Proficiency Assessment

H. A valid supervisor certificate from another state may substitute for the teaching experience, program in educational administration, and practicum (requirements I, C, D, and E).

I. See Secondary Education I, E, 1 and 2

II. Principal Certificate (Valid for six years; renewable)

A. Master's or more advanced degree from an accredited institution

B. Three years of verified teaching experience in grades PreK–12

C. Completion of a program in education administration for principals from an accredited institution including at least 30 graduate semester hours of educational administration courses

D. Practicum as a principal from an accredited institution or 2 years of verified experience as a principal or assistant principal in grades PreK–12

E. See Supervisor I, F and G

F. A valid principal certificate from another state may substitute for the teaching experience, program in educational administration, and practicum (requirements II, B, C, and D)

H. See Secondary Education I, E, 1 and 2

III. Superintendent (valid six years; renewable)

A. Master's or more advanced degree from an accredited institution

B. At least 60 graduate semester hours from an accredited institution

C. Three years of verified teaching experience in grades PreK–12

D. Completion of a program in educational administration for superintendents from an accredited institution including at least 36 graduate semester hours of educational administrative courses

E. Practicum as a superintendent from an accredited institution or documentation of 2 years of verified experience as a superintendent, assistant superintendent, or associate superintendent in grades PreK–12

F. See Supervisor I, F and G

G. A valid superintendent certificate from another state may substitute for the teaching experience, program in educational administration, and practicum (requirements III C, D, and E).

H. See Secondary Education I, E, 1 and 2

Arkansas

Requirements for Initial Certification

I. Bachelor's degree from a regionally or nationally accredited institution with an approved program.
    A. General education component to include study in language, mathematics, sciences, history, philosophy, literature, the arts, and health and wellness education
    B. Completion of a degree major in a teaching field
    C. Proficiency in oral and written communication and mathematics, with at least a grade of "C" in each course
II. Successful completion of a teacher education program approved by the National Council for the Accreditation of Teacher Education (NCATE) from an institution to include
    A. The requirement of no less than a 2.5 grade point average on a 4.0 scale to enter the program
    B. The requirement that students obtain acceptable scores on entrance tests into teacher education that assess competency in computation, reading, and writing, as well as on exit tests in professional knowledge and the academic teaching area
    C. Twelve weeks of student teaching
    D. Professional studies component should provide competencies specified by the Arkansas Department of Education
III. Passing scores on the National Teacher Examination (Professional Knowledge and appropriate area tests
IV. Criminal background check through the Arkansas State Police and the F.B.I., including a fingerprint check.

Elementary and Specialist

I. Standard Elementary Certificates and Specialist Certificates
    A. Six Year Elementary Certificates
        1. Professional Requirements
            a. Education—18 semester hours of elementary education, including (1) study of the school, of the learning processes, and elementary teaching, including a methods course in reading; and (2) six semester hours of directed teaching (3 years experience may be accepted for 6 semester hours)
        2. Specialization Requirements
            a. Public school art and crafts, semester hours 3
            b. Public school music, semester hours 3
            c. Geography, semester hours 3
            d. U.S. History, semester hours 3
            e. U.S. Government, semester hours 3
            f. Economics (designed for elementary teachers), semester hours 3

g.   Children's literature, semester hours 3

h.   Mathematics (designed for elementary teachers), semester hours.......... 6

i.   Elementary science (designed for elementary teachers),
      semester hours.. 3

j.   Elementary physical education (may count as part of general education
      requirements), semester hours.. 2

k.   Reading, semester hours 3

B.   Specialist Certificates K–6.

    1.   Professional Requirements

      a.   Education—18 semester hours of professional education, including (1)
      study of the school, of the learning processes, and of elementary teaching,
      including a methods course in reading; and (2) six semester hours of
      directed teaching

    2.   Specialization Requirements

      a.   Bachelor's degree in Elementary Education or Early Childhood Education
      which meets requirements for standard six year elementary certificate

      b.   Child Development, semester hours.. 3

      c.   Early Childhood Curriculum Methods and Materials,
      semester hours.. 6

      d.   Three semester hours of practicum in Kindergarten; 3 additional hours of
      practicum in K–3, or 3 years of successful teaching experience in grades
      K–3, in an accredited school. This is interpreted to mean that 6 semester
      hours of practicum is needed for a K–6 certificate. If a person has 3
      years of successful teaching experience in a K–3 situation in an
      accredited school, 3 semester hours of the total 6 semester hours may be
      waived.

C.   Elementary Physical Education Teacher

    1.   See Specialist Certificate, B, 1, above

    2.   Specialization requirements, semester hours.. 26

D.   Elementary Reading Teacher (Valid 6 years in grades K–6; based on bachelor's
      degree)

    1.   See Specialist Certificate, B, 1, above

    2.   Specialization requirements, semester hours.. 9

E.   Art K–12 (Valid 6 years; based on bachelor's degree)

    1.   Professional requirements—18 semester hours including: (1) study of the
      school, of the learning processes, and of teaching; and (2) 6 semester hours of
      direct teaching

    2.   Specialization requirements, semester hours.. 24

F.   Music K–12 (Valid 6 years; based on bachelor's degree)

    1.   Basic requirements, semester hours.. 26

      a.   Music theory (14), music history and literature (6), conducting (2), and
      piano (4)

    2.   Specialization requirements for Music Plan I (Vocal), semester hours 14

    3.   Specialization requirements for Music Plan II (Instrumental),
      semester hours 18

G. Physical Education K–12
   1. Prescribed course work, semester hours 32
   2. Meet one of the following two field experiences
      a. Three semester hours of student teaching must be completed at the elementary or middle school level, below the ninth grade, where the cooperating teacher is certified in Elementary Physical Education, *or*
      b. The student must complete a 3-semester-hour internship under the direct supervision of the staff of the Physical Education Department of the College or University

H. Reading Specialist K–12 (Valid 10 years, based on master's degree)
   1. Professional Requirements
      a. Must hold specialist, elementary, or secondary certificate
   2. Specialization requirements, graduate semester hours 12
   3. Minimum of 3 years of successful teaching experience

I. Professional Librarian
   1. Library Media Specialist (Valid 10 years)
      a. Must have current teaching certificate (specialist certificate will be issued at same level as on teaching certificate)
      b. For K–12 certification, candidates with either an elementary or secondary teaching certificate must complete
         1) Twelve additional hours in the area other than the level of the teaching certificate
         2) Practicum experience—50% in a unified elementary library media center and 50% in a unified secondary library media center
      c. Specialized Requirements
         1) Master's degree in an approved program including library science and educational media or a unified library media program offered by an accredited institution
         2) Twenty-four semester hours in library/media education designed to develop competencies in the following areas (a separate course in each area is not required)
            a) Relation of media to instructional systems
            b) Organization and administration of media programs
            c) Evaluation, selection, and organization of media and accompanying technology
            d) Utilization of media and accompanying technology
            e) Production of media
            f) Evaluation of media programs
            g) Leadership and professionalism
         3) Practicum of 3 semester hours
         4) Information on additional endorsements to this certificate available from the Arkansas Department of Education
   2. Library Media Administrator (Valid 10 years)
      a. Master's degree plus 30 semester hours. Must be certified as a Library Media Specialist, K–12

    b. Specialized Requirements
       1) An additional 30 semester hours in graduate education courses, including an appropriate distribution in administration, supervision and related fields
    c. Minimum of 4 years successful experience as a classroom teacher in an accredited elementary or secondary school and/or a library media center Specialist in a unified school library media center (a minimum of 2 of the 4 years experience must have been as a Media Center Specialist).

Middle School

I. Teachers teaching 9th grade students must hold a secondary certificate
    A. All teachers shall hold a high school or elementary teaching certificate based on a bachelor's degree. A teacher teaching in a departmental situation shall meet one of the following requirements
       1. Hold a secondary teaching certificate and have 18 semester hours in the field in which he/she is teaching and have at least 3 semester hours in human growth and development of children below adolescent age and have 3 semester hours of elementary or middle school methods of teaching,
           or
       2. Hold an elementary teaching certificate and have 18 semester hours in the field in which he/she is teaching
    B. Middle School certificates are available in the areas listed below
       1. Agriculture, business, English, French, Spanish, physical education, home economics, industrial art, math, science, and social studies

Secondary School

I. Secondary Teacher Certificates
    A. Professional Requirements
       1. Education—18 semester hours including: (1) study of the school, of the learning processes, and of teaching; and (2) 6 semester hours of direct teaching
    B. Requirements in teaching fields listed in Specialist Certificate

1.	Business education, semester hours	32
2.	Driver education—by endorsement, semester hours	6
3.	English, semester hours	24
4.	Foreign languages, semester hours	24
5.	Health education, semester hours	23
6.	Journalism, semester hours	24
7.	Mathematics, semester hours	21
	a. Algebra, semester hours	3
	b. Calculus, semester hours	3
	c. Geometry, semester hours	3
8.	Physical education, semester hours	26
9.	Coach—by endorsement, semester hours	11
10.	Reading—by endorsement, semester hours	9*

11. Science:
    a. General science, semester hours.. 24
    b. Biological science, semester hours.. 24
    c. Physical science, semester hours.. 24
    d. Chemistry, semester hours.. 24
    e. Physics, semester hours.. 24
12. Speech, semester hours 24
13. Social studies, semester hours 36**
    a. U.S. history, semester hours... 12
    b. World history, semester hours.. 6
        1) Arkansas history, semester hours...................................... 3
    c. Political science, semester hours.. 6
        1) Arkansas government, semester hours 3
    d. Geography, semester hours 6
    e. Economics, semester hours... 3
    f. Sociology, psychology, or anthropology, semester hours.................... 3

*   In addition to being certified in Reading, the teacher must be certified in English or Speech.

** In addition to being certified in Social Studies, the teacher must have a total of at least 6 semester hours in the subject he/she is assigned to teach.

Note: Anyone teaching Arkansas History must have at least one course in Arkansas History.

Administration

I. Administrator's (superintendent's) certificate, valid for ten years, may be issued to applicants meeting the following requirements
   A. Hold, or be qualified to hold, at the time of application, the six year high school or elementary teaching certificate
   B. Completion of 60 semester hours of graduate training with emphasis in school administration from an accredited institution authorized by the State Department of Education or accredited by NCATE to grant the Diploma of Advanced Study or Specialist's Degree in school administration. This work shall include the master's degree in school administration (or the equivalent), with a minimum of 30 semester hours in graduate education courses including an appropriate distribution of courses in administration, supervision, and related fields. Master's degree graduates from institutions not authorized to grant the Diploma of Advanced Study or Specialist's Degree in School Administration must submit a "deficiency and removal plan" to the Office of Teacher Education and Licensure, Arkansas Department of Education, for evaluation and approval, in order to receive the administrator's certificate.
   C. A minimum of 4 years experience as a teacher or administrator, 3 of which must be in the classroom

Note: An individual serving as an elementary and/or secondary principal should meet particular certification requirements to include, but not limited to: specific requirements related to the work of elementary or secondary principal; certification to teach at the elementary level for the elementary principal; and certification to teach at the secondary level for the secondary principal.

II.   Secondary school principal's certificate is valid for 10 years and may be issued to applicants meeting the following requirements
   A.   Hold, or be qualified to hold, at the time of application a six year high school certificate or a K–12 certificate
   B.   Completion of a minimum of 45 semester hours of graduate credit, inclusive of the master's degree in school administration (or the equivalent), from an institution authorized by the State Department of Education or accredited by NCATE to grant the Diploma of Advanced Study or Specialist's Degree in school administration. Master's degree graduates from institutions not authorized to grant the Diploma of Advanced Study or Specialist's Degree in school administration must submit a "deficiency and removal plan" to the Office of Teacher Education and Licensure, Arkansas Department of Education, for evaluation and approval, in order to receive the secondary principal's certificate.
   C.   Have a minimum of 4 years experience as a teacher or administrator, 3 of which must be in a secondary school classroom
III. Elementary School Principal's Certificate, effective September 1, 1989, is valid for ten years and may be issued to applicants meeting the following requirements
   A.   Hold, or be qualified to hold, at time of application, the six year elementary (K–6 or K–12) certificate. If not certified in K–6 Elementary, must have 6 hours elementary reading and 3 hours elementary math
   B.   Must have a minimum of 4 years teaching experience as a teacher or administrator, 3 of which must be in an elementary school classroom
   C.   Must have 45 semester hours graduate work in elementary-related field. Must include a master's degree in elementary administration or equivalent

Special Education

I.   The certificate should encompass present general education requirements as stipulated in *Arkansas Laws and Regulations for Certification of Teachers, Administrators and Supervisors, Bulletin VII.*
II.   Teachers preparing for any Special Education Certificate shall receive 15 hours of training in the following areas:
   A.   Child and adolescent development, semester hours 6
   B.   Principles of learning, semester hours 3
   C.   Application of behavior management principles, semester hours 3
   D.   Study of the school, semester hours 3
III. Certificates in Special Education will not require dual certification (Elementary, Secondary, and Special). Certificates will be in the following areas:
   A.   Generic special education–Mildly handicapped K–12
   B.   Moderately/Profoundly handicapped K–12
   C.   Severely emotionally disturbed K–12
   D.   Early childhood special education (Birth through 5 years)

IV. For each of the certifiable areas, students must take a minimum of 24 semester hours in addition to the 15 basic core hours as listed above

V. Students in preservice programs will complete appropriate field and teaching experience at both the elementary and secondary levels

VI. Early Childhood Special Education (new certificate)
   A. Bachelor's or graduate degree in the field from an approved institution
      or
      Bachelor's degree in an approved related field
   B. Professional education (12 semester hours): child development, behavior management, study of the school, and principles of learning (3 hours each)
   C. Practicum in early childhood special education (6 semester hours)
   D. An additional 18 semester hours addressing specified competencies related to teaching children with handicaps, birth through five years of age

Guidance Counselor

I. General Requirements
   A. Hold or be eligible to hold a 6 year teaching certificate
   B. One school year of full-time experience as a certified classroom teacher; experience may be continuous or accumulated
   C. One calendar year of nonteaching, paid employment; experience may be continuous or accumulated, full-time and/or part-time
   D. A program of study consisting of 36 or more graduate-level semester hours including or accompanied by a master's or higher degree; program of study must have professional accreditation by an accrediting agency recognized by the State Board of Education
   E. Educational and guidance foundations—24 semester hours, with at least 2 semester hours in each of the following areas:
      1. Introduction to guidance and counseling services
      2. Student development, kindergarten through adult
      3. Statistics, or statistics and research
      4. Group testing
      5. Counseling and consultation
      6. Group guidance and counseling
      7. Guidance information system, kindergarten through adult
      8. Vocational education

II. Elementary Guidance, K–6, Specialized Requirements
   A. Nine semester hours of laboratory and supervised experience with at least 2 semester hours in each of the following areas:
      1. Case management with simulated and/or actual experiences with Elementary students—including development and use of cumulative records, development and use of individualized educational plans, report writing, case conferences, placement, referral and follow-up
      2. Practicum—supervised experience with individuals and groups of elementary students, parents, teachers, administrators
         or

Internship—supervised experience in the delivery of guidance and counseling services in an elementary school setting(s)

III. Secondary Guidance, 7–12, Specialized Requirements
  A. Nine semester hours of laboratory and supervised experience with at least 2 semester hours in each of the following areas:
    1. Same as II, A, 1–3, except courses and experiences must be at the secondary level

IV. Reciprocity
  A. Applicants who hold a valid certificate from another state but who have not had any paid employment as a practicing school counselor (guidance worker) must meet all general and special requirements listed above.
  B. Applicants who hold a valid certificate from another state, when the certificate is based on a master's or higher degree from an accredited program, and who, in addition, have worked under contract one school year as a full-time counselor or 2 years as a half-time counselor may receive a certificate.

Advanced School Guidance/Counseling

I. General Requirements
  A. Hold or be eligible to hold a master's level school guidance/counseling certificate
  B. Have 3 school years of experience, at least half-time work each year, as a certificated school counselor (guidance worker)
  C. Completed post-master's program of study of 30 or more semester hours (Program of study must have professional accreditation by an accrediting agency recognized by the State Board of Education.)

II. Advanced Guidance Supervision, Specialized Requirements
  A. Administration/Supervision—12 semester hours, including at least 2 semester hours in each of the following areas: educational administration, supervision, curriculum, and vocational education
  B. Guidance/Counseling—12 semester hours
  C. Related areas—6 semester hours electives, related to work of a supervisor of guidance programs

III. Advanced Guidance/Counseling, Specialized Requirements:
  A. Guidance and Counseling—18 semester hours
  B. Electives—9 semester hours. Must be taken from: education, guidance and counseling, psychology, social work, sociology, vocational education
  C. Electives—3 semester hours. Must be related to the professional practice of a school counselor

Probationary Certification

An individual holding at least a bachelor's degree from a regionally accredited college or univer–sity may pursue the probationary route to certification as prescribed by the Arkansas Department of Education; see Appendix 1 for address.

California

Teaching Credentials

I. Multiple Subjects Teaching Credential—Commonly required for elementary school service

II. Single Subject Teaching Credential—Commonly required for secondary school service

III. Two Year Preliminary Credential (available only to candidates prepared outside of California and nonrenewable)

    A. Requirements

        1. Bachelor's or higher degree, except in professional education, unless the education degree was completed outside of California.

        2. Teacher preparation program, including student teaching completed with a grade of C or higher on a five point scale.

            a. If no professional preparation program was completed or if the grade in student teaching was less than C, the applicant may qualify if she or he can verify the completion of three years of successful full-time teaching in either single-subject teaching or multiple-subjects teaching (depending on the credential being sought) within the last ten years while holding or eligible for a full professional certificate based on a bachelor's or higher degree from the state in which the experience was obtained.

            b. Applicants meeting the requirements of the Interstate Agreement are considered to have successfully completed their teacher preparation program requirement (as well as the U.S. Constitution requirement in IV, A, 2 below).

        3. Basic skills examination (CBEST).*

IV. Five Year Preliminary Credential (nonrenewable)

    A. Requirements

        1. See III, A, 1–3.

        2. U.S. Constitution (course or examination).

        3. Subject matter competence.

            a. Verification of completion of approved subject-matter program (single subject) or liberal arts subject-matter program (multiple subjects) by California institution,
               or

            b. Passing score on the appropriate Praxis Series Subject Assessment or, for multiple subjects instruction, on the Praxis Series Multiple Subjects Assessment for Teachers.

        4. Completion of a course in the methods of teaching reading or passage (with a score of 680) of the Praxis Series Subject Assessment entitled "Introduction to Teaching of Reading."

        5. Multiple Subject Teaching Credential only: all applicants must pass the Reading

Instruction Competence Assessment (RICA). Applicants who hold, at the time they apply in California, a valid elementary teaching credential issued by another U.S. state based upon completion of a teacher preparation program are exempted from this requirement.

V. Five Year Professional Clear Credential (renewable every five years)
- A. Requirements
  1. See IV, A, 1–5.
  2. Fifth year of study beyond bachelor's degree.
  3. Health education—drug and alcohol abuse, nutrition, and training in cardiopulmonary resuscitation (CPR).
  4. Special education.
  5. Computer education.
  6. Recommendation of a California college or university with an approved multiple or single subject program (unless fifth year is completed outside California).
- B. Renewal Requirements
  1. Planned professional growth activities of at least 150 clock hours.
  2. One-half of one year of teaching experience.
- C. Authorization for Service
  1. A teacher authorized for multiple subject instruction may be assigned to teach in any self-contained classroom in grades preschool, K–12, and in adult education.
  2. A teacher authorized for single subject instruction may be assigned to teach any subject in his or her authorized fields, in any grade level: preschool, grades K–12, or adult classes.
     a. The statutory subjects available are agriculture, art, business, English, health science, home economics, industrial and technology education, language other than English, mathematics, music, physical education, science: biological sciences, science: chemistry, science: geosciences, science: physics, and social science.

VI. Five Year Professional Clear Specialist Instruction Credentials—Covers specialist areas requiring advanced professional preparation or special competencies including agriculture, bilingual cross-cultural education, early childhood education, gifted, mathematics, and reading and language arts.
- A. Requirements
  1. Hold or qualify for a valid California teaching credential which requires a bachelor's degree and a professional preparation program including student teaching.
  2. Fifth year of study beyond the bachelor's degree.
  3. Professional preparation in the specialist area.
  4. Recommendation of a California college or university with the specific, approved specialist program.
     a. Out-of-state applicants who meet requirements in VI, A, 1–3, may still be certified. Their student teaching or field work must have been completed with a grade of C on a five point scale.
     b. Out-of-state trained applicants for the Bilingual Cross-cultural Education

Specialist Credential must apply through and be recommended by a California college or university with an approved program.

    B. Authorization for Service
        1. The credential authorizes the holder to teach in the area of specialization in preschool, grades K–12, or adult classes.

VII. Designated Subjects Vocational Education Teaching Credential—Covers courses including, but not limited to, agricultural occupations, business and office occupations, health career occupations, home economics-related occupations, marketing and distributive occupations, technical occupations, or trade occupations which are part of a vocational educational program.

    A. Write the California Commission on Teacher Credentialing for complete list of subjects and detailed requirements (address in Appendix 1).

VIII. Education Specialist Instruction Credential—Covers the following specialization areas: mild/moderate disabilities, deaf and hard of hearing, visual impairments, physical and health impairments, and early childhood special education.

    A. Requirements for the Preliminary Level I Credential
        1. Bachelor's or higher degree from an approved institution.
        2. Professional preparation program in an education specialist category.
        3. Completion of at least a 3 semester unit course in non-special education pedagogy related to teaching basic academic skills and content areas.
        4. At least 1 semester unit of supervised field experience in regular education verified by transcript or 45 clock hours with non-special education students verified by the employing agency.
        5. Completion of a course in developing English language skills, including reading requirement or by passage (with a score of 690) of the Praxis Series Subject Assessment "Introduction to Teaching of Reading."
        6. Verification of subject matter competence (see IV, A, 3, a or b)
           a. Verification not required for the area of early childhood special education.
        7. CBEST*
        8. U.S. Constitution (course or examination)
        9. An offer of employment from a California school district, non-public school or agency, or county office of education.
      10. Recommendation of a California college or university with an approved program.
           a. For out-of-state applicants who meet requirements in A, 1–9, their approved program must have resulted in that state's certification and consist of a minimum of 24 semester units in a credential category comparable to an accredited California program, including successful completion of a supervised field study.

    B. A Professional Clear Level II Credential is also available.
    C. Authorization for Service
        1. The Education Specialist Instruction Credential authorizes the holder to teach in the area of specialization listed on the credential in the following settings: special day classes, special schools, home/hospital settings, correctional facilities, non-public school and agencies, and resource rooms.

Services Credentials

I. Five Year Preliminary Administrative Services Credential (nonrenewable)
   A. Requirements
      1. Possession of a valid California credential, which may be in teaching; designated subjects vocational teaching; pupil personnel services; librarianship; health services school nurse; or clinical rehabilitative services.
      2. Three years of successful, full-time experience in the public schools or private schools of equivalent status in any of the areas listed directly above in A, 1.
      3. Approved program of specialized and professional preparation in administrative services.
         or
         Approved one year administrative internship program from a California institution.
      4. Basic skills examination (CBEST).*
      5. Recommendation of a California college or university with an approved administrative services program.
         a. Out-of-state applicants who meet requirements in I, A, 1–4, may still be certified. Their approved program in school administrative services must have at least one year of postgraduate preparation and must include field work in a school situation (completed with a grade of C or better on an A to F grading pattern).
II. Five Year Professional Administrative Clear Credential
   A. Requirements
      1. Preliminary credential (See I, A, 1–5 above)
      2. Two years of successful full-time experience in a position requiring the preliminary credential.
      3. Approved California program of individualized advanced preparation designed in cooperation with the employing agency and the recommendation of the institution.
   B. Authorization for Service
      1. This credential authorizes the holder to serve as a superintendent, associate superintendent, deputy superintendent, principal, assistant principal, supervisor, consultant, coordinator, or in an equivalent or intermediate level administrative position.
III. Library Media Teacher Services
   A. Requirements
      1. A baccalaureate degree from a regionally accredited college or university.
      2. A valid prerequisite California teaching credential that requires a program of professional preparation including student teaching.
      3. Completion of either a or b:
         a. A Commission-approved library media teacher services program and the recommendation of the California college or university where the program was completed,
            or

  b. Completion of an out-of-state library media teacher services program of 30 graduate semester units approved by the appropriate state agency in the state where the program was completed.

 4. CBEST*

B. Authorization for Service

 1. The Library Media Teacher Services credential authorizes the holder to assist and instruct pupils in the choice and use of library materials; to plan and coordinate school library programs with the instructional programs of a school district; to select materials for school and district libraries; to conduct a planned course of instruction for those pupils who assist in the operation of school libraries; to supervise classified personnel assigned to school library duties; and to develop procedures for and management of the school and district libraries.

IV. Clinical-Rehabilitative

A. Requirements

 1. A master's or higher degree from an approved institution (except for orientation and mobility, which requires at least one year of applicable graduate-level course work which may or may not have resulted in an advanced degree).

 2. CBEST*

 3. A fifth year or its equivalent of college or university education.

 4. Such specialized and professional preparation resulting in the recommendation for the credential by the California college or university through which the program was completed.

  a. For out-of-state applicants who meet requirements in A, 1–3, their program must meet the certification requirements for authorization requested in the public schools of the state in which it was completed and must include a practicum with school-age children (completed with a grade of C or better on an A to F grading pattern).

B. Authorization for service

 1. This credential authorizes the holder to perform the service designated on the credential at any grade level. The following authorizations may be listed on the document: language, speech, and hearing; audiology; language, speech, hearing, and audiology; orientation and mobility; and language, speech, and hearing including special class authorization to teach aphasic children.

V. Pupil Personnel Services

A. Authorizations for Services

 1. This credential covers four different areas: school counseling, school social work, school psychology, and school child welfare and attendance services.

B. Requirements for School Counseling and School Social Work Authorizations

 1. Post-baccalaureate degree study consisting of a minimum of either 30 semester hours for school counseling or 45 semester hours for school social work in an approved professional preparation program (including a practicum with school-age children) in the respective specialization.

 2. CBEST.*

 3. Recommendation of a California institution with an approved program.

      a.   Out of state applicants must be eligible for a certificate in area of specialization in home state.

C.   Requirements for School Psychology Authorization
1.   Same as B, 1–3 directly above, except that the post-baccalaureate study must be in school psychology (60 semesters).

D.   Requirements for School Child Welfare and Attendance Services Authorization
1.   Professional preparation program specializing in school counseling, school social work, or school psychology, plus a professional preparation program specializing in school child welfare and attendance (including a practicum with school-age children).
2.   CBEST*
3.   Recommendation of a California institution with an approved program
      a.   Out-of-state applicants must also be recommended by a California institution with an approved program.

Application Procedures

Submission of a completed application form, the required $60.00 fee, duplicate set of fingerprint cards and $56.00 processing fee, a complete set of official transcripts, verification of teaching or administrative experience, official report of any examination scores, and copies of credentials that the candidate may hold in other states.

*   For initial issuance, all applicants must obtain a passing score on the California Basic Education Skills Test (CBEST). This requirement does not apply to applicants who are having their credentials renewed, reissued, or upgraded. Out-of-state applicants may be issued a one year, nonrenewable credential pending the passage of the CBEST if a California school district or county education office verifies that it cannot find a fully credentialed person to fill the position; that it has offered employment to the credential applicant; and that the applicant has passed the district basic skills test.

Colorado

All applicants for an initial Colorado license or authorization must submit a properly completed fingerprint card, oath form, and a fingerprint fee ($32). All initial applicants also must take and pass one or more of the PLACE assessments (Program for Licensing Assessments for Colorado Educators), for which varying fees are charged. There is an additional $64 fee to evaluate all applications for licenses, authorizations, and endorsements. To receive application materials please call Colorado's automated phone system at (303) 866-6628.

Program for Licensing Assessments for Colorado Educators

I. Basic Skills Assessment
   A. Passing scores required prior to student teaching in a Colorado educator preparation program
   B. Passing scores required for individuals seeking special services, principal, or administrative licenses who do not currently hold a Colorado teaching license
II. Liberal Arts and Sciences Assessment
   A. Passing scores required for individuals seeking teaching licenses
III. Professional Knowledge Assessment
   A. Passing scores on appropriate assessment field required for applicants for initial teaching licenses
      1. Fields: early childhood, elementary, middle school, and secondary
IV. Content Fields Assessments
   A. Passing scores required on assessment in the specific field in which a license is being sought
   B. Applicable for teaching, special services, principal, and administrator licenses (Contact the Department of Education or see testing bulletin for detailed list of content fields.)

General Requirements for Initial Licenses

I. Provisional Teacher License (valid three years; renewable)
   A. Completion of an approved program of teacher preparation or completion of an alternative teacher program
   B. Passing scores on the needed PLACE assessments
      1. A two year Temporary Authorization may be issued to an out-of-state applicant for a Provisional License so that the applicant can complete the PLACE assessments. All other requirements for the Provisional License must be met.
   C. Evidence of oral English proficiency
II. Provisional Special Services License (valid three years; renewable)

    A. Completion of an approved special services program

    B. See I, B and C directly above

III. Provisional Principal License (valid three years; renewable once)

    A. Completion of an approved graduate program for the principalship

    B. See I, B and C directly above

IV. Provisional Administrator License (valid three years; renewable once)

    A. Completion of an approved graduate program for school administration

    B. See I, B and C directly above

V. TYPE VI Temporary Authorization (valid two years, not renewable)

    A. Available to out-of-state applicants for the Provisional License who have met all the requirements for that license but have not been able to complete the PLACE assessments.

VI. Alternative Teacher License (valid one year; nonrenewable)

    A. Bachelor's degree from a regionally accredited institution of higher education

    B. Passing scores on the PLACE assessments including basic skills, oral English proficiency, liberal arts and sciences, and content knowledge

    C. Meet the subject matter requirements necessary for teaching in the appropriate endorsement area(s) through transcript review, standardized assessment, or portfolio review

    D. Agree to participate in an on-the-job, one-year alternative teacher training program

    E. Has received a contract from a school or high school district for one full academic year as an alternative teacher

VII. Reciprocity—A provisional Colorado license may be issued to an applicant who has met the following requirements

    A. Completion of the appropriate degree or educational level for the license and endorsement being sought

    B. Completion of a state-approved program at a regionally accredited out-of-state institution in the endorsement area sought

    C. Holds or is eligible to hold a standard certificate or license in another state

    D. Passing scores on the required PLACE assessments appropriate to the license

    E. Evidence of oral English proficiency

    F. The Department of Education may recognize other state authorized educator preparation programs for applicants who have completed such programs and have provided evidence of three or more years of full-time, satisfactory experience at the grade or developmental level and endorsement/specialty area being sought.

Advanced Licenses

I. Professional License (valid five years; renewable)

    A. Holds a valid Provisional License, *and*

    B. Successful completion of an approved induction program and recommendation for the Professional License by the district providing the induction program, *or*

    C. Certification by the National Board of Professional Teaching Standards

II. Master Certification (valid seven years; renewable)

    A. Voluntary certification held in conjunction with a Professional License

B. Holds National Board for Professional Teaching Certification or has developed a Colorado master certification portfolio of demonstrated excellence

Endorsements

I. Early childhood education (valid for ages 3–8)
II. Elementary Education (valid for K–6)
III. Middle school (valid for grades 5–9)
IV. Secondary endorsement areas (valid for grades 7–12)
    A. Agriculture and renewable natural resources, art,* business/marketing education, drama, driver education, English, foreign language(s), health, consumer and family studies, linguistically diverse (bilingual and ESL), mathematics, music,* physical education,* science, social studies, speech, and technical education
V. Special education endorsement areas—All areas may be approved on the basis of undergraduate or graduate level programs.
    A. Teacher 1—moderate needs
    B. Teacher 2—severe needs: cognitive, affective, vision, hearing, and communication
    C. Teacher 3—profound needs
    D. Teacher 4—early childhood special education
VI. Special services provider endorsement areas
    A. Audiologist, occupational therapist, orientation and mobility (peripatology), physical therapist, school nurse, school psychologist, school social worker, counselor, and speech/language pathologist
VII. Principal and Administrator licenses (not endorsed for specialization or grade levels)
VIII. Other endorsement areas
    A. Director of special education, reading teacher, reading specialist, and school library media

* Endorsements in areas with asterisks may be issued for elementary, middle school, secondary, or K–12.

Connecticut

Connecticut has made revisions in its certification requirements, which are effective until July 1, 2003, at which time further revisions are planned.

General Requirements

I. In addition to the specific requirements noted below, individuals seeking certification in Connecticut must fulfill the following teacher assessment requirements.
    A. Demonstrate essential skills in mathematics, reading, and writing by passing the PRAXIS I-Computer Based Tests or by receiving a waiver.
    B. Demonstrate subject matter competence by receiving a satisfactory evaluation on the PRAXIS II test for certification in specific subject areas (including elementary education and middle grades education).
    C. Demonstrate professional knowledge through the Beginning Educator Support and Training Program (BEST), consisting of assignment to mentor teachers or teams and performance assessments (completed prior to second level of certification).
II. Connecticut requires each candidate for certification to present the recommendation of the preparing institution for the certification sought in the absence of verified successful experience in the type of position to be covered (at least 2 years in an approved private school).

Early Childhood Education (Birth–3)

I. Initial Educator Certificate for Birth–K and N–3
    A. Bachelor's degree from an approved institution.
    B. General education, including study in five out of six of the following areas, as well as a survey course in U.S. history, semester hours 39
        1. English
        2. Science
        3. Mathematics
        4. Social studies
        5. Fine arts *or*
        6. Foreign language
    C. Completion of a minimum of 15 semester hours in human growth and development, including typical and atypical development, psychology of learning, and family studies (may be part of a subject area major or general academic courses).
    D. Completion of a major awarded by an approved institution in any one subject area (a major or courses in professional education may not be counted);
    or
    Completion of an interdisciplinary major consisting of 39 semester hours with a

concentration of at least 18 semester hours in human growth and development, including: typical and atypical development, psychology of learning, and family studies, with the remainder distributed among no more than three additional subjects related to human growth and development (a major or course work in professional education may not be counted).

   E. Professional education in early childhood education in each of the following areas, semester hours 36

      1. Foundations of education

      2. Curriculum and methods of teaching

         a. Required courses differ for Birth–K and N–3 endorsements; write the Bureau of Certification and Teacher Preparation for details (address in Appendix 1)

      3. Supervised student teaching at the level of the endorsement, semester hours 6–12

         a. Write the Bureau of Certification and Teacher Preparation for additional details.

  II. Provisional Educator Certificate

    A. Evidence of meeting the general conditions and requirements for an initial certificate.

    B. Completion of beginning educator support and assessment program as may be available from the Connecticut Board and ten school months of successful service under the interim or initial certificates or durational shortage area permit;
      or
    Thirty school months of successful teaching in the same area for which the provisional educator certificate is being sought, in a school approved by the appropriate governing body in another state, within 10 years prior to application.

 III. Professional Educator Certificate

    A. Thirty school months of successful teaching under the provisional educator certificate.

    B. Course work beyond bachelor's degree, semester hours 30
    To include:

      1. A planned program at an approved institution of higher education, related directly to the subject areas or grade levels of the endorsement or in an area or areas related to the teacher's ability to provide instruction effectively or to meet locally determined goals or objectives;
         or

      2. An individual program which is mutually determined or approved by the teacher and the employing agent of the board of education and which is designed to increase the ability of the teacher to improve student learning.

Elementary (1–6)

  I. Initial Educator Certificate

    A. See Early Childhood I, A and B.

    B. Completion of a major awarded by an approved institution in any one subject area (a major or courses in professional education may not be counted);
      or

Completion of an interdisciplinary major consisting of 39 semester hours, with a concentration of at least 18 semester hours in any one subject area and the remainder distributed among no more than three subjects related to the concentration (a major or courses in professional education may not be counted).

C. Professional education in each of the following areas, semester hours 30
1. Foundations of education
2. Educational psychology
3. Curriculum and methods of teaching
A. Must include 6 semester hours in language arts
4. Supervised observation, participation, and full-time, responsible student teaching, semester hours.. 6–12
5. Course of study in special education of at least 36 clock hours (Contact the Bureau of Certification and Teacher Education for additional details).

II. Provisional Educator Certificate
A. See Early Childhood II, A–B.
III. Professional Educator Certificate
A. See Early Childhood III, A–B.

Middle Grades

I. The middle grades subject-specific certificate or a secondary academic certificate authorizes the teaching of specific subjects in a middle school setting. Middle-grades certificates shall be endorsed for the subject in accordance with the recommendation of the preparing institution.

II. Initial Educator Certificate
A. See Early Childhood I, A and B.
B. Same as Early Childhood I, D, except at the middle grades level
C. Completion of study in any one of the following
1. A subject area major in any of the following areas: English, mathematics, biology, physics, chemistry, earth science, general science, social science, history, political science, economics, geography, anthropology, sociology; *or*
2. An interdisciplinary major in humanities, history/social science, or integrated science; *or*
3. Twenty-four hours of study in one of the subjects (except general science) listed directly above in C, 1
and either
a. Fifteen semester hours in a second subject in one of the subjects (except general science) listed directly above in C, 1, which will result in endorsements in two subject areas,
or
b. Fifteen semester hours in an all-level endorsement which will qualify for an additional teaching endorsement
D. See Elementary I, D.
E. For middle grades endorsement in English, history or social science, mathematics, humanities, and integrated science, additional special subjects are required. Contact

the Bureau of Certification and Teacher Preparation for additional information (address in Appendix 1).

III. Provisional Educator Certificate
    A. See Early Childhood II, A–B.

IV. Professional Educator Certificate
    A. See Early Childhood III, A–B.

Secondary Academic (7–12)

I. Initial Educator Certificate
    A. Bachelor's degree from an approved institution.
    B. General education, including a course in U.S. history and including study in five of the six following areas, semester hours 39
        1. English
        2. Natural sciences
        3. Mathematics
        4. Social studies
        5. Arts
        6. Foreign languages
    C. Completion of a subject area major awarded by an approved institution in the subject for which endorsement is sought (professional education majors may not be used to fulfill this requirement);
        or
        Completion of at least 30 semester hours in the subject for which certification is sought and a minimum of 9 semester hours in a subject or subjects directly related to the subject for which certification is sought (professional education majors or courses may not be used to fulfill this requirement or to fulfill the requirements for the specific endorsements listed below)
        1. General science endorsement—Major of at least 39 semester hours in science, including study in biology, chemistry, physics, and earth science
        2. History and social studies endorsement—Requirements may be met by completion of a major in one of the following areas
            a. History (including 18 semester hours in social studies)
            b. Political science, economics, geography, or anthropology/sociology (except that each must include at least 18 semester hours in U.S., Western, and non-Western history)
            c. An interdisciplinary major of at least 39 semester hours in subjects covered by the endorsement, with at least 18 semester hours in U.S., Western, and non-Western history and with at least one course each in psychology, political science, economics, geography, and anthropology/ sociology
        3. Business endorsement: Major awarded by an approved institution in business or in any one of the subjects covered by the endorsement or an interdisciplinary major consisting of 39 semester hours of credit in subjects covered by the endorsement.

       4.   Foreign language endorsement: 24 semester hours in the foreign language in which endorsement is sought.

  D. Completion of a planned pattern of study and experience in professional education, including study in the following areas, semester hours 18

       1.   Foundations of education

       2.   Educational psychology

       3.   Curriculum and methods of teaching

       4.   Supervised observation, participation, and full-time responsible student teaching, semester hours 6–12

          a.   One year of successful teaching experience at the secondary level may be accepted in lieu of this requirement.

       5.   Course of study in special education of at least 36 clock hours covering specific areas.

  II. Provisional Certificate

    A. See Early Childhood II, A and B.

 III. Professional Certificate

    A. See Early Childhood III, A and B.

Special Subjects

  I. Initial Educator Certificate (Special subject endorsements, taught at the elementary and secondary levels, are agriculture, art, health, home economics, technology education, music, and physical education.)

    A. Bachelor's degree from an approved institution.

    B. General education, semester hours 39

       1. See Secondary Academic I, B,

    C. Completion of a subject area major awarded by an approved institution in the subject for which endorsement is sought (professional education majors, except those in physical education and technology education, may not be used to fulfill this requirement);

      or

      Completion of at least 30 semester hours in the special subject or field for which certification is sought and a minimum of 9 semester hours in a subject or subjects directly related to the subject for which certification is sought (professional education majors or courses, except those in physical education and technology education, may not be used to fulfill this requirement).

    D. Professional education, semester hours 18

       1. See Secondary Academic I, C.

  II. Provisional Certificate

    A. See Early Childhood II, A and B.

 III. Professional Certificate

    A. See Early Childhood III, A and B.

School Library-Media (PreK–12)

I. Initial Educator Certificate
  A. Bachelor's degree from an approved institution.
  B. Holds or is eligible for a Connecticut teaching certificate.
  C. Ten months of successful teaching experience.
  D. Completion of at least 24 semester hours of credit in an approved graduate program of certification for school library media specialists in specified areas, including a course of study in special education of at least 36 clock hours.

Note: Connecticut has several alternative routes to initial certification in school-library media.

II. Provisional Certificate
  A. See Early Childhood II, A and B.
III. Professional Educator Certificate
  A. Thirty school months of successful teaching under the Provisional Certificate.
  B. Master's degree or a sixth-year program in school-library media at an approved institution;
      or
      Master's degree in another field from an approved institution, plus 30 semester hours of graduate credit in school-library media from an approved institution.

School Counselor

I. Initial Educator Certificate
  A. Holds a Professional Educator Certificate;
      or
      Holds or is eligible for an Initial Educator Certificate with 3 years of successful teaching experience;
      or
      Has completed a one-year, full-time supervised school internship as school counselor.
  B. Master's degree.
  C. Study in an approved institution, to include 30 semester hours in a planned program in school counseling.
  D. Recommendation by preparing institution of knowledge, skills, and understanding in the following areas: principles and philosophy of developmental guidance and counseling; psychological and sociological theory as related to children, youth, and family; career development theory and practice; individual and group counseling procedures; organizational patterns and relationship of pupil services to total school and community programs; pupil appraisal and evaluation techniques; and school-based consultation and practice.
  E. Evidence of progression of supervised experience in counseling and guidance through laboratory and practicum.
  F. Course of study in special education of at least 36 clock hours.
II. Provisional Educator Certificate

    A. See Early Childhood II, A and B, except that successful service must be in a school counseling capacity.

III. Professional Educator Certificate

    A. Thirty school months of successful service under the provisional educator certificate, interim educator certificate, or provisional teaching certificate.

    B. Completion of at least 45 semester hours of graduate credit at an approved institution in counseling and related courses.

Intermediate Administration or Supervision

I. Initial Educator Certificate for Intermediate Administration or Supervision (deputy or assistant superintendent, principal or assistant principal, etc.)

    A. Master's degree from an approved institution, as well as 18 semester hours of graduate credit in addition to the degree program.

    B. Completion of 50 school months of successful teaching or administrative service in public schools or approved nonpublic schools.

    C. Recommendation of an approved institution where the applicant has completed a planned program of preparation for administrative and supervisory personnel.

    D. Graduate study in the following areas:

        1. Psychological and pedagogical foundations of learning

        2. Curriculum development and program monitoring

        3. School administration

        4. Personnel evaluation and supervision

        5. Contemporary educational problems from a policy-making perspective

    E. Course of study in special education of at least 36 clock hours.

II. Provisional Educator Certificate for Intermediate Administration and Supervision

    A. Same as Early Childhood II, A and B, except that successful service must be in an administrative capacity.

III. Professional Educator Certificate for Intermediate Administration and Supervision

    A. Thirty school months of successful service under the provisional educator certificate, interim educator certificate, or provisional teaching certificate.

    B. Completion of at least 30 semester hours of graduate credit at an approved institution, in addition to the master's degree.

Other Certificates

I. Special Service Certificates

    A. In addition to school counselor, Connecticut also offers certificates for speech and language pathology, school nurse-teacher, school dental hygienist-teacher, school psychology, and school social work.

II. Special Education Endorsement

    A. Special Education, endorsed for grades 1–12, authorizes instruction to children who are mentally handicapped, either educable or trainable; physically handicapped; autistic, traumatically brain injured; socially and emotionally maladjusted; neurologically impaired; or learning disabled.

III.   Administrative Certificates
A.   In addition to intermediate administration or supervision, Connecticut also offers certificates for reading and language arts consultant, department chairperson, and superintendent of schools.

Please write to the Bureau of Certification and Teacher Preparation for the requirements for these certificates or see its Web page at <http://www.state.ct.us/sde>.

Delaware

For all certificates, candidate must successfully complete the PRAXIS 1 Skills Tests. Cut-off scores for paper and pencil tests (scores for computer based tests are in parentheses): Reading–175 (322); Mathematics–174 (319); Writing–173 (319). PRAXIS 2 testing requirements are pending. Please write the Department of Public Instruction (address in Appendix 1) for updated information.

Early Care and Education Standard Certificate (Birth–K)

I. Degree Requirements
    A. Bachelor's degree from a regionally accredited college in the field of education
       or
    B. Bachelor's degree from a regionally accredited college in *any* field
       1. General education, semester hours 45
          To include: English [one course each required in upper level composition and in literature] (9); science [one course each required in life/environment, earth/space, and physical sciences] (12); social sciences [world history, American geography, and geography] (9); mathematics (9); and fine arts (6)

II. Professional Education Requirements
    A. Approved program in early care and education, birth to kindergarten
       or
    B. Approved program in primary education, including 15 semester hours or the equivalent specific to the birth to kindergarten child with instruction in each of the following areas:
       1. Children's growth, development, and learning (ages 0–3); assessment of young children; language development and early literacy in young children; family development and service systems for children and families; and three additional semester hours taken in one of the four areas above or in another area specifically related to early care
       or
    C. Course work, semester hours 60
       1. Courses to be taken in addition to the degree if not part of the degree program, semester hours.. 45
          To include children's growth, development, and learning (6); identifying and teaching exceptionalities (6); parent/family/ community interactions (3); early childhood curriculum development, content, and implementation (15); professional issues in early childhood education (3); and student teaching and clinical experiences, with at least 100 clock hours of clinical experience (12).
       2. Courses specifically on children from birth to kindergarten, semester hours. 15
          a. See II, B, I above

Primary Standard Certificate (K–4)

I.   Degree Requirements
  A.   See Early Care and Education Certificate I, A–B
II. Professional Education Requirements
  A.   Approved program in primary education
       or
  B.   Approved program in elementary education, including 18 semester hours or the equivalent specific to the birth to kindergarten child with instruction in each of the following areas:
       1.   Children's growth, development, and learning (6); parent/family/ community interactions (3); early childhood curriculum development, content, and implementation (6); and professional issues in early childhood education (3)
       or
  C.   Approved program in early childhood education, birth through age 8, to include the following additional courses focusing on children in grades K–4:
       1.   Curriculum and methods in science, social studies, and mathematics, semester hours 9
       2.   Literacy, including reading, writing, and children's literature, semester hours 6
       or
  D.   Approved program in middle level education to include 15 semester hours in additional courses focusing on children in grades K–4: children's growth, development, and learning (3); parent/family/community interactions (3); early childhood curriculum development, content, and implementation (6); and professional issues in early childhood education (3)
       or
  E.   Course work, semester hours 60
       1.   Courses to be taken in addition to the degree if not part of the degree program, semester hours 45
            To include child development (6); identifying and teaching exceptionalities (3); effective teaching strategies (3); curriculum and methods (21); exploring contemporary cultural and social issues (3); student teaching and clinical experiences, with at least 100 clock hours of clinical experience (9); and electives related to K–4
       2.   Courses specifically on grades K–4, semester hours 15
            To include: children's growth, development, and learning (3); parent/family/community interactions (3); early childhood curriculum development, content, and implementation (6); professional issues in early childhood education (3); and electives related to the above areas or any area dealing with teaching K–4 students

Middle Standard Certificate (5–8)

Required for all teachers assigned to teach grades 5–8, except those certified with Middle School Content Area Certificates or Secondary Subject Area Certificates (who are required to take a 15 semester hour Middle School Endorsement)

I. Degree Requirements
    A. See Early Care and Education Certificate I, A–B
II. Professional Education Requirements
    A. Approved program in middle level education
       or
    B. Approved program or standard certificate in elementary education and an additional 15 semester hours related to the adolescent child including instruction in:
       1. Adolescent development and behavior; curriculum and instruction strategies for middle grades; classroom management techniques; student advising, mentoring, and counseling techniques; and reading in the content area
       or
    C. Approved program or standard certificate encompassing any segment of birth through age eight, and an additional 30 semester hours related to the adolescent child including:
       1. Adolescent development and behavior; curriculum and instruction strategies for middle grades; classroom management techniques; student advising, mentoring, and counseling techniques; and reading in the content area, semester hours 15
       2. Curriculum and methods in science, social studies, and mathematics, semester hours 9
       3. Literacy, including reading, writing, and children's literature, semester hours 6
       or
    D. Approved program or standard certificate in either primary or secondary education and an additional 15 semester hours to include each of the following areas related to the adolescent child:
       1. See II, B, 1 directly above;
       or
    E. Course work, semester hours 60
       1. Same as Primary Standard Certificate, II, E, 1, except that 12 (rather than 9) semester hours of student teaching and clinical experiences are required in place of electives, semester hours 45
       2. See II, C, 1 directly above, semester hours 15

Secondary School

I. Degree Requirements
    A. Bachelor's degree from an accredited college
II. Professional Education Requirements

A. Completion of a teacher education program in the endorsement area

or

B. Professional education, semester hours.. 27

    To include: human development, methods of teaching secondary English (to include written composition and oral communication), teaching of reading, identifying/treating exceptionalities, effective teaching strategies, multicultural education, and clinical experience/student teaching at the secondary (7–12) level

and

C. Course work in the specific teaching field

    1. Art (elementary, secondary, or comprehensive), semester hours 30

        a. Course work must focus on methods, materials, and student teaching at the appropriate level

    2. Drama, semester hours 30

    3. English (courses above 100 level), semester hours.. 36

    4. Foreign language (course above 200 level), semester hours.......................... 30

        a. Those holding one foreign language certificate are required to have only 24 semester hours for the second foreign language certificate.

    5. Health education, semester hours 30

    6. Home economics, semester hours 30

    7. Mathematics (algebra and above), semester hours 36

    8. Music (elementary, secondary, and comprehensive), semester hours 36

        a. Course work must focus on methods, materials, and student teaching at the appropriate level

    9. Natural science

        a. Biology, semester hours 39

        b. Chemistry, semester hours 42

        c. Earth science, semester hours 39

        d. General science, semester hours 36

        e. Physics, semester hours.. 45

        f. Physical science, semester hours.. 42

   10. Physical education (elementary, secondary, and comprehensive), semester hours 36

        a. Course work must focus on methods, materials, and student teaching at the appropriate levels

   11. Social studies, semester hours 54

Administration

I. Elementary School Principal or Assistant Principal

    A. Requirements

        1. Master's degree from an accredited college

        2. Minimum of three years' successful experience as an elementary school teacher, or two years' elementary teaching experience and one year of internship

    B. Specialized Professional Preparation

1. Master's degree from an accredited college in an approved elementary school administration program
or
2. Completion of approved graduate program in elementary school administration
or
3. Any master's degree with 2- or 3-semester-hour course at graduate level in each of the following: general school administration; elementary school administration; supervision; curriculum development; school business management

II. Secondary School Principal or Assistant Principal
  A. Requirements
    1 and 2. Same as I, A, 1 and 2, but at secondary school level
  B. Specialized Professional Preparation
    1 and 2. Same as II, B, 1 and 2, but for secondary school administration
    3. Any master's degree with a 2- or 3-semester-hour course at graduate level in each of the following: secondary school administration; supervision; curriculum development; school business management; administration and interpretation of tests

III. Administrative Supervisor
  A. Requirements
    1. Master's degree from an accredited college with a major in educational supervision and curriculum
    or
    2. Master's degree including:
      a. Advanced work with emphasis in area of supervision, semester hours 15–18
      b. Advanced work in professional education to include supervision and curriculum development, semester hours 15–18
    3. Three years' teaching experience in area to be supervised

IV. Superintendent
  A. Requirements
    1. Master's degree plus 30 graduate credits; *or* 60 graduate credits including a master's degree; or a doctor's degree from an accredited college or university
    2. Three years' teaching experience or 2 years of teaching and one year of supervised internship in a 60-semester-hour program for school administration
  B. Specialized Professional Preparation
    1. Major in school administration and its related areas such as curriculum, supervision, business administration, and personnel administration

Guidance Counselor

I. Elementary School Counselor
  A. Requirements
    1. Master's degree from an accredited college
    2. Completion of a graduate degree program in elementary school counseling

3. Three years' professional experience in an elementary school; *or* three years of appropriate experience approved by the Delaware State Department of Public Instruction; *or* one year of supervised school counseling internship (1,000 hours) in elementary school,
or
1. Graduate degree from an accredited college in any field, *plus*
2. Graduate course work, including the following, semester hours.................... 30
   a. Principles and practices of the guidance program; tools and techniques in counseling; counseling theory and interviewing; organization and administration of the guidance program; career information; testing and analysis; supervised practicum or internship
3. Experience as in A, 3, above

II. Secondary School Counselor
   A. Requirements—The same as for Elementary School Counselor, but at the secondary school level

Librarian/Media Specialist

I. Librarian/Media Specialist
   A. Requirements
      1. Bachelor's degree from an accredited college
   B. Professional Education
      1. Course work including human development and methods, semester hours ... 15
      2. Valid teaching certificate
   C. Specialized Professional Preparation
      1. Completion of a teacher education program with major in school library,
      or
      2. Master's degree with specialization in school librarianship from a library school accredited by the American Library Association
      or
      3. Library/Media education courses, semester hours 24
      4. Completion of a practicum in school library, credits.................................... 6
      5. One year of successful experience in a school library/media program, plus 6 additional semester hours of library science education

Exceptional Children
Standard Certificate

Required for teachers of special education in the areas of Mental Handicap, Serious Emotional Disturbance, Learning Disability, Physical Impairment, and Visual Impairment

I. Elementary Special Education (1–8)
   A. Bachelor's degree from a regionally accredited institution, and
   B. Completion of a teacher education program in the area of endorsement
   or

C.   Course work, semester hours (minimum)... 42
  1.   Core courses for all exceptional teaching certificates, semester hours........... 24
    a.   To include: methods in elementary reading; methods in elementary mathematics, classroom management, introduction to education of exceptional children; child growth/development; applied behavior analysis; student teaching with exceptional children (grades 1–8).
  2.   Specialized courses for all areas, semester hours 18
    a.   Courses vary for different areas; write the Delaware Department of Public Instruction for details
II.   Secondary Special Education (7–12)
  A.   See I, A and B directly above
  B.   Same as I, C directly above, except course work should be related to secondary level.
III.   A Limited Standard Certificate may be issued for up to 3 years to individuals to complete the requirements for the Standard Certificate; write the Delaware Department of Public Instruction for details

District of Columbia

General Requirements

I. Applying for certification
Applicants seeking teacher certification in the District of Columbia must file a completed application with the Director.
  A. The completed application consists of:
    1. An application for professional certification.
    2. Official transcript(s) bearing the seal and signature of the registrar and showing the degree and date conferred.
    3. Verification (notarized) of previous teaching experience furnished by the responsible officer of the school district (or state) on official stationery (if applicable).
    4. Affidavit of previous nonteaching and/or trade technical experience (if applicable).
    5. A passing score on the Praxis I Pre-Professional Skills Test (reading, writing, and mathematics).
  B. Eligible applicants will be issued one of two initial regular certificates:
    1. Standard.
    2. Provisional—valid for 18 months pending the satisfactory completion of license deficits and the attainment of a passing score on the Praxis II Subject Assessment Tests or on the National Teacher Examination Specialty Tests.
  C. Persons who are employed by the District of Columbia Public School System will be issued a professional certificate at the time permanent tenure is granted.

II. General education requirements for all teaching certificates
  A. Bachelor's degree from an accredited institution
  B. Completion of appropriate tests as mandated by the Board of Education
  C. A minimum of forty-eight (48) semester hours in a program of general and/or liberal education including each of the following fields
    1. Humanities, semester hours 12
      a. At least one course in English grammar and composition; in literature, art, music, philosophy; and in foreign languages
    2. Social sciences, semester hours 12
      a. At least one course in American history and in one of the following areas: history, anthropology, sociology, economics, political science, geography, psychology, world studies, or contemporary world cultures
    3. Natural sciences and mathematics, semester hours 12
      a. At least one course in laboratory science and in mathematics
    4. Health and physical education, semester hours 12
      a. Including course work in substance abuse education
    5. Additional course work in C, 1–3, semester hours 12

III. Professional education requirements for all teaching certificates
    A. Course work, semester hours... 18
        1. Human growth and development (6 semester hours)
        2. Curriculum and instruction (6)
        3. Foundations of education (6)
    B. Supervised classroom instruction
        1. At least six (6) semester hours in student teaching involving at least 200 clock hours in classrooms with a minimum of 120 clock hours in direct teaching activities in the senior year;
        or
        2. At least one (1) year of satisfactory teaching experience in the certificate area

Teaching Certificates

I. Early Childhood Education (PreK–3)
    A. See General Requirements I–III above
    B. Completion of a sequence of courses of at least thirty (30) semester hours, including fieldwork, which provides theoretical and research knowledge, as well as practical skills in the following:
        1. Human development, with special emphasis on the developmental processes from birth through age eight
        2. Historical, philosophical, psychological, and social foundations of early childhood education
        3. Roles of the teacher
        4. Curriculum for teaching young children, including course work in observing and recording their behavior
    C. Completion of six (6) semester hours in student teaching which consists of at least 150 clock hours spent in each of two different age groups, preprimary and primary
        or
        At least one (1) year of satisfactory teaching experience under appropriate supervision at the early childhood level
    D. Three endorsements are available for the early childhood certificate: Head Start Early Childhood, Early Childhood Special Education, and Montessori Primary Education (write the Division of State Services for details).
II. Elementary Education (1–6)
    A. See General Requirements I–III above
    B. Completion of at least sixty (60) semester hours of specialized course experiences appropriate for children at this level, distributed among the following subject areas:
        1. Mathematics (6), reading (6), language arts (12), social science (6), sciences (12), health and physical education (6), fine arts appreciation and expression (6), and electives to be chosen from the first five areas listed (6)
    C. Supervised planning, observation, and teaching experiences preferably at both the primary (1–3) and intermediate (4–6) grade levels; or one experience on the elementary level
        or

At least one (1) year of satisfactory teaching experience on the elementary level

D.   Certificates in Elementary Science Resource and Elementary Mathematics Resource are also available.

III.   Middle School Education (4–8)

A.   See General Requirements I–III above

B.   Completion of a sequence of courses of at least twenty-one (21) semester hours in the professional foundations and instructional knowledge of middle school education which provides theoretical and research knowledge, as well as practical skills in the following:

1.   Human growth and development of the young adolescent; modeling and incorporating positive skills; creating a positive and caring environment; program design; curriculum; assessment strategies; and active student involvement

C.   Supervised planning, observation, and teaching experiences, preferably at the intermediate (4–6) grade levels or middle school grades

or

At least one (1) year of satisfactory teaching experience in grades K–12

D.   An endorsement for Middle School Education is also available.

IV.   Certification in Secondary Subjects

A.   See General Requirements I–III above

B.   Specialized course work in individual subjects is required. Semester hours are given below.

1.   English (36), mathematics (33), general science (30), biology (30), chemistry (30), physics (30), computer science (30), social studies (33), home economics (45), industrial arts (42), business education (30), art (K–12) (42), modern or classical foreign language (K–12) (30), and health/physical education (52).

C.   Write the Division of State Services for details regarding distribution requirements for specialized course work, as well as for additional subject certification areas.

School Personnel

I.   School Counselor

A.   Master's degree in counseling from an accredited institution

1.   Graduate program must meet competencies specified by the Board of Education, including no less than three hundred (300) clock hours of graduate-level, university-supervised field experience in counseling in a school setting, PreK–12.

a.   This field experience requirement may be met by completion of a degree in school counseling from a program approved by the Council for Accreditation of Counseling and Related Educational Programs or by a National Board of Certified Counselors certificate.

B.   Minimum of two successful academic years of full-time experience in teaching

1.   One year may be satisfied by full-time work experience in a nonschool setting

II.   School Librarian/Media Specialist (K–12)

A.   Master's degree from an accredited institution

B. Completion of twenty-one (21) semester hours in library and/or information science which meet competencies specified by the Board of Education
C. Directed field experience in a school library media center with an experienced media specialist
    or
    Two years of successful teaching
    or
    One year of library experience

Reciprocity

I. Applying for certification by reciprocity
    A. Applicants who have been employed for at least 27 months under a standard certificate or are completing teacher training in approved programs at colleges/universities in one of 29 states may apply for certification under the Interstate Agreement on Qualifications of Educational Personnel.
    B. Applicants must:
        1. Present a valid certificate from a state listed below.
        2. File a completed application.
    C. The District of Columbia has signed reciprocity agreements with the following states:

Alabama	Massachusetts	South Carolina
California	Michigan	South Dakota
Connecticut	Nebraska	Tennessee
Delaware	New Hampshire	Utah
Florida	New Jersey	Vermont
Hawaii	New York	Virginia (including
Idaho	North Carolina	Dept. of Defense
Indiana	Oklahoma	Schools, Alexandria)
Kentucky	Ohio	Washington
Maine	Pennsylvania	West Virginia
Maryland	Rhode Island	

Note: Acceptance of experiential learning to satisfy specific license requirements will be determined by the Director of Teacher Education and Certification.

Florida

The Office of Testing and Evaluation, Florida Department of Education, has established scores for certain NTE/PRAXIS tests. Other areas still require that applicants take the Florida state tests. Please write the Bureau of Teacher Certification (address in Appendix 1) for complete information.

Professional Certificate
(Valid for five years, PreK–12)

I. General requirements
A certificate may be issued to an applicant who has met the following:
   A. Files a completed application, including official degree transcripts and a complete fingerprint report that has been cleared by the Florida Department of Law Enforcement and the FBI.
   B. Holds a bachelor's or higher degree from an acceptable institution of higher learning.
   C. Has an acceptable major in a single subject in which Florida offers certification or meets specialization requirements in the subject.
   D. Meets professional preparation requirements.
   E. Has completed at least 6 semester hours of appropriate college credit during the five-year period preceding the date of application for an initial temporary or professional certificate, or has completed two (2) years of full-time teaching experience during the five-year period preceding the date of application for an initial temporary certificate.
   F. Has obtained a 2.5 grade point average on a 4.0 scale in each subject shown on the certificate.
   G. Has received a passing score on the College Level Academic Skills Test (CLAST).
   H. Has received a passing score on the Professional Education Subtest of the Florida Teacher Certification Examination.
   I. Has received a passing score on a NTE/PRAXIS or Florida state-approved subject area examination for each subject or field shown on the certificate.
   J. Completes a state-approved program for demonstration of professional education competence.

II. Renewal
   A. Completion of 6 semester hours of appropriate credit or 120 approved Florida staff development points specific to the subject(s) shown on the certificate or training/course work related to the educational goals and performance standards outlined in Florida statutes during each five-year validity period.

III. Professional Preparation Requirements for Academic, Administrative, and Speciality Class Coverages (PreK–12)
   A. Complete an undergraduate teacher education program at an institution approved by the Florida State Board of Education or another state, or the National Council for the Accreditation of Teacher Education, *or* possess a valid full-time teaching certificate

issued by another state and meet the terms of the interstate agreement or Florida State Board Rule in regard to recognition of regular certificates from other states.
or

B. Complete 20 semester hours in professional preparation to include the following:
1. Foundations of education, to include both sociological and psychological foundations, total semester hours 6
2. General methods of teaching, semester hours 6
   a. Three semester hours to be at the level of certification being sought (elementary, secondary, etc.).
   b. All K–12 areas must have credit in both elementary and secondary methods.
3. Special methods
   a. Middle Grades (5–9).
      1) Methods of teaching the subject at the middle grades level, semester hours 2
   b. Secondary Grades (6–12).
      1) Methods of teaching the subject at the secondary level for each secondary subject on the certificate, semester hours 2
   c. Grades K–12.
      1) Methods of teaching the subject including credit covering the elementary and secondary levels for each of the following: art, computer science, health, foreign languages, humanities, and music, semester hours 4
   d. Credit in special methods is not required for certification in educational leadership, guidance, exceptional child education areas, media specialist, elementary education specialist in school psychology, school social worker, or physical education.
4. Practical Experience in Teaching
   a. One of the following:
      1) Six semester hours in a college student teaching program.
      2) Two years of full-time teaching experience.
   b. Each of the above must be done in an elementary or secondary school. (Teaching experience in a nonpublic school shall be acceptable provided the applicant held a valid full-time certificate issued by the state where the teaching experience was acquired.)

Elementary School

I. Requirements
   A. Bachelor's or higher degree with a major in elementary education which includes teaching reading at the elementary or primary level
      or
   B. Bachelor's or higher degree with semester hours in elementary education 24
      1. Competencies in teaching basic reading, diagnosing reading problems, and prescribing methods to improve reading skills, semester hours 3

2.   Materials for use with children; nature study or science; social studies; health and/or physical education; art; music; arithmetic, semester hours 21

Middle Grades (5–9)

I.   General Requirements
A.   General and professional preparation. See Professional Certificate.
II. Specific Requirements
A.   Middle Grades English: a bachelor's or higher degree major in middle grades English or a bachelor's or higher degree in another subject or field and 18 semester hours above the freshman level in English including specific courses in grammar, composition, and literature.
B.   Middle Grades Mathematics: a bachelor's or higher degree major in middle grades mathematics or a bachelor's degree in another subject or field and 18 semester hours in mathematics including specific courses in calculus, geometry, and probability.
C.   Middle Grades General Science: a bachelor's or higher degree major in middle grades general science or a bachelor's or higher degree in another subject or field and 18 semester hours in science including specific courses in biology, physical science, earth-space science, and philosophy of science.
D.   Middle Grades Social Science: a bachelor's or higher degree major in middle grades social science or a bachelor's or higher degree in another subject or field and 18 semester hours in social science including specific courses in history, economics, United States government, and geography.
E.   Middle Grades Integrated Curriculum:
1.   A bachelor's or higher degree with a degree major in middle grades education which includes a minimum of 12 semester hours in each of the following areas: English, mathematics, science, and social science;
or
2.   A bachelor's or higher degree with a degree major in a subject other than middle grades education and 54 semester hours in English, mathematics, science, and social science.
a.   18 semester hours to be completed in one of the four subject areas and at least 12 semester hours to be completed in each of the remaining subject areas.

Secondary School (6–12)

I.   General Requirements
A.   Bachelor's or higher degree
B.   General and professional preparation. See Professional Certificate.
II. Special requirements for subject fields: English, social science (general), economics, geography, political science, psychology, sociology, mathematics, biology, chemistry, earth-space science, and physics.
A.   Florida offers alternative plans for certification in the subject fields.

1. For all subject fields, applicants may qualify by having a bachelor's or higher degree with a major or 30 semester hours of specified courses in the field for which certification is being sought.
2. For English and the social science fields, applicants may also qualify by having a bachelor's or higher degree with at least 30 semester hours in the field or in related fields for which certification is being sought. (Contact Florida's Bureau of Teacher Certification for details on specific course distributions.)
3. For mathematics and the sciences, applicants may also qualify by two additional certification routes. In all cases, the applicant must have a bachelor's or higher degree with at least 30 semester hours of specified courses in the field or related fields for which certification is being sought. (Contact Florida's Bureau of Teacher Certification for details on specific course distributions.)

Administration

I. Educational Leadership, level one certificate
   A. Have three years of successful teaching experience in an elementary or secondary school.
   B. Hold a Master's or higher degree from an accredited institution.
   C. Successful completion of the Florida Educational Leadership Core Curriculum by specified options, including graduate courses covering
      1. Public School Curriculum and Instruction
      2. Organizational Management and Development
      3. Human Resource Management and Development
      4. Leadership Skills
      5. Communication Skills
      6. Technology
      7. Educational Law
      8. Educational Finance
   D. Graduate credit (or equivalent), semester hours.. 6
      In one area of emphasis:
      1. Early childhood/primary education/elementary education
      2. Middle school education
      3. Secondary school education
      4. Exceptional student education
   E. Passing scores on the Florida Educational Leadership Examination
II. School Principal, level two certificate
   A. Hold a valid professional certificate covering educational leadership, school administration, or school administration/supervision.
   B. Document successful performance of the duties of school principalship.
   C. Demonstrate successful performance of the competencies of the school principalship which shall be documented by the Florida district school superintendent.
III. Professional School Principal
   (Certification as professional school principal is a voluntary certification.)
   A. Hold a valid school principal certificate.

B. Have three years of successful experience as a principal in the same Florida public school district.
C. Superior performance documented by district school superintendent.

Educational Media Specialist (PreK–12)

I. Specialization requirements
A. Bachelor's or higher degree with a major in educational media
    or
B. Bachelor's or higher degree in another subject with work in educational media, including the following areas, semester hours 30
    1. Management of library media programs 3
    2. Management of school library media programs 3
    3. Instructional role of library media specialist 3
    4. Collection development 3
    5. Library media resources 6
    6. Reference sources and services 3
    7. Organization of collections 3
    8. Design and production of educational media, including a survey course 6

Guidance Counselor (Grades PreK–12)

I. Specialization requirements
A. Master's or higher degree with a graduate major in guidance and counseling or in counselor education which includes 3 semester hours in a supervised counseling practicum in an elementary or secondary school
    or
B. Master's or higher degree with 30 semester hours of graduate credit in guidance and counseling, including
    1. Principles and administration of guidance 3
    2. Student appraisal 3
    3. Education and career development 3
    4. Learning theory and human development 3
    5. Counseling theories and techniques 3
    6. Group counseling 3
    7. Consultation skills 3
    8. Legal and ethical issues 3
    9. Counseling techniques for special populations 3
    10. Supervised practicum 3

Note: Noncitizens, exchange teachers, and resident aliens and refugees may be issued a certificate on the same basis as a citizen of the United States, provided they meet exact and specific qualifications established by the Florida State Board of Education.

Georgia

Regulations Applicable to Certification of School Personnel

I. Certification through completion of an approved teacher education program in a field recognized by Georgia
   A. Teacher education program must be approved by the appropriate state authority.
   B. Professional recommendation for certification must be made by the authorized college official.

II. Certification by evaluation (for those not qualifying under approved program plan)
   A. The evaluation compares the applicant's official transcripts with the minimum course requirements listed for the provisional certificate desired.
   B. Conditions for evaluation
      1. Bachelor's degree or higher from a regionally accredited college or university.
      2. Minimum overall grade point average of 2.5 on a 4.0 scale.

III. Certification based on out-of-state certification
   A. Applicant must submit application, official transcripts, and verification of teaching experience completed within the last five years.
   B. Applicant must submit a legible photocopy (front and back) of any professional certificate(s) held or previously held in another state, District of Columbia, D.O.D.D.S., U.S. territory, or NBPTS.

IV. A $20.00 fee is required for each certificate application unless the applicant is employed in a Georgia public or private school or in a Georgia state agency.

Special Georgia Requirements

All applicable special Georgia requirements must be satisfied by an individual to complete the initial process of certification. These requirements include special course work, a subject matter assessment, and recent experience. An initial one-year professional certificate may be issued to allow the qualified out-of-state applicant to meet special course work and assessment certification test requirements.

I. Courses
   A. Introduction to Exceptional Children
      1. Any person certified as a teacher, administrator, media specialist, or counselor must complete course work in the Identification and Education of Children with Special Needs, quarter hours 5
   B. The Teaching of Reading
      1. Persons certified in elementary grades (P–8), early childhood grades (P–5), middle grades (4–8), English, and certain special education fields, must complete course work in the Teaching of Reading, quarter hours 5

II. Subject Matter Assessments
   A. Appropriate assessments are required of all persons seeking initial certification.

III. Experience
    A. School Experience
        1. Three years of acceptable school experience are required for all leadership fields and for teacher support specialist.
    B. Occupational Experience
        1. Two years of full-time employment in business or industry is required as a prerequisite to certification in vocational-technical teaching fields at levels below the bachelor's degree.
        2. One year of full-time employment is required as a prerequisite to certification in vocational-technical teaching fields at bachelor's degree level or above.

Supplementary Certification

Individuals may establish eligibility for supplementary certification by completing the preparation required to add a new field or type to the certificate.

Fields refer to one's areas of specialization. The following fields have been adopted by the Georgia Professional Standards Commission, and all have been classified according to one of three types of certificates: Teaching, Leadership, and Service.

Teaching Fields

(4), (5), or (6) indicates college degree level of initial certification.

Agriculture (4)

Art (4)

Behavior Disorders (4)

Biology (4)

Business (4)

Chemistry (4)

Chinese (4)

Dance (4)

Drama (4)

Early Childhood Education (P–5) (4)

Earth/Space Science (4)

Economics (4)

Elementary Grades (P–8) (4)

English (4)

Family & Consumer Science (4)

French (4)

Geography (4)

German (4)

Greek (4)

Health (4)

Health Occupations (4)

Health & Physical Education (4)

Hearing Impaired (4)

Hebrew (4)

History (4)

Interrelated Special Education (4)

Interrelated Teacher: Special Education
    Early Childhood (4)

Italian (4)

Japanese (4)

Latin (4)

Learning Disability (4)

Marketing Education (4)

Math (4)

Mental Retardation (4)

Middle Grades (4–8) (4)

Music (4)

Orthopedically Impaired (4)

Physics (4)

Political Science (4)

Reading Specialist (5)*

Russian (4)

Science (4)
Social Science (4)
Spanish (4)
Speech (4)

Technology Education (4)
Trade & Industrial Ed. (4)
Visually Impaired (4)

Leadership Fields

Educational Leadership (5)*
Director of Media Services (5)*
Director of Pupil Personnel Services (5)*

Director of Special Education (5)*
Director of Vocational Education (5)*
Instructional Supervision (5)*

Service Fields

Audiologist (5)
Media Specialist (5)
School Counselor (5)
School Nutrition Director (4)

School Psychologist (5)
School Social Worker (5)
Speech & Language Pathologist (5)

Endorsements
(Prerequisite certificate required)

Career Exploration (PECE)
Coordinator of Cooperative Education
  (CVAE)
Diversified Cooperative Training (DCT)
English to Speakers of Other Languages
  (ESOL)

Gifted (second field)
Preschool Special Education
Related Vocational Instructor (RVI)
Safety and Driver Education
Teacher Support Specialist (TSS)

* Prerequisite Certificate required.

Hawaii

Hawaii requires that a teaching license be issued only upon the employment of an individual as a teacher, school librarian, or counselor with the Hawaii State Department of Education. Unless an applicant's teaching field is in a critical shortage area (as identified by the Department), the applicant will need to be available in Hawaii over a period of time for school-level interviews after she or he has met all licensing requirements.

Teacher and Specialist Licenses

I. Method A
   A. Completion of a state-approved teacher education program from an accredited institution including student teaching or practicum experiences in a K–12 setting
   B. Passing scores on the PRAXIS II series: PPST, PLT (K–6, 5–9, or 7–12) and Subject Assessments tests (The Subject Assessment tests are required to be taken only if they are available for an applicant's major and are tests for which the Hawaii State Department of Education has established passing scores.)
II. Method B
   A. Possession of a valid license/certificate from any state,
   B. Three years of successful teaching experience within the past 7 years beginning after the issuance date of the valid certificate and in the teaching area indicated on the license/certificate
   C. See I, B
   D. License for the specialty fields of school counselor or school librarian cannot be awarded through Method B but instead must be issued on the basis of successful completion of a state-approved graduate specialist education program which includes practicum experiences in a K–12 setting.
III. Authorizations and Validity
   A. Elementary, secondary, special education, school counselor, and school librarian
   B. Valid for five years and renewable by continuing to meet the standards established by the Hawaii Teacher Standards Board

Teacher Credentials

I. A credential is an emergency or temporary license. It is issued upon employment, under the following circumstances:
   A. The person who completes a teacher preparation program but has not yet submitted all necessary documents to the Department will be issued a credential until all requirements for licensing are met. The pending documents may include
      1. Official transcript(s) bearing the school seal and indicating the degree(s) awarded and dates conferred; official passing PRAXIS Examination scores; and,

as appropriate, out-of-state teaching certificates, institutional recommendation(s), and verification of employment

II.   Valid for one school year and may be reissued annually up to three years if the credential holder continues to satisfy the Board's credentialing standards and actively pursues requirements for licensing

III. By law, a person who has not completed a teacher preparation program or equivalent training can be hired and issued a credential only if no suitable individual who meets the licensing requirements is available for the position.

Areas of Preparation

I.   The area of preparation category on a license may reflect either:
   A.   Completion of a state-approved teacher education (SATE) program, including a student teaching or practicum component with a major area of concentration, from an accredited institution
       or
   B.   An endorsement, which is a Department of Education program available to teachers with valid licenses who have exhibited successful performance and who have successfully completed the appropriate PRAXIS subject assessment tests or have earned credits in the endorsement area

II.   Specific areas of preparation, other than special education
   A.   Agricultural arts; arts; business education; school counselor;** early childhood; elementary education; English; school librarian;** guidance; Hawaiian language; Hawaiian language immersion; Hawaiian studies; health; health and physical education; home economics; industrial arts; industrial technical;* languages; marketing education;* mathematics; middle school music; office education;* physical education; reading science; social studies; speech; teaching English to speakers of other languages; technology education; vocational agriculture;* vocational home economics;* and other areas as determined by the Department

III. Special education areas of preparation
   A.   Mild/moderate; severe/profound; hearing impaired; visually impaired; orientation and mobility; orthopedically handicapped; deaf-blind; and others as determined by the Department

*   Trade experience is required for these vocational technical programs.

** This license is issued for areas other than regular classroom instruction.

Professional Certificates

I.   Professional Teacher
   A.   Completion of teacher preparation program at the graduate level or equivalent requirements
   B.   Possession of a valid teacher license

II.   Professional Educational Administrator
   A.   Completion of a graduate level program

      B.   Demonstration of 1 year of successful performance as an educational administrator within the Department of Education

      C.   Completion of 3 years of teaching experience or equivalent work experience

III.   Professional School Administrator

      A.   Possession of an Initial Administrator's Certificate

      B.   Successful completion of probationary vice-principal requirements

      C.   Successful completion of all requirements of the Department's school administrator training program

      D.   This certificate may also be issued to those who have demonstrated an acceptable level of competencies identified in the Department's Profile of an Effective School Administrator and earned tenure in the Department.

Idaho

Applicants for initial certification must have earned six (6) semester credit hours of college courses within the last five years. The National Teachers Examination (NTE) Battery is not required of applicants for an initial Idaho certificate.

Elementary School (Grades K–8)

I. Standard Elementary Certificate*
    A. Bachelor's degree.
    B. Professional requirements to include the following areas, total semester hours 24
        1. Philosophical, psychological, and methodological foundations of education.
        2. Elementary student teaching, semester hours 6
            or
            Three years of successful teaching in an elementary school.
        3. Developmental reading, semester hours 6
    C. General education, to include the following areas, total semester hours 44
        1. English, to include composition and literature 12
        2. Social science, including United States history and/or government............. 12
        3. Two or more areas of natural science.. 8
        4. Fine arts 3
        5. Fundamentals of mathematics (not methods)..................................... 6
        6. Methods of physical education and/or health 3

Secondary School (Grades 6–12)

I. Standard Secondary Certificate*
    A. Bachelor's degree.
    B. Professional requirements, semester hours 20
        1. Philosophical, psychological, and methodological foundations of education.
        2. Secondary student teaching, semester hours 6
            or
            Three years of successful teaching in a secondary school.
        3. Reading in the content area, semester hours.................................. 3
    C. Preparation in at least two fields of secondary teaching:
        1. Major subject, semester hours 30
            and Minor subject, semester hours 20
            or
        2. Preparation in a single area, in lieu of a major and minor, semester hours 45

The Exceptional Child

I. Standard Exceptional Child Certificate*
    A. Generalist (Educationally Handicapped) Endorsement
        1. Completion of a program in Special Education approved by Idaho State Board of Education, *or* by the State Educational Agency where the program was completed.
        2. Special education courses, semester hours 30
            a. To include developmental processes; evaluation; individualization of instruction for exceptional child; instructional experience; individual and group classroom management; knowledge of and coordination with other school personnel; knowledge of state and community ancillary services; work with parents.
    B. Specialized Endorsement (one or more)
        1. Hearing and visually impaired; physical disabilities; multiple disabilities; severe retardation; and seriously emotionally disturbed.
        2. Requirements
            a. Baccalaureate degree.
            b. Completion of approved program in area of endorsement, as recommended by the training institution.
    C. Consulting Teacher Endorsement*
        1. Valid Standard Exceptional Child Certificate.
        2. Valid Standard Elementary or Secondary teaching certificate.
        3. Completion of fifth-year or master's degree program.
        4. Three years of teaching experience, with at least two years in a special education classroom setting.
        5. Demonstration of competencies.
    D. Supervisor/Coordinator Endorsement
        1. Master's degree.
        2. Standard Exceptional Child Certificate, or Pupil Personnel Services Certificate, endorsed for School Psychologist, Communication Disorders Specialist, or School Social Worker.
        3. Three years of experience in special education.
        4. Demonstration of competencies.

Administration

I. Administrative Certificates
    A. School Principal Endorsement (K–12)*
        1. Master's degree from an accredited institution.
        2. Four years full-time experience (under certification) working with K–12 students while under contract in a school setting.
        3. Completion of an administrative internship or one year experience as an administrator.
        4. Completion of a state-approved program of at least 30 semester hours of

graduate study in school administration for the preparation of school principals at an accredited institution.

    a. To include competencies in supervision of instruction; curriculum development; school finance; administration; school law; student behavior management; and education of special populations.

    5. Institutional recommendation.

B. Superintendent Endorsement*

    1. Educational specialist or doctorate degree or a comparable post-master's sixth-year program at an accredited institution.

    2. See School Principal I, A, 2 and 3.

    3. Completion of a state-approved program of at least 30 semester hours of post-master's degree graduate study in school administration for the preparation of school superintendents at an accredited institution.

        a. In addition to the competencies required for the principal (see I, A, 4, a), this program will include competencies in advanced money management, budget, and accounting principles; district-wide support services; employment practices and negotiations; school board and community relations; and special services and federal programs.

    4. Institutional recommendation.

C. Director of Special Education Endorsement (K–12)

    1. See School Principal I, A, 1 and 2.

    2. Institutional verification of competencies in organization and administration of special services; school finance and school law as related to special education; supervision of instruction; practicum experience in special education administration; counseling parents of exceptional children; foundations of special education; curriculum and methods in special education and diagnosis and remediation in special education.

    3. Competency checklist forms from the applicant's institution may be requested by the Certification Division.

Pupil Personnel Services

I. Standard Counselor Endorsement (K–12)*

  A. Requirements

    1. Master's degree plus verification of completion of approved program of graduate study in school guidance and counseling from an institution approved by the Idaho State Board of Education or the state educational agency of the state in which the program was completed.

        a. The program must include successful completion of 700 hours of supervised field experience, one-half of which must be in a K–12 school setting.

    2. Institutional recommendation.

II. School Psychologist Endorsement*

  A. Requirements

    1. Graduate semester hours.. 60

                  a.   Master's degree program of 30 semester hours in education or psychology, plus 30 hours in school psychology,

                  b.   Sixty semester hours in master's degree program in School Psychology, *or*

                  c.   Sixty semester hours in School Psychology Specialist program which did not require a master's degree.

            2.   Laboratory experience.

            3.   A 300 clock-hour internship.

            4.   Institutional recommendation.

III.   Speech-Language Pathologist Endorsement*

    A.   Requirements

        1.   Completion of state-approved program in speech-language pathology.

        2.   Master's degree in speech language pathology.

        3.   Institutional recommendation.

IV.   Audiology Endorsement*

    A.   Same as for Speech-Language Pathologist Endorsement, but substitute "audiology" for "speech-language pathology."

V.   School Social Worker Endorsement*

    A.   Requirements

        1.   Master's degree in social work from an approved program, *or*

        2.   Master's degree in guidance and counseling, sociology, or psychology, plus graduate work in social work education, semester hours 30

        3.   Valid social work license issued by the Idaho Bureau of Occupational Licenses.

        4.   Institutional recommendation.

VI.   School Nurse Endorsement*

    A.   Requirements

        1.   Valid registered nursing license issued by the Idaho State Board of Nursing.

*   All these certificates are issued upon a single credential which is valid for five years and may be renewed upon completion of at least six semester credits of college courses within the period of validity.

Illinois

General Requirements

I. Teachers and supervisors in the public schools of Illinois must be of good character, good health, at least 19 years of age, and citizens of the United States.
II. All persons seeking elementary, high school, early childhood, special, school service personnel, or administrative certificates must pass both a test of basic skills and a test of subject matter knowledge. These are offered four times annually by the Illinois State Board of Education.
III. An applicant who holds or is eligible to hold another state's teacher, school service personnel, or administrative certificate may be granted a corresponding Illinois certificate if the requirements for the out-of-state certificate are comparable to the Illinois requirements.

Elementary School

I. Must have evidence of teaching experience or completion of an approved program either in Illinois or in another state.
II. Standard Elementary School Certificate (Grades K–9; valid for 4 years)
    A. Bachelor's degree from a recognized college and presentation of certified evidence of earned credits as given below.
    B. General education, total semester hours 71
        1. Communication skills, semester hours 9
            a. Oral (3) and written (6)
        2. Mathematics and science, semester hours 18
            a. Mathematics (6) and biological and physical sciences, including one laboratory course (12)
        3. Humanities,* semester hours 15
            a. American history** (3) and English (3)
            b. Any combination of history,** English, literature, foreign language, fine arts, linguistics, or philosophy (9)
        4. Social Science,* semester hours 9
            a. American government (3)
            b. Any combination of political science, anthropology, cultural geography, economics, psychology, or sociology (6)
        5. Health and physical development, semester hours 2
        6. Additional study, semester hours 18
            a. Courses may be in any of the disciplines listed under B, 2, 3, and 4, including a minimum of 9 semester hours of upper division course work

* At least one 3-semester hour course must be taken in non-Western or third world cultures from either humanities or social sciences.

** Courses in American history or history may be applied toward meeting either the humanities or social science requirements.

    C. Professional education, semester hours.. 16
        1. Educational psychology, including human growth and development,
            semester hours 2
        2. Methods and techniques of teaching on the elementary level, semester hours ... 2
        3. History and/or philosophy of education, semester hours............................. 2
        4. Methods of teaching reading, semester hours... 2
        5. Pre-student teaching clinical experiences of 100 clock hours at the grade
            level or in the area of specialization.*
        6. Course work equivalent to 3 semester hours on the psychology of exceptional
            children, identification of exceptional children, and methods of teaching
            exceptional children. Learning disabilities must be explicitly included in this
            course work.
        7. Student teaching, grades K–9, semester hours 5
        8. Electives in professional education may be taken from the above fields and/or
            guidance, tests and measurements, and instructional materials,
            semester hours 16
    D. General electives, to make a total of semester hours 120

* Those with successful teaching experience at appropriate level do not need to complete pre-student teaching.

High School

  I. Must have evidence of teaching experience or completion of an approved program in Illinois or in another state.
  II. Standard High School Certificate (Grades 6–12; valid for 4 years)
    A. See Elementary School, II, A.
    B. General education, total semester hours.. 47
        1. Communication skills, semester hours 9
          a. Oral (3) and written (6)
        2. Mathematics and science, semester hours 12
          a. Mathematics (3) and biological and physical sciences, including one
             laboratory course (9)
        3. Humanities,* semester hours... 15
          a. American history** (3) and English (3)
          b. Any combination of history,** English, literature, foreign language, fine
             arts, linguistics, or philosophy (9)
        4. Social Science,* semester hours.. 9
          a. American government (3)
          b. Any combination of political science, anthropology, cultural geography,
             economics, psychology, or sociology (6)
        5. Health and physical development, semester hours 2

* At least one 3-semester hour course must be taken in non-Western or third world cultures from either humanities or social sciences.

** Courses in American history or history may be applied toward meeting either the humanities or social science requirements.

C. Professional education, semester hours... 16
   1. Educational psychology, including human growth and development, semester hours 2
   2. Methods and techniques of teaching on the secondary level or in a teaching field, semester hours 2
   3. History and/or philosophy of education, semester hours............................. 2
   4. See Elementary II, C, 5.
   5. See Elementary II, C, 6.
   6. Student teaching, grades 6–12, semester hours...................................... 5
   7. Electives from the above fields and the following: guidance, tests, and measurements; methods of teaching reading; instructional materials (to complete 16 hours), semester hours.. 5
D. One major area of specialization, semester hours 32
   1. If area of specialization is the same as one of the general education categories, then the same courses may be used for both requirements.
   2. Areas of specialization: history, social science, English, Spanish, French, German, Hebrew, Italian, Latin, Russian, dance, speech, biological science, mathematics, chemistry, computer science, general science, physical science, physics, health, health occupations, family and consumer sciences, industrial technology education, agriculture, business/marketing/management, art (6–12), music (6–12), physical education (6–12), and theater arts.
E. Electives, to make a total of semester hours 120

Middle Grades Endorsement

I. This endorsement, which may be added to either the Elementary or High School Certificates, is valid for grades 5–8.
A. Professional education, semester hours... 6
   1. Educational psychology focusing on early adolescents and the role of the middle grade teacher in assessment, coordination, and referral of students to health and social services, semester hours.................................... 3
   2. Middle school philosophy, curriculum, and instructional methods, semester hours 3
B. Subject area of major teaching assignment, semester hours 18
   1. Subject area of second teaching assignment, semester hours....................... 9

Early Childhood

I. Must have evidence of teaching experience or completion of an approved program either in Illinois or in another state.
II. Early Childhood Certificate (Ages 0 to Grade 3; valid for 4 years)
A. Bachelor's degree from a recognized college.
B. General education, total semester hours.. 71
   1. Communication skills, semester hours 9
       a. Oral (3) and written (6)
   2. Mathematics and science, semester hours 18

       a.   Mathematics (6) and biological and physical sciences, including one laboratory course (12)

   3.   Humanities,* semester hours.. 12

       a.   American history** (3)

       b.   Any combination of history,** English, literature, foreign language, fine arts, linguistics, or philosophy (9)

   4.   Social Science,* semester hours.. 12

       a.   American government (3)

       b.   Any combination of political science, anthropology, cultural geography, economics, psychology, or sociology (9)

   5.   Health and physical development, semester hours 2

   6.   Additional study, semester hours.. 18

       a.   Courses may be in any of the disciplines listed under B, 2, 3, and 4, including a minimum of 9 semester hours of upper division course work

*   At least one 3-semester hour course must be taken in non-Western or third world cultures from either humanities or social sciences.

**   Courses in American history or history may be applied toward meeting either the humanities or social science requirements.

   C.   Professional Education, semester hours... 32

       1.   Child growth and development with emphasis on the young child 3

       2.   History and philosophy of early childhood education 3

       3.   Types of instructional methods, including types of activity/learning centers, individualization, educational play, and media and their utilization in extending the child's understanding of art, music, literature, reading instruction, mathematics, natural and social science................................... 4

       4.   Methods of teaching reading, with emphasis on the young child.................. 2

       5.   Techniques and methodologies of teaching language arts, mathematics, science and social studies at the primary level 4

       6.   The development and acquisition of language in young children 2

       7.   Child, family, and community relationships 3

       8.   Course work, equivalent to three (3) semester hours, on the psychology of exceptional children, identification of exceptional children and methods of teaching exceptional children. Learning disabilities must be explicitly included in this course work. 3

       9.   Pre-student teaching clinical experiences equivalent to 100 clock hours, including experience with infants/toddlers, preschool/kindergarten children, and primary school students.

      10.   Student teaching 5
           Those who have had five semester hours of student teaching at the primary grade level (K–3) and who have had teaching experience are not required to take another practicum at the preschool level.

      11.   Electives in professional education.. 3

   D.   General electives to total semester hours... 120

Special Subjects

I.   Must have evidence of teaching experience or completion of an approved program either in Illinois or in another state.

II. Standard Special Certificate (Grades K–12). Valid for 4 years.

    A.   Standard Special Certificate may be issued, valid for 4 years of teaching the special subject or subjects named on the certificate in grades K–12. Requirements are for the most part similar to the Standard High School Certificate A–E, except that the candidate should be prepared in methods and/or student teaching in the area of specialization.

III. Areas for Special Education—Areas A through G each require 32 semester hours of appropriate courses in the particular area.

    A.   Educable mentally handicapped

    B.   Learning disabilities

    C.   Social-Emotional problems

    D.   Trainable mentally handicapped

    E.   Blind and partially sighted

    F.   Deaf and hard of hearing

    G.   Physically handicapped

    H.   Speech and language impaired

        1.   Master's degree and completion of a course in communicative disorders and related disciplines.

        2.   Competencies in the area, professional education, and in the application of psychological principles.

        3.   Clinical practicum in communicative disorders.

IV. Supervisory Endorsement on Standard Special Certificate

    A.   Master's degree from a recognized institution of higher learning.

    B.   Graduate professional education, semester hours 8

        1.   To include 1 course in supervision of personnel and 1 course in administration and organization of schools.

    C.   Two years of appropriate teaching experience.

Administration

The Administrative Certificate, valid for 5 years for supervising and administering in the common schools, may be issued to persons who have graduated from a recognized institution of higher learning with a master's degree and who have been certified by these institutions of higher learning as having completed a program of preparation for one or more of these endorsements.

I.   General Supervisory Endorsement

    A.   This endorsement is required for supervisors, curriculum directors and other similar or related positions.

    B.   Minimum Requirements of Graduate Level Study:

        1.   Areas of Study

            a.   Curriculum, semester hours 3

      b. Educational research, semester hours 3
      (work in areas [a] and [b] combined must total eight [8]
      semester hours) 8
      c. Supervision and staff development, semester hours 8–9
      d. Schools and public policy, semester hours.................................. 8–9
      e. Clinical experience appropriate to the endorsement.
  C. Two years of full-time teaching experience or school service personnel experience.
  D. Successful completion of the required certification examinations.

II. General Administrative Endorsement
  A. This endorsement is required for the following positions: principal, assistant principal, assistant or associate superintendent, and other similar or related positions.
  B. Minimum Requirements of Graduate Level Study:
    1. Areas of Study
      a. Instructional leadership, semester hours 12
      b. Management of public schools, semester hours.............................. 9
      c. Schools and public policy, semester hours.................................. 4–6
      d. Clinical experience appropriate to the endorsement.
  C. Two years of full-time teaching experience or school service personnel experience.
  D. Successful completion of the required certification examinations.

III. Chief School Business Official Endorsement
  A. This endorsement is required for chief school business officials.
  B. Minimum Requirements of Graduate Level Study:
    1. Areas of Study
      a. School business management, semester hours....................................... 12
      b. School organization and administration, semester hours 3
      c. School finance and fiscal planning, semester hours 6
      d. Clinical experience appropriate to endorsement while holding a certificate of comparable validity.
  C. Two years school business management experience.
  D. Successful completion of the required certification examinations.
  E. Alternative route to certification
    1. Master's degree in business administration, finance, or accounting.
    2. Successful completion of the required certification examination.

IV. Superintendent
  A. This endorsement is required for superintendents of school districts.
  B. Minimum Requirements of Graduate Level Study:
    1. Areas of Study (semester hours of credit listed below must be beyond the master's degree level)
      a. Governance of public schools, semester hours 6
      b. Management of public schools, semester hours.................................... 6
      c. Educational planning, semester hours.. 6
      d. Additional graduate credit, semester hours.. 12
      e. Clinical experiences appropriate to the endorsement.
  C. Two years school supervisory or administrative experience and possession of the

General Supervisory or General Administrative Certificate or comparable out-of-state certificate.

D. Successful completion of the required certification examinations.

School Guidance Counselor

I.   Must have completed an approved program either in Illinois or in another state.
II. Requirements:
    A. Have or be qualified for a standard teaching certificate.
    B. Master's degree from a recognized teacher education institution.
    C. Approved course work, semester hours 39
        1. Human growth and development, semester hours 3
        2. Social and cultural foundations, semester hours.. 3
        3. The helping relationship, semester hours 6
        4. Groups, semester hours... 3
        5. Life style and career development, semester hours 3
        6. Appraisal of the individual, semester hours.. 3
        7. Research and evaluation, semester hours 3
        8. Professional Orientation, semester hours 3
        9. Environmental studies, semester hours... 6
      10. Supervised experience, semester hours 6
           a. To consist of 3 semester hours in a supervised counseling practicum and 3 semester hours in a postpracticum internship providing on-the-job experience in a school setting. Contact the Illinois State Board of Education for additional details.

Media Services—Librarian

I.   Media Professional—Library and Audio-visual
    A. Requirements:
        1. Appropriate teacher certificate.
        2. Library science—media, semester hours.. 18
        3. Professional preparation
           a. Four-year college and/or graduate level work in administration, organization, reference, and selection of materials at elementary and/or secondary levels.
II. Media Specialist
    A. Requirements:
        1. Standard Special Certificate with Library Science-Media endorsement.
        2. Work in field, semester hours.. 32
        3. See I, A, 3, above, plus production and communications.
III. Media Supervisor or Director
    A. Requirements:
        1. Supervisory or Standard Special Supervisory Endorsement, or the General Supervisory Endorsement with specialization in media.

Indiana

Early Childhood Education (Pre-Kindergarten)

I. Standard License (valid for 5 years)
   A. Baccalaureate degree from an institution of higher education accredited to offer programs in teacher education.
   B. Completion of undergraduate program of a minimum of 124 semester hours structured as follows:
      1. General education, semester hours 40
         To include language arts (always with children's literature), science, mathematics, and arts.
      2. Subject matter, semester hours 24
      3. Professional education, semester hours 40
         To include 10 weeks of student teaching, human growth and learning (infancy to age 8), laboratory experiences with individual children and parents, and curricula with reading readiness, ethnic, cultural and disability awareness.
      4. Electives, semester hours 20
   C. Recommendation for licensing by institution granting the degree.
   D. Successful completion of the NTE Core Battery and the NTE Specialty Area exam in Pre-Kindergarten Education.
II. Renewal
   The standard license may be renewed for the following five-year period if continuing education requirements are completed. These may include additional graduate or undergraduate semester hours and, if the applicant holds a master's degree or has completed 36 semester hours beyond the bachelor's degree, certification renewal units (CRUs) granted for approved professional experiences.
III. Professionalization (issued initially for 10 years). The Standard License may be professionalized upon
   A. Completion of 5 years teaching experience in accredited schools at the level covered by and subsequent to the issuance of the Standard License.
   B. Approved master's degree from accredited institution.
   C. Graduate level courses at a regionally accredited institution, semester hours 15
      1. Candidates with additional teaching areas or endorsements may professionalize these areas on completion of 3 semester hours of course work in subject matter area.
   D. Recommendation for Professional License by institution granting the master's degree.
IV. Additions
   A. The Standard or Professional License may be extended in subject area coverages upon completion of appropriate endorsement or teaching minors.

B. Before an addition can be made to the Professional License, candidate must complete course work requirements for endorsement or teaching minor being added.

Kindergarten–Primary (K–3)

I. Standard License (valid for 5 years)
   A. Baccalaureate degree.
   B. Completion of undergraduate program of a minimum of 124 semester hours structured as follows:
      1. General education to include: language arts, science, social studies, mathematics, and arts, semester hours.. 40
      2. Subject matter, semester hours 30
      3. Professional education, semester hours.. 30
         To include one semester full-time student teaching; foundations of education; educational psychology; methods and materials; classroom management; 6 semester hours of developmental, diagnostic, and corrective reading; and ethnic, cultural and disability awareness.
      4. Electives, semester hours... 24
   C. Recommendation for licensing by institution granting the degree.
   D. Successful completion of the NTE Core Battery and NTE Specialty Area exam in Early Childhood Education.
II. Renewal—see Early Childhood II.
III. Professionalization—see Early Childhood III.
IV. Additions—see Early Childhood IV.

Elementary Education
(Grades 1–6, and nondepartmentalized 7 and 8)

I. Standard License in Elementary Education (valid for 5 years)
   A. Baccalaureate degree from an institution of higher education accredited for programs in teacher education.
   B. Completion of undergraduate program of 124 semester hours structured as follows:
      1. General education and subject matter concentration, semester hours 70
         To include language arts; science; social studies; mathematics; arts; and electives such as physical and mental health; communicative exceptionality; safety education; recreation; physical activity; and nutrition.
      2. Professional education, semester hours.. 30
         To include foundations of education; educational psychology; methods and materials; specific and continuing pre-student teaching field experience; classroom management; developmental, diagnostic and corrective reading (6 semester hours); educational measurement and evaluation; ethnic, cultural and disability awareness; 10 weeks of full-time student teaching at level covered by this license.
      3. Electives, semester hours... 24
         To provide candidate with opportunity for self-determination of courses which shall add breadth and/or depth to undergraduate experience.

    C.   Recommendation for licensing by institution granting the degree.

    D.   Successful completion of the NTE Core Battery and the NTE Specialty Area exam in Elementary Education.

II.   Renewal—see Early Childhood II.

III. Professionalization—see Early Childhood III.

IV. Additions

    A.   The Standard Professional License may be endorsed for specific subjects (Grades 1–9) upon completion of

       1.   Course work in the subject, semester hours 18

       2.   Course work in junior high/middle school education, including a practicum, semester hours 6

          or

          One semester of junior high/middle school teaching experience prior to July 1, 1989.

Junior High/Middle School Education
(Departmentalized Grades 5–9)

I.   Standard License in Junior High/Middle School education.

    A.   See Elementary I, A.

    B.   Completion of undergraduate program of 124 semester hours structured as follows:

       1.   General education, semester hours 40

          a.   Humanities, semester hours 18–22
From among the following: literature; grammar; fine arts; foreign language; religion and philosophy; and always including 9 semester hours in oral and written expression.

          b.   Life and physical science, semester hours 8–12
From among the following: biology; physics; chemistry; physical geography; geology; astronomy; and mathematics.

          c.   Social and behavioral sciences, semester hours 8–12
From among the following: history; economics; sociology; government; anthropology; psychology; and geography.

       2.   Subject matter concentration.
To include a primary area of 24 semester hours and supporting area(s) of 18 semester hours.

          a.   Language arts, semester hours 18–24
To include world and American literature; language structure and basic communicative skills; and 3 semester hours in fundamentals of reading.

          b.   Science, semester hours 18–24
To include biology; chemistry; physics; and earth-space science.

          c.   Social studies, semester hours... 18–24
To include economics; U.S. history; world civilization; geography; government; and current social problems.

          d.   Mathematics, semester hours 18–24

To include college level mathematics such as statistics; probability; finite math; geometry; and number theory, adapted to junior high/ middle school.

    e. Foreign language, semester hours 18–24
To develop basic communication skills and understanding of culture, history and life style of people whose language they are studying.

    f. Home Economics, semester hours 36
To include textiles and clothing (6); consumer education and home management (6); foods and nutrition (9); housing, equipment and furnishings (6); human development, child development, family health and family relations (9).

    g. Industrial Arts, semester hours.. 42
To include principles, philosophy, organization and coordination of industrial education (6); industrial materials and processes (15); industrial communications (12); industrial power (9).

  3. Professional Education, semester hours 27

    a. To include foundations of education; educational psychology; methodology and organization; special methods; sociology of education; classroom management; reading; laboratory experience; and 10 weeks of student teaching at appropriate level.

  4. Electives, semester hours... 15

    a. See Elementary I, B, 3.

C. See Elementary I, C.

D. Successful completion of the NTE Core Battery and NTE Specialty Area Exams in appropriate areas.

II. Candidates for Standard License in Junior High/Middle School Education may also qualify when they have completed either A or B below, and always C.

A. Hold Standard or Professional License in Elementary Education, and have completed semester hours 15

  1. To include curriculum of junior high/middle school; adolescent psychology; practicum at grade level covered by the license; directed electives.

  2. Semester hours in content areas listed in I, B, 2 18

B. Hold Standard or Professional License in Secondary Education, plus semester hours... 15

  1. To include psychology and growth development from childhood to early adolescence.

  2. Curriculum, development and organization of junior high/middle school.

  3. Methods and techniques of individualized and inter-disciplinary learning.

  4. Practicum at grade level covered by this license.

C. Recommendation for licensing by institution of higher education where program was completed.

III. Renewal—see Early Childhood II.

IV. Professionalization—see Early Childhood III.

V. Additions—see Early Childhood IV.

Secondary School Education
(Grades 9–12)

I. Standard License in Secondary Education
    A. See Elementary I, A.
    B. Completion of undergraduate program of 124 semester hours as follows:
        1. General education, semester hours 40
            a. See Junior High/Middle School, I, B.
        2. Subject matter concentration
            a. Major, semester hours 36–52
            b. Minor (optional), semester hours 24
        3. Professional education, semester hours 24
            a. See Junior High/Middle school, I, B, 3.
        4. Electives (no specific number required)
    C. See Elementary I, C.
    D. See Junior High/Middle School Education I, D.
II. Renewal—see Early Childhood II.
III. Professionalization—see Early Childhood III.
IV. Additions—see Early Childhood IV.

Senior High, Junior High, and Middle School Education
(Grades 5–12)

I. Standard License in Senior High, Junior High, and Middle School Education
    A. See Elementary I, A.
    B. Completion of undergraduate program of 124 semester hours as follows:
        1. General education, semester hours 40
            a. See Junior High/Middle School I, B.
        2. Subject matter concentration
            a. See Secondary School, I, B, 2.
        3. Professional education, semester hours 27
            a. See Junior High/Middle School I, B, 3.
        4. Electives (no specific number required)
    C. See Elementary I, C.
    D. See Junior High/Middle School Education I, D.
II. Renewal—see Early Childhood II.
III. Professionalization
    A. See Early Childhood III, A.
    B. See Early Childhood III, B.
    C. Graduate level courses at a regionally accredited institution, semester hours 6
    D. Completion of appropriate course work in the major, minor, or endorsement areas.
IV. Additions—see Early Childhood IV.

Note: Applicants may also qualify for the standard license in this area if they hold a *valid* Indiana license in secondary education and have completed either one semester of junior high/middle school teaching experience prior to July 1, 1989, or six semester hours of course work in junior high/middle school education, including a practicum.

All Grade Education

I.   This license is available only in the following areas: hearing impaired, music, physical education, recreation, school media services, special education, and visual arts.
   A.   See Elementary I, A.
   B.   Completion of undergraduate program of 124 semester hours as follows:
      1.   General education, semester hours 40
         a.   See Junior High/Middle School I, B.
      2.   Subject matter concentration, semester hours 36–52
      3.   Professional education, semester hours 24
         a.   See Junior High/Middle School I, B, 3 (except student teaching must be in the subject area of major).
II. Renewal—see Early Childhood II.
III. Professionalization
   A.   See Early Childhood III, A.
   B.   See Early Childhood III, B.
   C.   Graduate level courses in professional education, semester hours 6
   D.   Graduate level courses in all grade major, semester hours................................... 6

Administration

I.   Elementary Administration and Supervision—Elementary, Middle or Junior High School
   A.   Requirements for Administrative Standard License—Elementary Administration and Supervision.
      1.   Hold Professional License in Early Childhood, Kindergarten–Primary, Elementary, Junior High/Middle School, or All Grade Education.
      2.   Graduate credit from a regionally accredited teacher preparation institution, semester hours 45
         To include elementary administration; elementary supervision; elementary curriculum; elementary guidance; philosophy of education; psychology and evaluation; school-community relations; cultural awareness of minority groups; human relations; school law.
      3.   Recommendation of institution where approved qualifying program was completed.
   B.   Renewal—see Early Childhood II.
   C.   Professionalization
      1.   Five years experience as an administrator and/or supervisor in an accredited elementary, junior high, or middle school subsequent to issuance of Standard License.
      2.   Graduate credit in school administration or cognate area from a regionally accredited institution, semester hours... 60

3. Recommendation for Professional License by institution where professionalization program was completed.

II. Secondary Administration and Supervision—Junior High, Middle, or Secondary Schools
   A. Requirements for Administrative Standard License—Secondary Administration and Supervision.
      1. Hold Professional License in Junior High/Middle School, Secondary School, or All Grade Education.
      2. Same as Elementary Administration and Supervision, I, A, 2, except at Secondary School level.
      3. Recommendation of granting institution.
   B. Renewal—see Early Childhood II.
   C. Professionalization
      1. Five years of experience as an administrator and/or supervisor in accredited junior high, middle, or secondary schools subsequent to issuance of Standard License.
      2 and 3. See Administration I, C, 2 and 3.

Counselor

I. School Services Standard License—Counselor
   A. Requirements
      1. Completion of one of the following professional experiences:
         a. Two years of creditable teaching experience,
            or
         b. Valid out-of-state school counseling license and one year experience as a school counselor,
            or
         c. A one year school counseling internship, under the supervision of an institution of higher education approved for training school counselors.
      2. Master's degree in counseling or a related field from a regionally accredited institution and the completion of 30 semester hours in counseling and guidance at the graduate level.
      3. Knowledge or competencies in the following areas: counseling theory; human growth and development; social and cultural foundations; the helping relationship; group dynamics; lifestyle and career development; appraisal of the individual; research and evaluation; and professional orientation.

II. Coverage
   A. Holder of a School Services License—Counselor is eligible to serve as a counselor at all levels.

III. Renewal
   A. School Services Standard License—Counselor may be renewed for one 5-year period upon completion of 6 semester hours of graduate work in counselor education directed toward professionalization of this license and with recommendation of the institution where renewal credit was earned.

IV. Professionalization

A. School Services Standard License—Counselor may be professionalized when the holder has completed 5 years of experience in accredited schools as a school counselor subsequent to the issuance of the Standard License, with at least half-time in counseling.

B. Completed 18 or more graduate hours in counselor education beyond the hours required for the Standard License, including 4 additional areas from the following: evaluation and accountability; consultation; advanced practicum; statistics; supervision of counseling programs; human potential; program management; and family counseling.

C. Recommendation for the Professional License by the institution where the approved professionalization program was completed.

Iowa

Types of Certificates

I. Provisional Certificate (valid two years; renewable for a second two-year term)
    A. Baccalaureate degree from an approved institution.
    B. Completion of an approved teacher education program.
    C. Completion of an approved human relations component.
    D. Completion of requirements for one of the teaching endorsements.
    E. Meets the recency requirement listed under the One-Year Conditional License (V, A, 3 directly below).

II. Educational Certificate (valid five years; renewable)
    A. See I, A–E.
    B. Two years of successful teaching experience (based on a local evaluation process).

III. Professional Teacher's Certificate (valid five years; renewable)
    A. Holder of or eligible for an educational certificate.
    B. Five years of teaching experience.
    C. Master's degree in an area of one of the teaching endorsements.
    D. Meets the recency requirement listed under the One-Year Conditional License (V, A, 3 directly below).

IV. Professional Administrator's Certificate (valid five years; renewable)
    A. Holder of or eligible for an educational license.
    B. See III, B and D.
    C. Completion of requirements for one of the administrative endorsements.

V. One-Year Conditional Certificate (valid one year; not renewable)
    A. Issued to applicant under the following conditions:
        1. Has not completed all required components in the professional education core.
        2. Has not completed an approved human relations component.
        3. Recency: meets requirements for a valid license but has less than 160 days of teaching during last 5-year period.
        4. Degree not granted until next regular commencement.

Teaching Endorsements

I. Subject area (K–6 and 7–12)
    A. See Provisional Certificate I, A–C.
    B. Professional education core.
        1. Completed course work or evidence of competency in: structure of American education; philosophies of education; professional ethics and legal responsibilities; psychology of teaching; audiovisual/media/computer technology; evaluation techniques; human development; exceptional learner; classroom management; instructional planning; curriculum; methods of

teaching; prestudent field-based experiences; and student teaching in desired subject area and grade level.

    C.   Curriculum content

        1.   Teaching major that must include the requirements for at least one subject endorsement, semester hours 30

  II.   Elementary (1–6)

    A.   See Provisional Certificate I, A–C.

    B.   See Subject area I, B.

    C.   Curriculum content.

        1.   Methods and materials of teaching a variety of elementary subjects.

        2.   Prestudent teaching experience in at least two different grades.

        3.   Specialization in a single discipline or a formal interdisciplinary program of at least 12 semester hours.

  III.   Prekindergarten/kindergarten

    A.   See Provisional Certificate I, A–C.

    B.   See Subject area I, B.

    C.   Curriculum to include courses related to young children.

  IV.   English as a second language (K–12)

    A.   See Provisional Certificate I, A–C.

    B.   See Subject area I, B.

    C.   Completion of 24 semester hours of course work in ESOL.

  V.   Elementary counselor (K–6)

    A.   Master's degree.

    B.   Holder of or eligible for one other teaching endorsement.

    C.   One year of successful teaching experience.

    D.   Completion of 27 semester hours focusing on guidance and counseling on the elementary level, including

        1.   practicum in elementary school counseling.

  VI.   Secondary Counselor (7–12)

    A.   Requirements are identical to those for elementary counselor, except that course work and practicum focus on the secondary level.

  VII.   Reading specialist (K–12)

    A.   Master's degree.

    B.   Holder of or eligible for the educational certificate and a teaching endorsement.

    C.   One year of experience which included the teaching of reading as a significant part.

    D.   Completion of 27 semester hours focusing on reading, including

        1.   practicum on reading.

  VIII.   Elementary school media specialist (1–6)

    A.   See Provisional Certificate I, A–C.

    B.   Completion of 24 semester hours in school media course work, including

        1.   practicum in an elementary school media center.

  IX.   Secondary school media specialist (7–12)

    A.   Requirements are identical to those for elementary school specialist, except that course work and practicum focus on the secondary level.

  X.   School media specialist (K–12)

A. See Provisional Certificate I, A–C.
B. Master's degree.
C. Completion of 30 semester hours in school media course work, including
    1. practicum at both the elementary and secondary levels.

Administrative Endorsements

  I. Elementary principal (PreK–6)
    A. Master's degree.
    B. Completion of at least 27 semester hours of course work in elementary administration, supervision, and curriculum.
    C. Five years of teaching experience, at least 3 of which were on the PreK–6 level.
  II. Secondary principal (7–12)
    A. Requirements are identical to those for elementary principal, except that course work and experience must be on the 7–12 level.
  III. Superintendent (PreK–12)
    A. Master's degree, plus at least 30 semester hours of planned graduate study in administration beyond the master's degree. Overall, at least 45 semester hours of course work must be in school administration and related subjects.
    B. Three years' experience as a building principal or other PreK–12 district-wide education agency administrative experience.

Note: Graduates from institutions in other states who are seeking initial Iowa certification and an administrative endorsement must also meet the requirements for the educational certificate.

Special Education Endorsements

  I. Program requirements for special education teaching endorsements
    A. See Provisional Certificate I, A–C.
    B. Twenty-four semester hours in special education, as well as other specific requirements, are necessary for teaching endorsements in the areas of mental and learning disabilities, hearing and visual impairment, the physically handicapped, and early childhood-special education.
  II. Special education support personnel
    A. Requirements for endorsements in this category vary greatly. Often a master's degree is necessary, and several endorsement areas have alternative routes for authorization. Requirements for school psychologist, school audiologist, speech and language clinician, school social worker, and other support personnel are available from the Board of Examiners.

Reciprocity

Iowa has signed an exchange certification agreement with Missouri, Nebraska, Kansas, South Dakota, Oklahoma, and Arkansas (MINKSOA) which allows individuals certified in one of the member states to be eligible for a two-year exchange certificate in any of the participating states.

Kansas

The State Board is validating a new test to replace the National Teacher Examination. Contact the Certification Office (address in Appendix 1) for the latest information.

Initial Certification

I. Baccalaureate degree and completion of an approved program
   A. Minimum cumulative grade point average of 2.5 on a 4-point scale
II. If applicant does not hold an advanced degree, completion of 8 semester hours of recent college credit or one year of recent, approved or accredited experience is required.
   A. If applicant holds an advanced degree, completion of 6 semester hours of recent college credit or 1 year of recent approved or accredited experience is required.
III. Recommendation from the head of the college, department, or school of education of the teacher education institution
   A. The official submitting the recommendation may certify that the applicant has demonstrated proficiency equivalent to the stated semester hour requirement; the recommendation may be substituted for specific hour requirements or for subject and field requirements.
IV. Passing scores on the precertification examination:
   A. Pre-Professional Skills Test
      1. Reading, passing score 173
      2. Mathematics, passing score 174
      3. Writing, passing score 172
   B. National Teacher Examination, Professional Knowledge, passing score 642
   C. Exemptions from the precertification examination are given in certain situations; write the Certification Section, Kansas State Department of Education (address in Appendix 1) for details.
V. Validity and renewal
   A. The initial certificate is valid for 3 years and is renewable thereafter, when requirements are met, for 5 year terms.
VI. Exchange Certificate
   A. Applicants for an initial Kansas teaching certificate, who hold a valid certificate with one or more full endorsements issued by a state which has been approved by the state board of education for exchange certificates, may be issued a two-year certificate (if the endorsements are based on completion of a state-approved program in the other state).

Teaching Endorsements

I. Requirements
   A. Completion of a state-approved program in the area
   B. Recommendation by a teacher education institution

II. Specific Endorsements
   A. Aerospace education; art; bilingual-multicultural education; business education; computer studies; driver education; early childhood; elementary; English, middle-level English; English as a second language; middle-level foreign language; foreign or classical language; health; home economics; middle-level home economics; mathematics; general mathematics; middle-level mathematics; music; adapted physical education; physical education; general science; middle-level science; biology; chemistry; earth and space science; physical science physics; U.S. history, U.S. government, and world history; economics; anthropology and sociology; geography; comprehensive social studies; middle-level social studies; social studies; speech communication; drama (theater); journalism; psychology; and principles of technology
   B. Write the Certification Section, Kansas State Department of Education for information on endorsements in vocational education.

School Support Personnel Endorsements

I. School Counselor
   A. Successful completion of a state-approved graduate degree school counselor program which includes course work and a supervised practicum at the level at which endorsement is sought
   B. Documentation of 2 years of teaching experience
   C. Recommendation by a teacher education institution
   D. Provisional endorsement (1 year)
      1. See I, A
      2. Completion of 1 year of accredited teaching experience
      3. Recommendation by a teacher education institution
      4. One year supervised field experience in school counseling arranged with the recommending teacher education institution
II. Library Media
   A. Successful completion of a state-approved library media program which includes graduate-level course work
   B. Holds a valid teaching certificate
   C. Recommendation by a teacher education institution

Administrator Endorsements

I. District School Administrator
   A. Graduate degree
   B. Completion of a state-approved administrator program
   C. Three years of experience as a certified educational professional in an approved or accredited school
   D. Recommendation by a teacher education institution
II. Building Administrator (Elementary or Secondary)
   A. Same as I, A–D, except experience must be at the level for which endorsement is sought

Kentucky

General Requirements

I. There shall be a recency of preparation prerequisite for the issuance of certificates. The program of preparation shall have been completed within the 5 year period preceding the date of receipt of the certificate application form, or else the applicant shall have completed 6 semester hours of additional graduate credit within this 5 year period. For applicants who do not meet the recency of preparation prerequisite, and who have not previously held a regular Kentucky teaching certificate, but who otherwise qualify for certification, the certificate shall be issued for a 1 year period ending June 30 of the next calendar year and with the condition that 6 semester hours of graduate credit applicable toward the usual renewal requirements be completed by September 1 of the year of expiration. Thereafter the further extension of the certificate shall be in compliance with the usual renewal requirements.

II. Teaching certificates shall be issued for a duration period of 5 years and with provisions for subsequent 5 year renewals, except that the initial certification for the beginning teacher internship shall be issued for a duration period of 1 year and initial certification for applicants who do not meet the recency of preparation prerequisite shall be issued for a duration period of 1 year. Upon successful completion of the beginning teacher internship as judged by majority vote of the beginning teacher committee, the 1 year certificate shall be extended for the remainder of the 5 year period. The certificate shall be renewed for subsequent 5 year periods upon completion by September 1 of the year of expiration of 3 years of successful teaching experience or upon completion by September 1 of the year of expiration of at least 6 semester hours of graduate credit or the equivalent, except that persons who have not yet completed the planned fifth year program, shall complete at least 15 semester hours of graduate credit applicable to the program for the first renewal and the remainder of the program for the second renewal. Credits for certificate renewal shall be earned after the issuance of the certificate, and any credits earned in excess of the minimum requirements for any renewal period shall accumulate and be carried forward to apply toward subsequent renewals.

III. An applicant having completed 2 or more years of acceptable teaching experience outside of the Commonwealth of Kentucky who otherwise qualifies for certification shall not be required to take the written tests or to participate in the beginning teacher internship program. An applicant who has held a regular Kentucky teaching certificate which has lapsed for failure to meet renewal requirements shall not be required to take the written tests or to participate in the beginning teacher internship program.

IV. Prerequisites for the issuance of a 1 year certificate for the beginning teacher internship shall include

    A. The completion of an approved program of preparation which corresponds to the certificate desired.

B. Passing scores on the PRAXIS II Subject Assessment appropriate for each content area in which certification is requested.

C. Evidence of full-time employment in a Kentucky school as attested by the prospective employer.

V. Upon successful completion of the approved program of preparation and upon completion of the designated tests with acceptable scores, the Education Professional Standards Board shall issue a statement of eligibility for employment which shall serve as evidence of eligibility for the 1 year certificate once a teaching position is secured. The statement of eligibility shall be valid for a 5 year period.

Approved Programs

The Commonwealth of Kentucky follows the "approved program" approach to certification. An individual should follow the program in effect at the college or university with the guidance of the college advisor and meet General Requirements (see above). Applicants interested in certification should write the Division of Certification (address in Appendix 1) for the latest information.

I. Interdisciplinary Early Childhood Education (Birth to Primary)

II. Elementary School (Primary through Grade 5)

III. Middle School (Grades 5 through 9)
A. Preparation includes two teaching fields selected from the following fields: English and communications, mathematics, science, and social studies.
1. Candidates who choose to prepare simultaneously for teaching in the middle school and for teaching exceptional children are required to complete only one middle school teaching field.

IV. Secondary School (Grades 8 through 12)
A. Preparation includes one or more of the following specializations: English, mathematics, social studies, biological science, or physical science.

V. Middle/Secondary School (Grades 5 through 12)
A. Preparation includes one or more of the following specializations: agriculture, business and marketing education, home economics, or industrial technology.

VI. Elementary/Middle/Secondary School (Primary through Grade 12)
A. Preparation includes one or more of the following specializations: art, foreign language (French, German, Latin, Russian, or Spanish), health, physical education, music, or school media librarian.

VII. Exceptional Children (Primary through Grade 12, and for collaborating with teachers to design and deliver programs for pre-primary children)
A. Preparation includes one or more of the following specializations: learning and behavior disorders, moderate and severe disabilities, hearing impaired, visually impaired, or communication disorders.

VIII. Endorsements to Certificates (Primary through Grade 12)
A. Computer science, English as a second language, gifted education, driver education, and reading and writing.

IX. Professional Certificate for Instructional Leadership
A. Certification is offered for the following positions: Supervisor of Instruction, Level

1; Supervisor of Instruction, Level 2; Principal, All Grades, Level 1; Principal, All Grades, Level 2; and School Superintendent.

Principal, All Grades

I. Requirements for Principals, All Grades, Level I
   A. As prerequisites for the Level I program of preparation for the initial Professional Certificate for Instructional Leadership, the candidate shall
      1. Have been admitted to the preparation program on the basis of criteria developed by the teacher education institution.
      2. Have completed 3 years of full-time teaching experience.
      3. Have completed the master's degree, plus 18 semester hours of graduate credit.
      4. Qualify for a Kentucky teaching certificate, although certificates issued or endorsed for speech and communication disorders shall not satisfy this prerequisite.
   B. The certificate shall be issued and renewed in accordance with the testing and internship provisions and related regulations.
   C. The initial Professional Certificate for Instructional Leadership shall be issued for a duration period of 1 year upon successful completion of Level I preparation and the tests prescribed and upon obtaining employment for an internship position as principal or assistant principal. During the period of validity of the one-year certificate the internship program for school principals as outlined shall be completed. Upon successful completion of the internship, the certificate shall be extended for 4 years.
   D. The certificate shall be renewed subsequently for 5 year periods. The first renewal shall require the completion of the 12 semester hour graduate curriculum identified as the Level II program in the curriculum standards. Each 5 year renewal thereafter shall require the completion of 2 years of experience as a principal, or 3 semester hours of additional graduate credit related to the position of school principal, or 42 hours of approved training selected from programs approved for the Kentucky Effective Leadership Training Program.
   E. If a lapse in certification occurs for lack of completion of the Level II preparation, the certificate may be reissued for a 5 year period upon successful completion of the Level II preparation. If a certificate lapses with Level II preparation, but for lack of the renewal requirements, the certificate may be reissued after the completion of an additional 6 semester hours of graduate study appropriate to the program.
   F. Persons applying for the Professional Certificate for Instructional Leadership who satisfy the curriculum requirements and all other prerequisites, and who have completed at least 2 years of successful full-time experience, including at least 140 days per year, as an early elementary school principal, grades K–4, within a 10 year period prior to making application, will be exempt from the internship requirements for school principals, but shall be required to pass the written examinations.
II. Standards for School Principal
   A. Individuals must meet the standards for principals taken from the Standards for School Leaders developed by the Interstate School Leaders Licensure Consortium

(ISLLC). Please contact the Kentucky Division of Certification for additional information.

Guidance Counselor

I. Provisional Certificate Requirements
   A. Hold a Kentucky teaching certificate.
      1. Guidance counseling grades K–8 requires a teaching certificate at the elementary level.
      2. Guidance counseling grades 5–12 requires a teaching certificate valid for grades 5–8, 7–12, or 9–12.
   B. Out-of-state applicants who have completed an approved master's degree preparation-certification program for guidance counseling which does not require classroom teaching certification and teaching experience may satisfy A, 1 and 2 with 3 years of experience as a guidance counselor.
   C. One year of successful, full-time, classroom teaching experience.
   D. Master's degree, including the essentials of the curriculum outlined in areas 1–12 below
      1. History, philosophy, and principles of guidance and personnel services.
      2. Organization and administration of guidance and personnel services.
      3. Appraisal, assessment, and understanding of the individual.
      4. Developmental processes, personality, and behavior change.
      5. Theories and methods of individual counseling.
      6. Career development and vocational planning.
         a. There should be an emphasis on the career-related developmental tasks and on methods and materials in career development appropriate to the school level for which certification is sought (elementary, middle, or secondary grades).
      7. Group processes and procedures.
      8. Legal and ethical issues.
      9. Social and personal issues.
      10. Supervised experiences in guidance and counseling (practicum).
      11. Research and evaluation procedures.
      12. Electives from general and/or professional education.
   E. Valid for 5 years and renewable upon completion of 9 semester hours of graduate credit every 5 years, leading to Standard Guidance Certificate.
II. Standard Certificate Requirements
   A. One year of experience as a full-time guidance counselor.
   B. Graduate program of 60 semester hours which includes
      1. Master's degree.
      2. Advanced instruction in areas 1–12 listed in I, C.
      3. Additional course work designed to increase skills and knowledge related to school counseling.
   C. Valid for 5 years and renewable for 5 year periods upon completion (by September 1 of the year of expiration) of 60 clock hours of appropriate training.

Librarian and School Media Librarians

I. Provisional Certificate for School Media Librarian (K–12)
    A. Validity cycle is the same as for a Provisional Early Childhood, Middle Grades, or Secondary Grades Certificate.
    B. Curriculum
        1. General education component the same as required for Provisional Teaching Certificate.
        2. Professional preparation, semester hours 25
            To include at least 150 clock hours of clinical and field experiences, and a supervised practice in a school media center for 12 weeks.
        3. Specialization component to consist of a major including the following areas, semester hours 30
            School media organization and administration; media classification and processing; literature by content and age level; computer applications; reference and bibliographic services; special users; media design and production.
        4. Semester hour credits in a minor or in two academic subject fields 21
II. Standard Certificate for School Media Librarian
    A. Eligible for provisional certificate for school media librarian.
    B. See I, A above.
    C. Master's degree or a 32 semester hour planned fifth year program to include
        1. Specialization in media library study, semester hours.................................. 12
        2. Research and methodology, semester hours 12

School Psychologist

I. Standard Certificate for School Psychologist
    A. A master's degree consisting of at least 60 semester hours.
    B. One year of supervised internship experience (first year of service).
    C. Professional requirements
        1. Graduate credit, semester hours... 60
            To include psychological foundations (12); education foundations (9); assessment and intervention which includes preparation in referral and assessment of students who experience problems of learning and adjustment, and preparation in planning and implementing direct and indirect interventions including counseling, instructional and behavioral management, and consultant and other prevention approaches (15); professional school psychology which includes the history and foundation of school psychology, legal and ethical issues, professional issues and standards, and roles and functions of the school psychologist (3); research, evaluation, and statistics (9).
    D. Valid for 5 years and may be renewed for subsequent 5 year periods upon completion within each period of at least 3 years of experience as a school psychologist which includes attendance and participation in 72 hours of continuing professional development.

II. Provisional Certificate for School Psychologist
   A. Issued to an applicant who has completed 48 semester hours of the 60 hour program for the Standard Certificate (see I, C, 1). Valid for 1 year.
III. For either certificate, a passing score of 630 is required on the National Teacher Examination specialty exam 40.

Teacher for Gifted Education

I. Standards for a certificate endorsement
   A. A classroom teaching certificate.
   B. One year of teaching experience.
   C. The completion of an approved graduate level curriculum
      1. At least 9 semester hours of credit giving emphasis to the following content
         a. Nature and needs of gifted education.
         b. Assessment and/or counseling of the gifted.
         c. Curriculum development for the gifted.
         d. Strategies and materials for teaching the gifted.
         e. Creative studies.
      2. At least 3 semester hours of credit in a supervised practicum for gifted education; however, with two years experience as a teacher for gifted, the practicum requirement may be waived.

Louisiana

Teachers seeking initial employment in the Louisiana public school system must complete, in addition to the requirements below, the Louisiana Teacher Assessment Program to be eligible for a Type A or Type B Certificate.

Standard Certificates

I. Type C
   A. Baccalaureate degree, including an approved teacher education program and student teaching.
   B. Credits distributed among general, professional, and specialized academic education, as provided.
   C. Appropriate NTE scores for initial certification.
   D. Valid for three years; renewable.

II. Type B
   A. Baccalaureate or higher degree, including completion of an approved teacher education program.
   B. See I, B, above.
   C. Three years of successful teaching experience in certified field.
   D. Successful completion of the State Teacher Assessment Program.
   E. Valid for life for continuous service.

III. Type A
   A. Baccalaureate degree including completion of an approved teacher education program.
   B. See I, B, above.
   C. Master's or higher degree from an approved institution.
   D. Five years of successful teaching experience in certified field.
   E. Successful completion of the State Teacher Assessment Program.
   F. Valid for life for continuous service.

Early Childhood (N–K)

I. General education, semester hours 46
   A. To include: English (12); social studies (12); science (12); mathematics (6); health and physical education (4).

II. Professional education, semester hours 27
   A. To include history of education, introduction to education, foundations of education, and/or philosophy of education (3); educational psychology and/or principles of teaching and learning (3); student teaching or practicum (9); professional courses for teaching children under age six (12).

III. Specialized academic education, semester hours 39
   A. To include 21 additional semester hours in the following: art; children's literature; safety and first aid; Louisiana history and/or Louisiana geography; music; speech; teaching of reading (9); nutrition; methods and materials and/or creative activities for young children.
   B. Home economics, semester hours 18
IV. Other routes to authorization or certification for early childhood teaching
   A. Authorization to teach at the nursery school level may be added to the elementary school certificate upon completion of specialized preschool work (9 semester hours), including a practicum (3 semester hours) at the preschool level.
   B. Authorization to teach kindergarten may be added to the elementary school certificate upon completion of specialized kindergarten work (9 semester hours), including a practicum at the kindergarten level, as well as student-teaching in elementary grades.
   C. Authorization to teach nursery school (not kindergarten) may be added to the home economics certificate upon completion of work in child development (9 semester hours), including observation and participation in the nursery school.
   D. An early childhood education certificate may be granted upon completion of a master's degree in early childhood education from an institution with a program in the area approved by the State Board of Elementary and Secondary Education.

Elementary School

I. General education, semester hours, to include 46
   A. English (including 3 semester hours in grammar, 3 semester hours in composition), total semester hours 12
   B. Social studies, semester hours 12
   C. Science (including 3 semester hours in biological science and 3 semester hours in physical science), total semester hours 12
   D. Mathematics, semester hours 6
   E. Health and physical education, semester hours 4
II. Professional education, semester hours, to include 30
   A. History of education, introduction to education, foundations of education, and/or philosophy of education, semester hours 3
   B. Educational psychology and/or principles of teaching, semester hours 3
   C. Introduction to the study of exceptional children, semester hours 3
   D. Professional teacher education at appropriate level: child psychology (3), teaching of reading (6), reading practicum (3), semester hours 12
   E. Student teaching elementary level, semester hours 9
III. Specialized academic education
   A. Children's literature, semester hours 3
   B. Speech, semester hours 3
   C. Nutrition education, semester hours 2
   D. Louisiana history and/or Louisiana geography, semester hours 3
   E. Art for elementary school, semester hours 3

    F.   Music for elementary school, semester hours 3

    G.   Health and physical education, semester hours 4

Secondary School

I.   General education, semester hours 46

    A. See Elementary School, I, A–E, above.

II. Professional education, semester hours 24

    A. To include history of, introduction to, foundations of, and/or philosophy of education (3); educational psychology and/or principles of teaching (3); appropriate professional education courses (3); adolescent psychology (3); teaching of reading (3); student teaching in subject field (9).

III. Additional specialized academic education, in semester hours: agriculture (50); business and office education (36); computer literacy (9); computer science (18); dance (30); distributive education (29), to include 24 semester hours in technical courses (marketing, merchandising, and management) and 5 semester hours in professional distributive education, and a minimum of 2,000 hours of work experience; English (30), to include 27 in English and 3 in teaching of reading; foreign language (36); home economics (42); industrial arts (48); journalism (15); mathematics (20), to include 1 semester of calculus and 1 of college geometry; general science (32), including 8 each in biology, chemistry, earth science, and physics; biology (20), to include botany, zoology, and microbiology; chemistry (20), to include general, organic, and quantitative analysis or physical chemistry; earth science (20), to include physical and historical geology; physics (20); environmental science (30); social studies (33), to include U.S. and world history, U.S. government, geography, economics, sociology; speech (30); art (36); health (22); physical education (24); health and physical education (37); vocal music (62); instrumental music (62).

Teachers of Exceptional Children

I.   Mild/Moderate Impairment

    A. General education, semester hours 46

        To include English (12); social studies (12); science (12); mathematics (6); health and physical education (4).

    B. Professional education, semester hours 27

        To include history of education (3); educational psychology and/or principles of teaching (3); student teaching in a mild/moderate classroom.

        1. For mild/moderate, elementary: 9 semester hours of professional teacher education courses, including child psychology (3), teaching of reading (9), a practicum (3).

        2. For mild/moderate, secondary: 9 semester hours of professional teacher education courses, including adolescent psychology (3) and teaching of reading (6).

    C. Specialized academic education: Elementary and secondary

        1. Mild/moderate, semester hours 33

           a. General knowledge (3); methods and materials (9); management (6);

practicum in assessment (3); mainstreaming/inclusive education practicum (3); and professional electives (9).

II.   Severe/Profound Impairment
   A.   General education, semester hours.. 46
      1.   See I, A, above.
   B.   Professional education, semester hours.. 30
      To include history of education (3); educational psychology and/or principles of teaching (3); student teaching in severe/profound classroom (9); professional teacher education courses (15).
   C.   Specialized academic education, semester hours.. 33
      To include general knowledge (6); instructional strategies (9); learning principles and classroom/behavior management (3); assessment and evaluation (6); methods of working with paraprofessionals (3); parent, family and community involvement (3); and communication strategies (3).
III.   Please contact the Louisiana Department of Education for information on certificates in the following areas:
   A.   Early interventionist, visually impaired, hearing impaired, and in speech, language, and hearing disorders.

Administrators, Supervisors, and Special Service Personnel

I.   Elementary School Principal
   A.   Valid Type A Louisiana Teaching Certificate for elementary school.
   B.   Master's degree from an accredited institution.
   C.   Five or more years of elementary classroom teaching experience.
   D.   Graduate credit, semester hours 30
      To include educational administration (9); professional education (21)—18 semester hours of educational research, history or philosophy of education, elementary school curriculum, school law, school finance, school personnel administration; 3 semester hours of electives.
   E.   Passing score of 620 on the National Teacher Examination Educational Administration area test.
II.   Secondary School Principal
   A.   Valid Type A Louisiana Teaching Certificate for secondary school.
   B.   Master's degree from an accredited institution.
   C.   Five or more years of secondary classroom teaching experience.
   D.   Same as I, D, above, but at secondary level.
   E.   Same as I, E, above.
III.   Ancillary Elementary School Principal and Ancillary Secondary School Principal
   A.   A provisional elementary school principal ancillary certificate or a provisional secondary school principal certificate may be issued to an applicant who has met the requirements of I, B–E directly above and who is employed as an elementary (or a secondary) school principal in a Louisiana school system.
   B.   Upon employment as a principal, an individual with provisional certification must enroll in the two-year Principal Internship Program.

    C.   A secondary school principal ancillary certificate will be issued upon satisfactory completion of the two-year Principal Internship Program.

  IV. Parish or City School Supervisor of Instruction.

    A.   Valid Type A Louisiana Teaching Certificate.

    B.   Master's degree from an accredited institution.

    C.   Graduate courses, semester hours 33

        To include educational administration and supervision (15); professional education (15); practicum in instructional supervision or internship in instructional supervision (3).

   V. Parish or City School Superintendent

    A.   Valid Type A Louisiana Teaching Certificate.

    B.   Master's degree from an accredited institution.

    C.   Five years of successful experience as superintendent, assistant superintendent, supervisor of instruction, or principal in a state-approved system.

    D.   Graduate credit, semester hours 48

        To include educational administration and supervision of instruction (30); professional education (12); electives from cognate fields (6).

  VI. Assistant Superintendents are required to meet the same standards as superintendents.

Guidance Counselor*

   I. Elementary School Counselor (Provisional)

    A.   Valid Louisiana Elementary Teaching Certificate.

    B.   Three years of successful experience at elementary level.

    C.   Master's degree in Guidance and Counseling from an accredited institution, or a master's degree with equivalent hours and courses required for a Master's degree in Guidance and Counseling.

    D.   Professional courses, semester hours 21

        To include one course in each of the following basic areas: principles and administration of elementary school guidance; analysis of the elementary school pupil; counseling theory and practice; orientation to the world of work; group processes in the elementary school; elementary guidance practicum; child growth and development.

    E.   Requests for certification must be accompanied by recommendation from the institution where above requirements were completed.

   II. Permanent endorsement may be added upon completion of 9 semester hours of additional work from the list for professional counselor, below:

    A.   Human growth and development; social and cultural foundations; the helping relationship; groups (group theory, types, methods and practices); career development; individual appraisal; research and evaluation; supervised experiences; specialized studies.

  III. Secondary School Counselor (Provisional)

---

* Effective September 1, 2001, Louisiana will offer a Provisional Counselor in the School Setting endorsement that will be valid for grades K–12.

A.   Valid Louisiana Secondary Teaching Certificate.

B.   Three years of successful experience at secondary level, or two years at secondary level and one year of accumulated occupational experience.

C.   Master's degree in Guidance and Counseling from an accredited institution, or a master's degree with equivalent hours and courses required for a master's degree in Guidance and Counseling.

D.   Professional courses, semester hours 21
To include one course in each of the following basic areas: principles and administration of guidance; occupational and educational information; individual analysis; vocational guidance; counseling theory and practice; guidance practicum, group processes.

E.   See Elementary Counselor, I, E.

IV.   Please contact the Louisiana Department of Education for information on certification as Ancillary Counselor K–12. (Address in Appendix 1)

School Librarian

I.   Requirements

A.   Elementary or secondary school teaching certificate.

B.   Library science courses, semester hours 21
To include elementary and/or secondary school library materials (9); organization, administration and interpretation of elementary and/or secondary school library services (6); elementary and/or secondary school library practice (3); audiovisual education (3).

Regulations for Out-of-State Application for Classroom Teacher

I.   Requirements for Type C Certificate

A.   Bachelor's degree from an accredited institution, completion of an approved teacher education program and a regular certificate from the state where the applicant completed the program;
or
Bachelor's degree from an accredited institution, a regular certificate from another state, and three years of teaching in certified field.

B.   If applicant has not taught within five years immediately preceding date of application, he must complete 6 hours of resident credit, or extension credit, in areas relative to his field.

C.   Appropriate NTE scores.

D.   These certificates are governed by laws and regulations applying to certification in Louisiana.

E.   An applicant who lacks the appropriate NTE scores but meets all other requirements may be issued a one-year nonrenewable certificate.

Maine

Teacher and Educational Specialist Certificates

I. Conditional Certificate (valid for 1 year; renewable only with approval)
   A. Maine offers this certificate to applicants who have not completed all professional requirements for a particular position.
   B. Applicants are expected to complete all requirements during the term of this certificate.

II. Provisional Certificate (valid for 2 years; renewable)
   A. Bachelor's degree from an approved institution (except for vocational education teachers and school nurses).
   B. Completion of an approved preparation program for educational personnel with the formal recommendation of the institution.
   C. Qualifying scores on the National Teacher Examination (NTE) Core Battery.
   D. Fulfillment of requirements for one or more endorsements (for teachers) or for one or more of the educational specialist certificates.

III. Professional Certificate (valid for 5 years; renewable)
   A. Holder of a provisional certificate.
   B. See II, D.
   C. Recommendation for a professional certificate from the support system following the successful completion of a Teacher Action Plan, including 6 classroom observations.

IV. Master Certificate (valid for 5 years; renewable)
   A. Holder of a professional certificate.
   B. Demonstration of exemplary professional skills.
   C. Knowledge of current theories of effective instruction.
   D. Has made outstanding contributions to the teaching profession in curriculum design; staff development; clinical supervision of student teachers or peer observation of teachers; or educational leadership.
   E. Recommendation for a master certificate from the support system following completion of a Teacher or Educational Specialist Action Plan, including 6 classroom observations.

Endorsements

I. Elementary Teacher (K–8)
   A. Bachelor's degree from an accredited institution in an approved program for the education of elementary teachers which is comprised of at least 60 semester hours in liberal arts which includes at least 6 semester hours in each of the four content areas (math, English, science, social sciences), together with the formal recommendation of the preparing institution;
      or

Bachelor's degree from an accredited institution with 60 semester hours in liberal arts which includes at least 6 semester hours in each of the four content areas noted above.

B. Professional education courses, semester hours.. 33
   1. Knowledge of the learner and the learning process.
   2. Teaching exceptional children in the regular classroom.
   3. Effective instruction through content area methods.
      a. At least 12 semester hours to include all of the following: mathematics, reading, science/health, and social studies.
      b. At least 3 semester hours from one of the following: language arts, process writing, children's literature, and whole language.
   4. Curriculum design and methods of program evaluation.
   5. Computer literacy and computer application in the classroom.
   6. Early and on-going experience or practicum.
   7. One academic semester or 15 weeks of full-time student teaching experience.

C. Renewal.
   1. Completion of 6 hours of approved study, preferably academic study in the endorsement area.

II. Secondary Level (7–12): Endorsements for English/language arts, mathematics, life science, physical science, and social studies

A. Bachelor's degree from an accredited institution in an approved program for teachers in the relevant subject area which includes a major in that subject area, together with the formal recommendation of the preparing institution;
or
Bachelor's degree from an accredited institution with a concentration in the liberal arts, plus
   1. At least 36 semester hours of credit in the relevant subject area for English/language arts, mathematics, social studies (with specific course concentrations in some areas), and science (with at least 18 semester hours of credit in either life science or physical science, as well as specific course concentrations in some areas).

B. Professional education courses, semester hours.. 24
   1. Knowledge of the learner.
   2. Knowledge of the learning process.
   3. Teaching exceptional children in the regular classroom.
   4. Content area methods.
   5. Curriculum design and program evaluation.
   6. Early and on-going experience or practicum.
   7. One academic semester or 15 weeks of full-time student teaching experience.

C. Renewal.
   1. See Elementary Teacher I, C, 1.

Administration Certificates

I. Superintendent Certificate (valid for 5 years; renewable)
A. Bachelor's degree and master's degree (at a minimum) from an accredited institution.

It is recommended, but not required, that the master's degree be in educational administration.

    B. Evidence of 3 years of satisfactory teaching experience or 3 years of equivalent teaching experience in an instructional setting.

    C. Evidence of 3 years of previous administrative experience in schools or equivalent experience as an administrator in an institutional setting.

  *D. Evidence of a basic level of knowledge appropriate to the certificate demonstrated by course work in the following areas:
community relations; school finance; supervision and evaluation of personnel; civil rights and education laws; organizational theory and planning; educational leadership; educational philosophy and theory; effective instruction; curriculum development; staff development; the exceptional student; cultural differences; discriminatory and nondiscriminatory hiring practices; and knowledge of the learner and the learning process.

    E. Completion of an approved internship or practicum in a school setting
1. Graduate level, state-approved administrator internship or practicum program of at least 15 weeks;

     or

     One full year of employment as an assistant supervisor or a superintendent;

     or

     Mentorship program lasting one academic year in which the mentor is a school superintendent.

II. Assistant Superintendent Certificate (valid for 5 years)
    A. See Superintendent Certificate, I, A–D, except that only one year of previous administrative experience (or an approved one-year administrative internship) is required.

III. Principal Certificate (valid for 5 years)
    A. See Superintendent Certificate, I, A, B, D, and E, except that internship options are on principal level.

IV. Assistant Principal Certificate (valid for 5 years)
    A. Bachelor's degree from an accredited institution.

    B. Evidence of 3 years of satisfactory public school teaching experience or 3 years of equivalent teaching experience.

    C. Evidence of a basic level of knowledge appropriate to the certificate demonstrated by course work in the following areas: civil rights and Maine school laws; supervision and evaluation of personnel; and organizational theory and planning.

* Past experience—such as performance upon examinations or completion of specialized programs approved for this purpose—may be accepted, upon documentation, in lieu of one or more of these course requirements.

School Guidance Counselor (K–12)

I. Requirements
    A. Master's degree or doctorate from an accredited institution and an approved program

to prepare school guidance counselors, together with the formal recommendation of the preparing institution.

B. Graduate credit, semester hours 33
   1. To include: profession of school guidance; educational philosophy and school operations; consultation skills; individual and group counseling skills; human development and behavior; career development; assessment and testing; research skills related to guidance; and a K–12 internship under the supervision of a certified guidance counselor or equivalent.
C. Completion of an approved graduate-level, K–12 internship of one academic year which relates to the duties of a school guidance counselor in a school setting.
D. Two full years of work experience.
E. Renewal.
   1. Completion of 6 hours of approved study, preferably academic study in the certificate area.

Library-Media Specialist (K–12)

I. Academic Requirements
    A. Holder of a Maine provisional or professional level certificate with a subject area endorsement.
    B. Completion of an approved graduate program for the preparation of school library-media specialists;
       or
    C. Graduate credit, semester hours 36
       1. To include: teaching of research techniques; administration of unified library-media programs; evaluation, selection, and organization of library-media materials; prescription and provision of materials and services to classroom teachers; curriculum design and development; technology applications; cataloging and classification; children's and adolescent's literature; and teaching exceptional children.
II. Professional Requirements
    A. Completion of 24 semester hours in the following areas:
       1. Knowledge of the learner; knowledge of the learning process; teaching exceptional students in the regular classroom; content area methods; curriculum design and methods of program evaluation; and a practicum.
III. Renewal
    A. See School Guidance Counselor, I, E, 1.

Maryland

Types of Certificates

I. Professional Eligibility Certificate and Standard Professional Certificate I
   A. Definitions
      1. The Professional Eligibility Certificate (valid for 5 years; renewable) is the initial certificate issued to an applicant who meets all certification requirements but is not employed.
      2. The Standard Professional Certificate I (valid for 3 years and renewable once) is issued to an applicant who meets all certification requirements and is employed by a Maryland local school system or an accredited nonpublic school.
   B. Requirements
      1. Receives a bachelor's degree or a higher degree from an institution of higher education ("higher degree," here and below, refers to a degree, such as a master's or doctorate, following the bachelor's degree)
         and
      2. Completes a Maryland-approved, NCATE-approved, or Interstate-approved program
         or
      3. Completes a state-approved program from a regionally accredited institution
         or
      4. Completes a Maryland Resident Teacher program (available through a participating local school district)
         or
      5. Completes specific course requirements (determined by content mastery) outlined in Maryland regulations
         or
      6. Meets the Interstate Contract criteria for experienced professionals
         a. Holds a valid certificate in the area to be recognized for reciprocity from a participating state and has taught in the subject area a total of 3 years (27 months) within the past 7 years in any member state
      7. An applicant qualifying under any of options 1–5 must have completed at least 6 semester hours of credit within the last 5 years.
      8. An applicant must take the following tests in the National Teachers' Examinations and obtain qualifying scores
         a. Communication Skills (score: 648), General Knowledge (645), Professional Knowledge (648), and the appropriate Specialty Area Test (varies by area)
         b. An applicant presenting an out-of-state professional teaching certificate with at least 2 years (18 months) of satisfactory full-time teaching experience in the certification area at the appropriate level is exempt from the testing requirement.

   c. An applicant presenting a current out-of-state professional teaching certificate and verification that a qualifying score on a comparable valid state certification test was submitted to receive the certificate is exempt from the testing requirement.

II. Standard Professional Certificate II (valid 7 years; not renewable)
   A. Completes the Standard Professional Certificate I
   B. Verifies 3 years of satisfactory professional experience, 2 consecutive
   C. 6 semester hours of acceptable credit
   D. Submits a professional development plan for the Advanced Professional Certificate

III. Advanced Professional Certificate (valid 5 years; renewable)
   A. Verifies 4 years of full-time professional school-related experience (2 years must be consecutive) within the last 7 years
   B. Has master's degree
       or
   C. Completes 36 semester hours of post-baccalaureate course work (including 21 hours of graduate credit, 6 hours of which must be related to the professional's discipline)

IV. Provisional Certificate (valid 1 year; may be reissued)
   A. Issued at the request of the local superintendent of schools to an employed individual who has a bachelor's or higher degree from an accredited institution but fails to meet requirements for the Standard Professional certificate.
       1. There is a limit to the number of provisional certificates an educator may hold.

V. Resident Teacher Certificate (valid 1 year)
   A. Issued to teacher candidates selected by a local school system to participate in a specialized program leading to professional certification

Early Childhood Education (Nursery-Grade 3)
(Requirements for Certification by Content Mastery)

I. Requirements
   A. General Education
       1. Bachelor's or higher degree from an IHE with a major in interdisciplinary studies or a major in an academic field taught in early childhood education, including course work (semester hours) in mathematics (12), science (12), social studies (9), and English (9)
           or
       2. Bachelor's or higher degree from an IHE and no less than 48 semester hours of content course work, including mathematics (12), science (12), social studies (9), and English (9)
   B. Professional Education
       1. Twenty-seven semester hours of course work, including a course in each of the following at the appropriate age or grade level of the certificate: child or adolescent development; human learning; teaching methodology; inclusion of special needs student populations; assessment of students; and 12 semester hours of specific course work in reading instruction
       2. Teaching Experience

      a. Supervised experience in a public or accredited nonpublic school setting at the nursery or kindergarten and primary age/grade level
        or
      b. Two years of successful full-time teaching experience in a public or accredited nonpublic school setting at the nursery or kindergarten and primary age/grade level

C. At least 50% of the course work in I, A and B, must be taken at the same institution or consortium of institutions, and each course submitted to fulfill a credit requirement must be completed with a grade of C or better.

Elementary Education (Grade 1-6) and Middle School
(Requirements for Certification by Content Mastery)

I. Requirements

  A. Identical to Early Childhood I, A–C, except professional education courses should be at the elementary and middle school level

  B. Teaching Experience

      a. Supervised experience in a public or accredited nonpublic school setting at the appropriate age or grade level

      b. One year of successful full-time teaching experience in a public or accredited nonpublic school setting at the appropriate age or grade level.

Secondary Education (Grade 7–12)
(Requirements for Certification by Content Mastery)

I. Certification Areas

  A. Agriculture/agribusiness; art (N–12); biology; business education; chemistry; computer science; earth/space science; English; foreign language (classical); foreign language (modern); geography; health education; history; home economics; industrial arts/technology; mathematics; music (N–12); physical education (N–12); physical science; physics; speech communication; and theater

II. Requirements

  A. General Education

    1. Bachelor's or higher degree from an IHE with a major in a certification area
      or
    2. Bachelor's or higher degree from an IHE and no less than 36 semester hours of content course work in one of the certification areas

  B. Professional Education

    1. Twenty-one semester hours of course work, including a course in each of the following at the appropriate age or grade level of the certificate: adolescent development; human learning; teaching methodology; inclusion of special needs student populations; assessment of students; and six semester hours of specific course work in reading instruction.

    2. Teaching Experience

      a. Supervised experience in a public or accredited nonpublic school setting at

the appropriate age or grade level and in the subject area for which the applicant is seeking certification
or

b. One year of successful full-time teaching experience in a public or accredited nonpublic school setting at the appropriate age or grade level and in the certification subject area

C. See Early Childhood I, C

Administration

I. Administrator I (supervisor)
  A. Master's degree from an accredited institution
  B. Twenty-seven months of satisfactory teaching performance or satisfactory performance as a specialist
  C. Completion of one of the following:
    1. A Maryland State Department of Education–approved program in administration and supervision;
      or
    2. An approved program in school administration having an on-site review as listed in the interstate contract approved programs;
      or
    3. An approved administration program using state approved standards or programs in school administration approved by other states for certification on the official list kept by the Assistant State Superintendent of Certification and Accreditation;
      or
    4. Eighteen semester hours of graduate course work (twelve of which must be taken at the same institution) taken at an accredited institution in administration and supervision to include school administration; clinical and/or instructional supervision; curriculum design; group dynamics; school law; and verification of a practicum/internship

II. Administrator II (school principal)
  A. Completion of requirements for Administrator I certification
  B. Qualifying score on the School Leaders Licensure Assessment

III. Superintendents
  A. Eligibility for a professional certificate in early childhood education, elementary education, or secondary education
  B. Master's degree from an accredited institution
  C. Three years of successful teaching experience and two years of administrative and/or supervisory experience
  D. Successful completion of a two-year program with graduate courses in administration and supervision in an approved institution. Must have a minimum of 60 semester hours of graduate work

Guidance Counselor

I. Requirements (Option 1)
   A. Master's degree in school guidance and counseling
   B. National Board of Certified Counselors (NBCC) certificate
   C. Two years of satisfactory performance as a teacher or school counselor in a school setting

II. Requirements (Option 2)
   A. Master's degree from a program in school guidance and counseling approved on-site using state-approved standards
   B. Two years of satisfactory performance as a teacher or counselor;
     or
     Supervised practicum of 500 clock hours in school guidance and counseling

III. Requirements (Option 3)
   A. Master's degree in school guidance and counseling from a program approved by the Council for Accreditation of Counseling and Related Educational Programs (CACREP)

IV. Requirements (Option 4)
   A. Master's degree in school guidance and counseling from an approved program under the Interstate Contract agreement for support services
   B. Two years of satisfactory performance as a teacher or school counselor

Educational Media (Audio-Visual/Library)

I. Education and Experiences for Associate (Level I)
   A. Bachelor's degree and, as part of or in addition to the degree, 18 semester hours in specific basic media education, including
     1. Introductory knowledge of educational systems
     2. Introductory knowledge of media and information systems
   B. Practicum, or 2 years of successful teaching, or 2 years of successful media-related experience

II. Education and Experience for Educational Media Generalist (Level II)
   A. Master's degree in media education or 36 semester hours of equivalent graduate credit (of which 15 must be completed at one institution), including
     1. Knowledge of educational systems
     2. Knowledge of media and information systems
   B. See I, B, above.

III. Education and Experience for Educational Media Specialist (Level II)
   A. See II, A, 1, above.
   B. The specialist program must be designed to develop full professional competency in a special or media-related field.
   C. See I, B, above.

IV. Education and Experience for Educational Media Administrator (Level III)
   A. Master's degree in a media program from an accredited institution
   B. An additional 15 semester hours of graduate credit or equivalent

       1.   Must include 6 semester hours in administration and supervision, with remaining credits chosen from management, planning, research, human relations

C.   Three years of successful school media program experience. Upon recommendation, 2 years of related successful experience may be substituted for 2 years of school media experience.

D.   Eligibility for a professional certificate as Educational Media Generalist (Level II)

Massachusetts

Each stage of certification and each certificate in Massachusetts have specific requirements and expectations in the area in which educators must demonstrate competency. For provisional certification with advanced standing there are seven Common Teaching Competencies and five Common School Administrator Competencies from which the competencies for specific certificates are drawn. The competencies for standard certification are essentially the same but the requirements are more stringent and the expected skill levels higher. Please write the Department of Education (address in Appendix 1) for details.

Common Teacher Competencies

I.   Subject Matter Knowledge
II. Communication Skills
III. Instructional Practices
IV. Evaluation
V.   Problem Solving
VI. Equity
VII. Professionalism

Teaching Roles

I.   Early Childhood (PreK–3)
II. Elementary (1–6)
III. Middle School (5–9)
IV. Teaching Fields (5–9, 9–12)
  A. English, social studies, history, mathematics, general science, physics, chemistry, biology, and earth science
V.   Teaching Fields (PreK–9, 5–12)
  A. Foreign language, English as a second language, Latin and classical humanities, health education, physical education, technology education, music, visual arts, and students with special needs
VI. Teaching Fields (All Levels)
  A. Reading, transitional bilingual education, home economics, performing arts, students with intensive special needs, students with vision impairments, deaf and hard-of-hearing students, and students with speech, language, and hearing disorders
VII. Other Areas
  A. Library media specialist (all levels), instructional technology specialist (all levels), school adjustment counselor (all levels), school guidance counselor (PreK–9, 5–12), school psychologist (all levels), and school nurse (all levels)

Stages of Certification for Teaching Roles

I. Provisional Certificate (valid for five years; not renewable)
  A. Bachelor's degree from an accredited college or university with a major in the arts or sciences or an interdisciplinary major appropriate to the instructional field
  B. Qualifying Score on the Two-Part Certificate Examination which covers communication and literacy skills and subject matter knowledge appropriate to the certificate sought
  C. Evidence of sound moral character
  D. Meets Competency 1 Subject matter knowledge for the field and level
II. Provisional Certificate with Advanced Standing (valid for five years; not renewable)
  A. Meets the requirements for provisional certification
  B. Successful completion of course work or other experience addressing the field of knowledge competencies in Competency I for the certificate sought, semester hours... 24
  C. Successful completion of course work, including pre-practicum field experience, or other experiences directly related to the Common Teaching Competencies II–VII, semester hours.. 18
    1. The pre-practicum must be a minimum of 75 clock hours of monitored field-based training in a school setting.
  D. Successful completion of a practicum of at least 150 hours at the level and area of the certificate and directly related to the Common Teaching Competencies
  E. Any combination of the Provisional Certificate and the Provisional with Advanced Standing Certificate is valid only for a total of five years.
III. Standard Certificate (valid for five years; renewable)
  A. Holds a Provisional Certificate with Advanced Standing (Advanced Provisional Certificate)
  B. Completion of an approved master's degree program or its equivalent, including clinical experience and a research project (unless otherwise specified) at the post-baccalaureate level and directly related to the Common Teaching Competencies is required for the Standard Certificate.
    1. The clinical experience option must be at least 400 clock hours or one full semester as defined by the field site.

Common School Administrator Competencies

I. Specific Field of Knowledge
II. Educational Leadership
III. School Management
IV. Professional Development
V. Equity

Administrator Roles

I. School principal/assistant principal (PreK–6, 5–9, 9–12), superintendent/assistant (all levels), supervisor/director (all levels), administrator of special education (all levels), and school business administrator (all levels)

Stages of Certification for Administrative Roles

I.   Provisional Certificate with Advanced Standing (valid for five years; not renewable)
  A. Successful completion of a master's degree or equivalent district or other program
  B. Holds at least a Provisional Certificate with Advanced Standing in some other role
  C. Three years of employment in a role in which the candidate holds a certificate in a school-based or an alternative instructional setting
  D. Successful completion of course work at the graduate level, including pre-practicum field experiences, or other equivalent experiences directly related to Competency I and the Common Administrator Competencies II–V, semester hours.................... 18
  E. Successful completion of a half-practicum or an internship or equivalent experience, demonstrating ability to perform in the area of the certificate, Competency I, and the Common Administrator Competencies II-V

II. Standard Certificate
  A. Successful completion of a clinical experience (except for superintendent/assistant superintendent, for which two years of employment in that role are required)

Routes to Certification

I.   Programs at Institutions of Higher Education
  A. Holding a bachelor's degree in the arts and sciences from an accredited college or university but not having completed an educator preparation program, a candidate is eligible for a Provisional Certificate.
  B. Having completed a state-approved educator program in a Massachusetts college or university, candidates are eligible for an Advanced Provisional Certificate.

II. District-Based Programs
  A. Holding a Provisional Certificate, candidates may prepare for an Advanced Provisional Certificate by participating in an educator preparation program offered by a specific school district.
  B. Holding an Advanced Provisional Certificate, candidates may prepare for a Standard Certificate by participating in an educator preparation program offered by a specific school district.

III. Certification Review Panel
  A. An alternative route to Advanced Provisional Certification for candidates with substantial experience and formal education relevant to the certificate sought, but who do not meet all of the specific certification requirements.

IV. Individual Programs
  A. Candidates who have not completed an approved institutional program or a district-based program, but believe they can prove they have acquired the competencies listed under the certificate sought, can present their case to the Department of Education and may qualify for certification.

V.   Interstate Agreement Program
  A. Candidates who successfully have completed an approved program at a college or university in a state with which Massachusetts has signed the Interstate Agreement Program may qualify for Advanced Provisional Certification.
  B. Candidates who are fully certified in states with which Massachusetts has signed the

Agreement and who have had three years of experience within the past seven years may qualify for Advanced Provisional Certification.

VI. Regional Credential

    A. Candidates who hold a regional educator certificate from New York State or one of the New England states with which Massachusetts has signed a contract, may qualify for Advanced Provisional Certification.

Michigan

Elementary School

I. Authorization. Elementary certificates issued since September 1, 1988 are valid for all subjects in grades K–5 and are valid in areas of certification (subject area majors and minors) in grades 6–8. Teachers assigned to self-contained classrooms may also teach all subjects in grades 6–8.

II. State Elementary Provisional Certificate (valid 6 years)
   A. Bachelor's degree and recommendation from an approved teacher training institution
   B. Academic requirements
      1. Three minors of 20 semester hours each, two of which shall be in substantive fields which may include a group minor of 24 semester hours and one of which may be a combination of methods and content appropriate to elementary education; *or* major of 30 semester hours (or group major of 36 semester hours) and one minor of 20 semester hours in other fields relevant to elementary education
   C. Teaching of reading, semester hours 6
   D. Professional requirements, semester hours in education...................................... 20
      To include courses focusing on:
      1. Developmental needs of preadolescents and early adolescents, including the needs of the exceptional child
      2. Structure, function, and purposes of educational institutions in our society
      3. Methods and materials of elementary and middle level instruction
      4. Directed teaching at the elementary level (at least 6 of the 20 semester hours)

III. State Elementary Professional Education Certificate
   A. Holds a state provisional certificate
   B. Three years of successful teaching following the issuance of the state provisional certificate
   C. Completion of a planned program of 18 semester hours of appropriate credit, subsequent to issuance of the provisional certificate (not required for those holding a master's or higher degree)
   D. Completion of six semester hours of teaching reading (required even for those holding a master's or higher degree)

Secondary School

I. Authorization. Secondary certificates issued after September 1, 1988, are valid in areas of certification (subject area majors and minors) in grades 7–12.

II. State Secondary Provisional Certificate (valid 6 years)
   A. Bachelor's degree and recommendation from an approved teacher training institution
   B. Academic requirements

      1.   Major subject, semester hours 30
          (or a group major of 36 semester hours)
      2.   Minor subject, semester hours 20
          (or a group minor of 24 semester hours)
  C. Teaching of reading, semester hours 3
  D. Professional requirements—Same as Elementary, II, D, 1–4, except courses and teaching should focus on middle and secondary levels
III. State Secondary Professional Certificates
  A. Same as Elementary, III, A–D, except provisional certificate is at secondary level and only 3 semester hours of teaching reading are required

Endorsements

I. Holders of certificates may qualify for another certificate endorsement by completing one of the following planned programs with a minimum of 18 semester hours.
  A. Early childhood
  B. Bilingual language area
  C. General elementary
  D. Middle school
  E. Areas appropriate to the secondary grades

Administrator Certification

Michigan no longer requires administrator certification.

Guidance Teacher and Counselor

Valid Michigan teaching certificate with endorsement in guidance. Such endorsement requires a minimum of 18 semester hours of appropriate guidance credit, including practicum. (Such guidance credit must be in addition to requirements for the requisite basic teaching certificate. Guidance is not an acceptable major or minor for such a teaching certificate.)

Librarian
(Requires a valid Michigan teaching certificate)

A major (30 semester hours) or minor (20 semester hours) in Library Science may be one of the majors or minors presented to meet the general requirements for either the elementary or secondary provisional certificate. A person presenting a minor may be certified as a teacher-librarian at the level of his Michigan certificate, but a person presenting a major may receive a K–12 Librarianship endorsement on a basic elementary or secondary level provisional or continuing certificate.

Minnesota

All applicants are required to complete an approved, competency-based human relations program and to pass the PRAXIS I Pre-Professional Skills Test (Reading–173, Writing–172; and Math–169) or the PRAXIS I Computer-Based Test (Reading–320, Writing–318, and Math–314). Teachers from other states who have not completed one or both of these requirements, but who otherwise meet all licensure requirements may be granted up to a one-year nonrenewable license, during which time these requirements must be met to qualify for the two year entrance license.

Elementary School

I. Requirements
  A. Degree from the College of Education of the University of Minnesota, the University of Minnesota at Duluth, University of Minnesota at Morris, a state university, or a liberal arts college accredited for teacher education on the elementary level.
    1. License valid for elementary schools and kindergarten when applicant has had special training for kindergarten.
  B. Professional requirements: completion of a teacher education program including credit in professional education for elementary school.
    1. For kindergarten teachers, a course in kindergarten education such as Early Childhood Education. Not less than one-half of student teaching shall be on kindergarten level.
  C. Applicant who did not complete a teacher education program where the degree was granted may complete a teacher education program as prescribed by an accredited teacher preparing institution and be recommended by such institution on completion of program including the number of education credits prescribed by the Minnesota State Board of Teaching.
  D. Programs completed in another state must have been completed at a regionally accredited college or university and must be essentially equivalent in content to programs offered by Minnesota teacher preparation institutions.

Secondary School

I. Requirements
  A. Degree from the College of Education of the University of Minnesota, the University of Minnesota at Duluth, University of Minnesota at Morris, a Minnesota state university, or a liberal arts college accredited as a teacher education institution.
    1. License valid for teaching in any secondary school, grades 7–12.
  B. Academic requirements and special fields
    1. Major as determined by the State Board of Teaching for full-time teaching in a subject.

2.   Minor for teaching in a subject half-time or less. Minors issued only in a few areas.
C.   Professional requirements: completion of a teacher education program including credit in professional education for secondary schools, semester hours................18
D.   Any secondary school applicant certified to teach after September 1, 1966, with minor preparation, shall within seven years after the initial certification acquire the minimum established by the State Board of Teaching for major preparation in order to continue to be licensed to teach in the subject or field.
E.   See Elementary School I, C and D.

Administration

I.   Licenses are issued for superintendent of schools and K–12 principal.
II.   Requirements
A.   Satisfactory completion of a program in school administration appropriate for license requested, approved by the Department of Education, *and*
1.   which results in a specialist or higher degree,
or
2.   which results in completion of 45 quarter hours credit or equivalent beyond a master's degree.
B.   Evidence shall be provided to the state Department of Education by those responsible for the training program to show that competency-based programs submitted for approval have been developed with appropriate participation from school administrators, teachers, school board members, and citizens.
C.   Three years of successful teaching experience on a license valid for the position in which experience was obtained.
III.   Renewal of Entrance License
A.   One year of successful experience in the licensed administrative role during the time that the applicant holds an appropriate administrative entrance license.
IV.   Renewal of Continuing License
A.   Persons holding standard or provisional licenses for one of the administrative roles, whose first license for this role was issued prior to September 1, 1967, may be issued a continuing administrative certificate upon the next renewal.
B.   The continuing license may be renewed according to general regulations of the state board of education pertaining to continuing education, 125 clock hours of pre-approved administrative continuing education.

Media Generalist

I.   Requirements for entrance certificate (valid for two years)
A.   Valid certificate to teach in the elementary or secondary schools of Minnesota.
B.   Two years of successful teaching experience.
C.   Completion of approved program in media and related fields of at least 36 quarter hours or their equivalent.
II.   Renewal of the Media Generalist certificate (valid for five years)

A. One or more years of successful full-time experience

or

Two or more years of successful half-time experience as a Media Generalist while holding the Media Generalist certificate.

Guidance Counselor

I. Requirements for Secondary School Counselor
    A. Valid teaching license based on bachelor's degree.
    B. Completion of a program of counselor education leading to a master's degree, including 54 quarter hours at graduate level.
        1. At least one course shall be taken in each of the following seven areas: principles and practice in guidance, personality structure and mental hygiene, measurement and research methods, appraisal techniques, occupational and training information and material, counseling procedure, practice in guidance and counseling.
        2. At least one course shall be chosen from the following: group guidance, organization and administration of guidance services, psychology of learning.
        3. Not more than 6 credits may be in undergraduate courses.
    C. At least one year of successful teaching experience.
    D. At least one year of cumulated work experience.
II. Requirements for Elementary School Counselor
    A. Valid teaching license based on bachelor's degree.
    B. One year of successful elementary teaching experience.
    C. Master's degree, including 54 quarter hours at graduate level.
        1. Competencies must be developed in areas of coordination, counseling, consultation, developmental guidance, diagnosis, and human relations.

Mississippi

Scores for the NTE Communications Skills Test and General Knowledge Test taken after July 1, 1997, are no longer accepted for licensure. A score on the NTE Professional Knowledge Test taken after August 1, 1997, is also no longer accepted for licensure. After these dates, applicants must take the PRAXIS I or PRAXIS II, Principles of Learning and Teaching tests. These changes are applicable to all licensure requirements below.

Standard Educator Licenses

I. Approved Program Route
  A. Class A Standard Educator License (valid for 5 years; renewable)
    1. Bachelor's degree in teacher education from a state-approved or a National Council for Accreditation of Teacher Education (NCATE)-approved program from a regionally/nationally accredited institution of higher learning
    2. Passing scores on PRAXIS II (Principles of Learning and Teaching Test) *or* NTE (Professional Knowledge Test)
    3. Passing scores on PRAXIS II (Specialty Area Test) *or* NTE (Specialty Area Test)
  B. Class AA Standard Educator License (valid for 5 years; renewable)
    1. See I, A, 1–3
    2. Master's degree in the endorsement area in which license is requested
  C. Class AAA Standard Educator License (valid for 5 years; renewable)
    1. See I, A, 1–3
    2. Specialist degree in the endorsement area in which license is requested
  D. Class AAAA Standard Educator License (valid for 5 years; renewable)
    1. See I, A, 1–3
    2. Doctoral degree in the endorsement area in which license is requested
II. Reciprocity
  A. Class A Standard Educator License (valid for 5 years; renewable)
    1. Valid out-of-state Standard Class A (bachelor's level) License in a Mississippi endorsement area
    2. Two years of out-of-state teaching or educational administration/leadership experience
  B. Class AA Standard Educator License (valid for 5 years; renewable)
    1. Valid out-of-state Standard Class AA (master's level) License in a Mississippi endorsement area
    2. Two years of out-of-state teaching or educational administration/leadership experience
  C. Class AAA Standard Educator License (valid for 5 years; renewable)
    1. Valid out-of-state Standard Class AAA (specialist level) License in a Mississippi endorsement area

2. Two years of out-of-state teaching or educational administration/leadership experience
   D. Class AAAA Standard Educator License (valid for 5 years; renewable)
      1. Valid out-of-state Standard Class AAAA (doctorate level) License in a Mississippi endorsement area
      2. Two years of out-of-state teaching or educational administration/leadership experience
III. Standard Educator License with Special Requirements–Guidance and Counseling
   A. Class AA Option One (valid 5 years; renewable)
      1. Hold a standard teaching certificate
      2. Complete a master's degree program in guidance and counseling; *or* hold a master's degree in another area and complete an approved program for guidance and counseling
      3. Passing score on NTE (Specialty Area for Guidance Counselor) *or* on Praxis II (Specialty Area for Guidance Counselor)
   B. Class AA Option Two (valid 5 years; renewable)
      1. Complete an approved master's degree program for guidance and counseling which includes a full year internship; *or* hold a master's degree in another area and complete an approved program for guidance and counseling which includes a full year internship
      2. Passing score on Praxis I (Pre-Professional Skills Test–PPST) or on Praxis I (Computer Based Assessment–CBT); *or* on National Teacher Exam–NTE (Communication Skills Test and General Knowledge Test)
      3. Passing score on NTE (Professional Knowledge Test) *or* on Praxis II (Principles of Learning and Teaching Test)
      4. Passing score on NTE (Specialty Area Test) *or* on Praxis II (Specialty Area Test)
   C. Class AAA (valid 5 years; renewable)
      1. Meet requirements for Class AA License (III, B, 1–4)
      2. Specialist degree in guidance and counseling
   D. Class AAAA (valid 5 years; renewable)
      1. Meet requirements for Class AA License (III, B, 1–4)
      2. Doctoral degree in guidance and counscling

Special Alternate Route Educator License
(Effective August 1, 1999)

I. Special Alternate Route Educator License—Master of Arts in Teaching Program (valid 3 years; nonrenewable): issued to applicant with a bachelor's degree who has not completed a state or nationally accredited teacher education program and who is enrolled in an approved Master of Arts in Teaching Program
   A. Bachelor's degree from a regionally/nationally accredited institution of higher learning
   B. Passing score on one of the following:
      1. Praxis I (Pre-Professional Skills Test–PPST); Praxis I (Computer Based Assessment–CBT); or National Teacher Exam–NTE (Communication Skills Test and General Knowledge Test)

C.   Content Mastery Exam for Educators (CMEE)
D.   Complete 6 hours pre-teaching course requirements from an approved Master of Arts in Teaching Program
E.   Institutional Recommendation
F.   During the 3 year term, applicant is expected to complete 6 semester hours, including the internship prescribed by the participating institution, in order to convert to a Class A Standard Alternate Route Educator License.

II.   Class A Alternate Route—Master of Teaching Program (valid for 5 years; renewable)
A.   Meet all requirements to convert the Special Alternate Route Educator License to a Standard Class A Alternate Route Educator License
B.   Institutional recommendation

III.   Class AA Alternate Route (valid for 5 years; renewable)
A.   Hold a Standard Class A Alternate Route Educator License
B.   Hold a Master of Arts in Teaching Degree from an approved program
C.   Institutional recommendation

Administrator Licenses

I.   Nonpracticing Administrator License (Class AA, AAA, or AAAA; renewable): issued to an educator not currently employed in an administrative position
A.   Completion of an approved master's, specialist, or doctoral degree in educational administration/leadership from a state-approved or regionally/nationally accredited institution of higher learning
B.   Successful completion of Principal's Licensure Assessment (Educational Testing Service)
C.   Validity is based upon validity of period of standard license currently held

II.   Entry Level Administrator License (AA, AAA, or AAAA; nonrenewable): issued to an educator employed as a beginning administrator
A.   Completion of an approved master's, specialist, or doctoral degree in educational administration/leadership from a state-approved or regionally/nationally accredited institution of higher learning
B.   Successful completion of Principal's Licensure Assessment (Educational Testing Service)
C.   Valid for 5 years in which time applicant is expected to complete requirements to obtain Career Level Administrator License

III.   Alternate Route—Entry Level Administrator License (Class AA; nonrenewable): issued to an applicant who has not completed an educational administration/leadership program and is limited to entry-level administrative positions, such as assistant principal or assistant coordinators
A.   Completion of one of the following:
1.   Master of Business Administration; Master of Public Administration; or Master of Public Planning and Policy
B.   Passing score on one of the following:
1.   Praxis I (Pre-Professional Skills Test–PPST); Praxis I (Computer Based Assessment–CBT); or National Teacher Exam–NTE (Communication Skills Test and General Knowledge Test)

    C. Passing score on one of the following:
        1. PRAXIS II (Principles of Learning and Teaching Test) or the NTE Professional Knowledge Test
    D. Five years of administrative/supervisory experience
    E. Successful completion of School Leaders Licensure Assessment (Educational Testing Service)
    F. Valid for 5 years in which time applicant is expected to complete requirements to obtain Standard Career Level Administrator License

IV. Standard Career Level Administrator License (Class AA, AAA, or AAAA; renewable)
    A. Completion of an approved master's, specialist, or doctoral degree in educational administration/leadership from a state-approved or regionally/nationally accredited institution of higher learning
    B. Successful completion of School Leaders Licensure Assessment (Educational Testing Service)
    C. Completion of School Executive Management Institute (SEMI) Entry-Level Requirements
    D. Completion of Mississippi Administrator Assessment Instrument (MAAI) Portfolio
    E. Institutional recommendation
    F. Valid for 5 years

Missouri

Missouri is planning a major revision of its requirements for certification for early childhood education and for early childhood special education which will become effective after September 1, 1999. Please write the Missouri Department of Elementary and Secondary Education for details (address in Appendix 1).

Early Childhood (PreK–3)

I. General Requirements
  A. Baccalaureate degree from an approved college or university.
  B. Recommendation of designated official for teacher education.
  C. Overall grade point average of 2.5 on a 4.0 scale.
  D. Completion of General Education and Basic Requirements:
    1. General requirements as determined by the recommending college or university.
    2. Basic requirements to include the following, which may be met in whole or part in the general education requirements. (Each course must be a minimum of 2 semester hours.)
      a. Humanities. Must include one course* from two of the following: music, art, foreign language, Western and non-Western cultures, philosophy, literature, classical studies, and theater and drama.
      b. Communication skills. Must include two courses* in English composition and one in oral communication.
      c. Social studies. Must include courses* in U.S. history and U.S. government, and one additional course selected from geography, economics, sociology, anthropology, and psychology.
      d. Natural science. Must include one course* in a physical or earth science and one course* in a biological science, with at least one of these courses having a laboratory component.
      e. Mathematics. A college level math course.*
  E. Completion of the National Teacher Examination (NTE) Specialty Area Test in the major area with a score equal to the Missouri qualifying score.
II. Professional Requirements (figures below reflect *minimum* requirements; no grade to be lower than a "C")
  A. Professional preparation, semester hours.. 60
    1. Foundations for teaching, semester hours.. 10
      a. To include foundations of education; school organization and management; personalized teaching strategies; self awareness and human relations; early childhood growth and development;* psychology of learning; psychology and education of the exceptional child;* and behavior management techniques.

     2.   Teaching methods, semester hours 15

     3.   Clinical experiences, semester hours 10

        a.   Minimum of 2 semester hours of field experience prior to student teaching, and a minimum of 8 semester hours in early childhood student teaching.

  B.   Early Childhood Special Courses

     1.   Required courses, minimum semester hours 15

        a.   Language acquisition and development;* utilizing family and community resources;* curriculum methods and materials;* screening, diagnosis and prescribing instruction;* health;* perceptual motor development;* mathematics (minimum 3 semester hours).

     2.   Practicum, semester hours 4

  C.   Optional courses

     1.   Principles of early childhood education; teaching/learning strategies; instructional media/learning environments; philosophy and issues; administration of early childhood programs; history and theory of early childhood education; study of infant programs.

*   Required course of at least 2 semester hours.

Elementary—Grades 1–6

I.   General Requirements

  A.   See Early Childhood, I, A, B, C, and D.

II.   Professional Requirements, semester hours 60

  A.   See Early Childhood, II, A, 1 and 2.

     1.   Clinical Experiences—same as Early Childhood, II, A, 3, but for elementary grades.

  B.   Elementary School Special Courses

     1.   Requirements

        a.   Mathematics: 2 courses appropriate for elementary, minimum total semester hours 5

        b.   Economics, geography, health, art or music.

        c.   Area of concentration, semester hours 21

Middle School—Grades 5–9

I.   General Requirements

  A.   Same as Early Childhood, I, A, B, C, and D, except 2 college level mathematics courses appropriate for middle level teachers are required.

II.   Professional Requirements (figures below reflect *minimum* requirements; no grade to be lower than a "C"), minimum semester hours 32

  A.   Foundations for teaching, semester hours 12

     1.   Pupil/Society (8 semester hours): personalized teaching strategies; adolescent psychology or psychology of the middle level child;* psychology or education

of the exceptional child;* techniques of classroom management; tests and measurements.

    2.   School/Society (4 semester hours): middle school philosophy, organization, and curriculum;* legal, philosophical, and sociological foundations of education.

B. Middle school methods, semester hours 10

    1.   Methods of teaching (5 semester hours); reading in content fields; middle level curriculum and instruction; teaching of writing; methods of teaching specialty area(s).

C. Clinical experiences, semester hours 10

    1.   A minimum of 2 semester hours of field experience prior to student teaching and a minimum of 8 semester hours of teaching in grades 4–8 are required. Teachers meeting certification requirements for Early Childhood elementary, PreK–grade 3, elementary grades 1–6, or secondary grades 9–12 must complete a practicum with middle level students. This practicum may be integrated within appropriate required courses.

III. Subject Certification

    A. Must have a grade point average of 2.5 on a 4.0 scale in the certificate subject area.

    B. There are 3 different ways to receive certification in a middle level subject area; please write to the Missouri Department of Elementary and Secondary Education for details.

       1.   Areas of concentration: language arts; mathematics; science; and social science.

       2.   Endorsement areas: agricultural education; family and consumer science; industrial technology; speech; drama; and business education.

       3.   K–9 endorsements which may be used at the middle school level: art; foreign language; health; physical education; and music.

*   Required course of at least 2 semester hours.

Secondary Teacher's Certificate

I. General Requirements

    A. Baccalaureate degree from a college or university having an approved teacher education program.

    B. Recommendation of designated official for teacher education.

    C. Must have an overall grade point average of at least 2.5 on a 4.0 scale.

    D. Completion of the National Teacher Examination (NTE) Specialty Area Test in the major area with a score equal to or greater than the Missouri qualifying score.

    E. Completion of General Education as determined by the recommending institution.

    F. Basic requirements: see Early Childhood I, D, 2.

II. Professional Requirements (no grade to be lower than a "C"), minimum semester hours 26

    A. Foundations for teaching, semester hours 8

       1.   Pupil/Society: adolescent growth and development; adolescent behavior

management techniques; psychology of learning (must include adolescent learning); adolescent interaction with others; psychology and education of the exceptional child* 6

    2. School/Society: legal foundations of education; historical foundations of education; philosophical foundations of education; sociological foundations of education 2

B. Secondary methods and techniques, semester hours.. 8

    1. Basic reading techniques for secondary teachers;* instructional strategies for secondary teachers; curriculum, methods, and techniques in subject area specialty;* measurement and evaluation; and microcomputer applications in education.

C. Clinical experience, semester hours.. 10

    1. To include student teaching at appropriate level.

* Required course of at least 2 semester hours.

III. Subject Matter Requirements for specific areas (9–12, except where noted)

A. Agriculture Education, semester hours 45
B. Art, semester hours 30
C. Business Education, semester hours 30
D. Driver Education, semester hours (endorsement only) 21
E. English, semester hours... 30
F. Family and Consumer Science, semester hours 30
G. Foreign Language (K–12), semester hours 30
    Plus demonstrated proficiency in language to be taught.
H. Health (7–12), semester hours... 30
I. Industrial Technology, semester hours 36
J. Journalism, semester hours 30
K. Mathematics, semester hours 30
L. Music (K–12)
    1. Instrumental (Band-Orchestra), semester hours........................ 36
    2. Vocal/Choral, semester hours 36
M. Physical Education, semester hours 30
N. Unified Science , semester hours... 39
    1. This certificate, which allows the holder to teach introductory courses in the sciences, requires the holder to have one of the specific science endorsements listed below. The endorsement allows the holder to teach advanced courses in the specific subject. The course work for the endorsement is *in addition to* the course work required for the Unified Science certificate
        a. Biology endorsement, semester hours................................ 20
        b. Chemistry endorsement, semester hours............................. 20
        c. Physics endorsement, semester hours 20
        d. Earth Science endorsement, semester hours 20
O. Social Science, semester hours 40
P. Speech and Theater, semester hours.. 30

These semester hours are total hours required. Each subject matter has detailed requirements within its discipline. A grade point average of 2.5 on a 4.0 scale in the subject area is required.

Administration

I. Elementary and Secondary Principal
    A. Initial Certificate (valid for 5 years)
        1. A valid Missouri teaching certificate (at appropriate level).
        2. A minimum of two years teaching experience (at appropriate level).
        3. Completion of a course in psychology and education of the exceptional child.
        4. Master's degree.
        5. Recommendation for certification from the designated official of a college or university. The approved graduate credit shall include 2 semester hours in:
            a. Specific courses:
                1) Foundation of educational administration.
                2) Elementary administration.
                3) Elementary curriculum.
                4) School supervision.
            b. Directed field experiences in administration at appropriate level of at least 2 semester hours.
            c. Knowledge and/or competency in each of the following areas: Instructional management systems; teaching-learning processes; instruction in communication skills (reading, writing, spelling, listening, speaking); educational measurements; evaluation of teachers; administration and coordination of special programs and services; school law; school business and facilities management; student discipline; public relations; administration and coordination of school activities programs; philosophy of vocational education (secondary only).
        6. Successful completion of Administrator's Assessment Center—Building Level.
    B. Renewal of Certificate
        1. The principal's initial certificate may be renewed only one time for five years by earning 15 graduate semester hours toward a two-year graduate program for principals approved by the Missouri Department of Elementary and Secondary Education.
II. Advanced Elementary and Secondary Principal
    A. Initial Certificate (valid for 10 years)
        1. Completion of all the requirements listed under the five-year Initial Certificate requirements for a principal's certificate.
        2. Completion of a two-year graduate program for preparation of principals approved by the Missouri Department of Elementary and Secondary Education.
        3. Recommendation for certification from the designated official of the college or university.
    B. Renewal of Certificate
        The Principal's advanced certificate may be renewed for ten years by persons meeting the following requirements:

1. A minimum of five years experience in school administration during the previous ten years.
2. Completion of a Professional Development Agreement. (Write the Missouri Department of Elementary and Secondary Education for details.)

III. Middle School Principal

A. A principal meeting the following requirements may request an additional certificate as a middle school principal.

1. Elementary Principal Endorsement
   a. Meet the requirements for an elementary principal's certificate or an elementary principal's advanced certificate.
   b. Have completed a planned program of at least 6 graduate semester hours in education courses focusing on middle school philosophy, organization, and curriculum, and the intellectual, physiological, emotional, and social development of the transescent child (10- to 14-year-olds).
   c. Have a recommendation for certification as a middle school principal from the designated official of the college or university approved to train principals by the Missouri Department of Elementary and Secondary Education. The recommendation shall be based upon the completion of the planned program.

2. Secondary Principal Endorsement
   a. Meet the requirements for a secondary principal's certificate or a secondary principal's advanced certificate.
   b. See above III, A, 1, b, Elementary Principal Endorsement.
   c. See above III, A, 1, c, Elementary Principal Endorsement.
   d. Have earned undergraduate or graduate credit as follows:
      1) Reading—two courses with one course to be techniques of teaching reading in content fields; a minimum total of five semester hours;
      2) Mathematics—one course of at least two semester hours in the methods of teaching elementary mathematics.

IV. Superintendent

A. Initial Certificate (valid for 10 years)
   1. A valid regular Missouri teaching certificate.
   2. Four years of teaching, supervisory, or administrative experience, or any combination thereof, in elementary and/or secondary schools approved by the Department of Elementary and Secondary Education.
   3. Completion of a course in psychology and education of the exceptional child.
   4. Completion of a two-year graduate program approved by the Missouri Department of Elementary and Secondary Education for preparation of the superintendent which shall include knowledge and/or competency in specified areas.
   5. Recommendation for certification from the designated official of the college or university.
   6. Successful completion of Administrator's Assessment Center—District Level.

B. Renewal of Certificate (valid for 10 years)
   1. Five years experience in school administration during the previous ten years.

2.   Completion of a Professional Development Agreement. (Write the Missouri Department of Elementary and Secondary Education for details.)

Counselor

I.   Initial Elementary Counselor Certificate (K–8) (valid for 5 years)
  A.   A valid regular Missouri teaching certificate.
  B.   Two years of approved teaching experience.
  C.   Master's degree with an emphasis on guidance and counseling from an approved institution.
  D.   One year of accumulated paid employment (other than teaching or counseling).
  E.   Completion of a course in psychology and education of the exceptional child of at least 2 semester hours.
  F.   Recommendation for certification from the designated official of an approved college or university based upon the completion of a planned program of 24 semester hours of approved graduate credit in guidance and counseling courses, with at least 12 semester hours focused on the elementary level. This program must include completion of one course of at least 3 semester hours in *each* of the following areas:
    1.   Personal and professional development in counseling
    2.   Foundations of elementary and secondary school guidance
    3.   Theories and techniques of elementary and secondary school counseling
    4.   Elementary school child and school learning problems
    5.   Theories and techniques of group counseling
    6.   Practicum in counseling
  G.   Supervised practice in an elementary school guidance program for 3 semester hours.
II.   Renewal of Elementary Counselor Certificate (valid for 5 years)
  A.   Two years experience in counseling at the elementary level during the previous five years.
  B.   Completion of an approved Professional Development Program. (Write the Missouri Department of Elementary and Secondary Education for details.)
III.   Initial Secondary Counselor Certificate (7–12) (valid for 5 years)
  A.   See I, A–E.
  B.   See I, F, 1, 2, 3, 5, and 6, except that 12 of 24 semester hours must be focused on counseling and guidance on the secondary level.
  C.   Supervised practice in a secondary school guidance program for at least 3 hours.
IV.   Renewal of Secondary Counselor Certificate (valid for 5 years)
  A.   See II, A and B, except that focus must be on the secondary level.

Library Media Specialist (K–12)

I.   General Requirements
  A.   See Early Childhood I, A–E.
II.   Professional Requirements
  A.   See Secondary Teacher's Certificate II, A–C.
III.   Valid Missouri teacher's certificate and 2 years of teaching experience.

IV. Library Concentration Requirements (figures below reflect minimum requirements in hours; grade point average of 2.5 on a 4.0 scale required), semester hours.................. 26
    A. Introductory seminar (1), library media administration (3), selection and acquisition (3), cataloging (3), reference (3), materials production (3), children's or adolescent literature (2), information technologies (3), utilization and integration (3), and a practicum (2).

Special Education*

I. General Requirements (Grades K–9, 7–12, and K–12)
    A. See Secondary Teacher's Certificate I, A–E.
II. Professional Requirements. Vary according to the area of specialization.

* The certification requirements for Learning Disabled Students, Behaviorally Disordered Students, Mentally Handicapped Students, Orthopedically and/or Health Impaired Students, Blind and Partially Sighted Students, Severely Developmentally Disabled Students, Early Childhood Special Education Students, Deaf and Hearing Impaired Students, Special Reading Teachers, and Speech and Language Specialists are varied. For exact requirements, consult Missouri State Board of Education (see Appendix 1).

Reciprocity

Missouri has signed an exchange certification agreement with Iowa, Nebraska, Kansas, South Dakota, Oklahoma, and Arkansas (MINKSOA) which allows individuals certified in one of the member states to be eligible for a two-year exchange certificate in any of the participating states.

Montana

All new applicants for initial class 1, 2, or 3 certification must provide evidence of having completed one of the following tests: the Pre-Professional Skills Test (Reading–170, Writing–170, Mathematics–170) or the Computer Based Test (Reading–316, Writing–314; Mathematics–315), or any basic skills tests required in another state either for entrance into a teacher education program or for certification in that state (requires written verification).

Elementary School

I. Class 5 (Provisional) Certificate (3 years—nonrenewable)
    A. The Provisional Certificate may be issued to applicants who have a bachelor's degree and a partially completed program in elementary education. Minimum requirements must be met. Written recommendation of appropriate official(s) is required.
II. Class 2 (Standard) Certificate (5 years—renewable)
    A. Completion of approved bachelor's program in elementary teacher education.
III. Class 1 (Professional) Certificate (5 years—renewable).
    A. Eligibility for Standard Certificate plus completion of an approved master's degree or planned fifth year program.
    B. Three years of successful teaching experience, the majority of which must have been at the K–12 level.

Junior High School

I. Certification
    A. Holders of Class 5, 2, or 1 certificates endorsed at elementary level may teach grades 7 and 8. Subject matter endorsements may be required to satisfy accreditation/funding requirements in certain school organizational patterns, i.e., middle schools and junior high schools.
    B. Holders of Class 5, 2, or 1 certificates endorsed at secondary level (5–12) may teach in grades 5–9 in any subject for which their certification is endorsed.

Secondary School (5–12)

I. Class 5 (Provisional) Certificate (3 years—nonrenewable)
    A. Bachelor's degree which must include the following:
        1. Major preparation (30 semester credits) in a subject commonly taught for credit in secondary schools in Montana.
        2. Six semester hours in a planned program of professional education and admittance to the secondary teacher education program of an accredited college.

B. Written recommendation of appropriate official(s) is required.
II. Class 2 (Standard) Certificate (5 years—renewable)
   A. Completion of approved bachelor's program in secondary teacher education at an accredited college or university, the program to include the following:
      1. Teaching major, semester hours.. 30
      2. Teaching minor, semester hours 20
      or
      3. Extended major, semester hours 40
      4. Professional sequence, including student teaching or equivalent experience, semester hours (at minimum) 16
III. Class 1 (Professional) Certificate (5 years—renewable)
   A. Eligibility for Standard Certificate plus completion of an approved master's degree or planned fifth year program.
   B. Three years of successful teaching experience, the majority of which must have been at the K–12 level.
IV. Secondary certification may be extended to grades 5 and 6 for teachers and administrators who have completed or are completing an approved 5–12 program. Within this program, emphasis must be on student growth and development, behavior, and the teaching of reading and writing skills. Student teaching and observation periods, when combined, must cover both 7–12 and 5–6 grade levels.

Administration

I. Class 3 Administrative Certificate (5 years—renewable)
   A. Superintendent
      1. Master's degree in school administration or the equivalent.
      2. Must be eligible for class 1 or 2 teaching certificate.
      3. Full eligibility for a principal endorsement in Montana.
      4. Graduate credits beyond the master's degree, to include, semester hours 8
         a. School management/facilities
         b. School negotiation
         c. School finance (advanced course)
         d. Public relations
      5. Graduate credits in elementary education to include elementary administration and elementary curriculum if endorsed at the secondary level; graduate credits in secondary education to include secondary administration and secondary curriculum if endorsed at the elementary level; semester hours.................... 8
      6. Experience:
         a. One year of administrative experience as an appropriately certified administrator (principal, assistant principal, supervisor), *or*
         b. One year of a supervised internship as superintendent.
   B. Principal
      1. Master's degree in school administration or the equivalent.
      2. Must be eligible for Class 1 or 2 teaching certificate with proper endorsement.

3. Verification of a minimum of 3 years of successful experience as an appropriately certified and assigned teacher at the proper level.
4. At least 14 graduate semester credits in education or the equivalent to include:
   a. General school administration
   b. Specific area administration as appropriate (elementary or secondary)
   c. Administration of guidance services
   d. Supervision of instruction/evaluation at the appropriate level
   e. School curriculum at the appropriate level
   f. School finance (basic course)
   g. School law

II. Class 5 Provisional Administrative Certificate (3 years—nonrenewable)
   A. Superintendent (Option A)
      1. Must be eligible for Class 1, 2, or 5 teaching certificate.
      2. Experience:
         a. Three years of successful experience as an appropriately certified and assigned teacher and one year of administrative experience as an appropriately certified administrator (principal, assistant principal, or supervisor),
            or
         b. One year of a supervised administrative internship.
      3. Master's degree in school administration or the equivalent.
      4. The plan of intent leading to regular certification must have in the program 8 graduate semester credits in administration beyond the master's degree to include:
         a. General school administration
         b. Elementary and secondary administration
         c. Administration of guidance services
         d. Supervision of instruction
         e. School curriculum, K–12
         f. Basic and advanced school finance
         g. School law
         h. School management/facilities
         i. School negotiations
         j. Public relations
      5. If the applicant does not qualify for the elementary teaching endorsement, 8 graduate semester credits in elementary education are required; if the applicant does not qualify for the secondary teaching endorsement, 8 graduate semester credits in secondary education are required.
   B. Principal
      1. Must be eligible for class 1, 2, or 5 teaching certificate at the appropriate level
      2. Three years of successful teaching experience as an appropriately certified and assigned teacher
         and
      3. Have a master's degree in school administration or the equivalent
         or

Hold an out-of-state administrative certificate and have 3 years of successful teaching experience as an appropriately certified and assigned teacher.

4. Within the term of the Class 5 certificate, the applicant must complete an approved master's degree in school administration to include the following state specified courses:
   a. General school administration
   b. Specific area administration as appropriate (elementary or secondary)
   c. Administration of guidance services
   d. Supervision of instruction/evaluation at the appropriate level
   e. School curriculum at the appropriate level
   f. School finance (budgeting)
   g. School law

Vocational

I. Class 4 (Vocational) Certificate
The vocational certificate is issued to applicants presenting training and experience required by the United States Office of Education or by the special needs required in the vocational area. Requirements vary with the situation.

Guidance and Counseling

I. Endorsement on a teaching certificate will require, in addition to an approved guidance and counseling K–12 program and a valid Montana teaching certificate, verification of 3 years of successful teaching experience or the equivalent.
II. The majority of the experience must be obtained in a school organization consistent with Montana's K–12 pattern.

Librarian

I. Requirements
   A. Valid Montana teaching certificate.
   B. Completion of an approved K–12 program in library science from an accredited institution, with a minimum of 20 semester hours.

Specialists

I. Class 6 (Specialist) School Psychologist Certificate
   A. Master's degree in school psychology or equivalent related areas, to include specific courses in education, psychological methods, and techniques.
II. Class 6 (Specialist) School Counselor Certificate
   A. Master's degree in guidance and counseling (K–12) or equivalent.
      1. To include an internship of at least 600 hours in a school or school-related setting.
   B. Teaching experience or certification as a teacher are not required.

Renewal Requirements

I. Class 1 (5 years)
   A. Verification of one year of successful teaching experience and 4 semester credits (60 renewal units) during the valid term of the certificate.
II. Class 2 (5 years)
   A. Verification of one year of successful teaching experience and 60 renewal units (40 of which must be earned by college credit).
III. Class 3 (5 years)
   A. Verification of one year of successful experience in the area of endorsement and 4 semester credits (60 renewal units) during the valid term of the certificate.
IV. Class 4 (5 years)
   A. Verification of one year of successful teaching experience and 4 semester credits (60 renewal units) during the valid term of the certificate.
V. Class 5 (3 years—nonrenewable)
VI. Class 6 (5 years)
   A. Verification of one year of successful specialist experience and 4 graduate semester credits during the valid term of the certificate.

Nebraska

Fingerprints (and a fingerprint fee of $40) must be submitted with an application for Nebraska certification if the applicant has not had five years of continuous residency in Nebraska prior to the date of application or if the applicant has never held a Nebraska certificate.

Teaching Certificates

I. Initial Teaching Certificate (valid 5 years)
   A. Evidence of scholarship, sound mental and physical health, good citizenship, and moral character (no felony conviction)
   B. Baccalaureate degree
   C. Completion, within 3 years prior to application, of the requirements of an approved program for the preparation of teachers
   D. Passing scores on the Pre-Professional Skills Test (PPST): reading, 170; mathematics, 171; writing, 172; *or* a satisfactory scaled score of 850 or higher on the Content Mastery Examinations for Educators Basic Skills Test
   E. Completion of an approved course in human relations skills
   F. Completion of 3 hours of credit in special education at a standard institution of higher education or equivalent training or experience demonstrated to the Department of Education's satisfaction
   G. Six semester hours of college credit, within 3 years prior to application, which meets all or part of the requirements for an endorsement
      1. If an applicant who has never held a regular certificate in any state applies more than 5 years after the completion of the approved program (see I, C), the applicant must have 15 semester hours of college credit within 3 years prior to application.
II. Standard Teaching Certificate (valid 7 years)
   A. See I, A, D, E, and F
   B. Possession of a Nebraska initial teaching certificate *or* of a comparable and equivalent certificate
   C. Experience teaching half-time or more for 2 successive school years in an approved setting within 5 years prior to application
III. Professional Teaching Certificate (valid 10 years)
   A. See I, A, D, E, and F
   B. Teaching requirements
      1. Hold or qualify for a Nebraska standard certificate, *or* hold a comparable and equivalent certificate, *or*
      2. Verify 2 years of teaching experience during the period of validity of a regular certificate
   C. Course work requirements

1. Master's degree, *or*
2. Completion of a fifth year program from a standard institution of higher education in the same area as the applicant's area of endorsement completed at the baccalaureate level, *or*
3. Completion of a 6 year specialist's certificate, or a doctorate, from a standard institution of higher education in an area related to the applicant's area of endorsement completed at the master's degree or fifth year level

D. Six semester hours of graduate credit, within 3 years prior to application

IV. Provisional Commitment Teaching Certificate (valid 1 year; renewable twice)
   A. Submission of a written request for issuance of the certificate from the superintendent of schools
   B. See I, A, B, D, E, and F.
   C. Completion of at least one-half of the pre-student teaching requirements of an approved program for the preparation of teachers
   D. Fulfillment of at least one-half of the requirements for the elementary education teaching endorsement or at least three-fourths of the requirements for at least one subject or field endorsement
   E. Submission of a statement of intent to fulfill the remaining program requirements

Special Service Counseling Certificates

I. Standard Special Services Counseling Certificate (valid 7 years)
   A. See Teaching Certificates I, A, B, and E
   B. Completion of a program in school psychology or speech pathology from a standard institution of higher education
   C. Hold or qualify for a school psychology endorsement
   D. Six semester hours of college credit, within 3 years prior to application, which meets all or part of the requirements for an endorsement

II. Provisional Commitment Special Services Counseling Certificate (valid 1 year; not renewable)
   A. Submission of a written request for issuance of the certificate from the superintendent of schools
   B. See Teacher Certificates I, A, B, and E
   C. Completion of at least three-fourths of a program in school psychology from a standard institution of higher education, *or* completion of a baccalaureate degree in speech-language pathology
   D. Submission of a statement of intent to fulfill the remaining program requirements

Administrative Certificates

I. Standard Administrative Certificate (valid 7 years)
   A. See Teaching Certificates I, A, D, E, and F
   B. Hold or qualify for a Nebraska standard or professional certificate, *or* hold a comparable and equivalent certificate
   C. Master's degree, *or* 36 semester hours of credit toward a 6 year specialist's certificate

(or toward a doctorate), in educational administration from a standard institution of higher education with an approved program for the preparation of school administrators in the area(s) of endorsement sought by the applicant

    D.   Hold or qualify for one or more educational administration endorsements

    E.   Six semester hours of graduate credit, within 3 years prior to application, which meet all or part of the requirements for an endorsement, *or*, within 5 years prior to application, have administered half-time or more for 2 successive school years in another state in which the applicant held a standard administrative certificate or its equivalent

    F.   Certificate will be valid for the position of superintendent of schools only if so endorsed

  II. Professional Administrative Certificate (valid 10 years)

    A.   See Teacher Certificates I, A, D, E, and F

    B.   Completion of a 6 year specialist's certificate or a doctorate degree in educational administration from a standard institution of higher education with an approved program for the preparation of school administrators in the area(s) of endorsement sought by the applicant

    C.   Hold or qualify for one or more educational administration endorsements

    D.   Six semester hours of graduate credit, within 3 years prior to application, which meet all or part of the requirements for an administrative endorsement, *or*, within 5 years prior to application, have administered half-time or more for 2 successive school years as a certificated school administrator in the same approved school system or other approved educational setting while holding a Nebraska standard administrative certificate or a comparable and equivalent certificate

    E.   See I, F directly above

 III. Provisional Administrative Certificate (valid one year; not renewable)

    A.   Contact the Nebraska Department of Education (address in Appendix 1) for details

Nevada

Elementary School

I. Authorization
   A. An elementary license permits the holder to teach all subjects from kindergarten through grade 8 in any public school or private school with a Nevada state license.

II. Elementary License
   A. Requirements (Complete 1 or 2.)
      1. Bachelor's degree and completion of a State Board of Education approved program of preparation for teaching in elementary grades, to include: Teaching of reading, reading skills, or phonics skills, semester hours.......................... 6
      2. Completion of the following:
         a. Bachelor's degree.
         b. Elementary professional education, semester hours 30
            1) Supervised teaching, semester hours.. 8
            2) Teaching methods, not including reading...................................... 8
            3) Reading (see II, A, 1), semester hours 6
   B. Term—Five years, renewable upon completion of 6 hours credit.

III. Professional Elementary License
   A. Requirements
      1. Meet all requirements for Elementary License.
      2. Master's degree.
      3. Three years of elementary teaching experience in state-approved schools.
   B. Term—Six years for master's degree, eight years for specialist's degree, ten years for doctor's degree. Six year renewable upon 6 semester hours credit or equivalent. Eight and ten year renewable upon evidence of professional growth during the term of the certificate.

IV. Limited Elementary Endorsement
   A. Requirements
      1. Bachelor's degree.
      2. Professional elementary education, semester hours 18
         a. Methods of teaching the basic elementary subjects, including literacy or language arts (6), mathematics (3), science (3), and social studies (3).
      3. Supervised teaching in grades K–8, semester hours 8
   B. Term—Five years, not renewable. Must complete requirements for Elementary License.

V. Elementary License Endorsement
   A. Credit within the area of endorsement, semester hours 12
      1. Recognized endorsement areas are: art; use of computers; English; health; mathematics; reading; science; social studies; early childhood education; and physical education

a. Endorsement for English requires 3 semester hours of credit in each of the following: advanced composition, descriptive grammar, and speech.
b. Endorsement to teach pupils who are enrolled in a program of bilingual education requires the applicant pass an examination, if the examination is available, and complete 12 semester hours of credit in an approved course of study.

VI. Substitute—Elementary Grades
   A. Credit from accredited college or university, semester hours 62
      1. To include, elementary education course work, semester hours 6
   B. Term—Five years, renewable.
   C. Limited to 60 days of consecutive service, except an additional 30 days may be granted in extenuating circumstances at the discretion of the State Superintendent.

Secondary School

I. Authorization
   A. A license endorsed in a recognized teaching field is required for teaching in departmentalized seventh and eighth grades, junior high schools, senior high schools, and designated and approved middle schools. Endorsements are dependent upon the applicant's field of specialization or concentration, usually designated as majors or minors or areas of concentration.

II. Teaching Endorsements
   A. Recognized Teaching Fields*: art, English, math, music, occupational educational, physical education, science, and social studies.
   B. Comprehensive fields of concentration
      1. Majors, semester hours 36
      2. Minors, semester hours 24
   C. Single subject majors and minors
      1. Majors, semester hours 30
      2. Minors, semester hours 16

III. Initial Secondary License
   A. Requirements (Complete 1 or 2.)
      1. Bachelor's degree and completion of an approved program of preparation for secondary school teaching, including multicultural education.
      2. Bachelor's degree and completion of the following:
         a. A teaching field major.
         b. Secondary professional education, semester hours 22
            1) Supervised teaching and/or teaching internship 8
            2) A course in methods and materials in field of specialization.
   B. Term—Five years, renewable upon 6 semester hours credit.

IV. Professional Secondary License

---

* For detailed information in each of the specialized teaching fields, please write to the Nevada Department of Education (see Appendix 1).

    A. Requirements
       1. Meet all requirements for Secondary Endorsement.
       2. Master's degree.
       3. Three years of teaching in state-approved secondary schools.
    B. Term—See Elementary III, B.

V. Substitute—Secondary Grades
    A. Requirements
       1. Credit from accredited institution; semester hours 62
         a. To include secondary education course work, semester hours 6
       2. Secondary education course work, semester hours 6
    B. Term—Five years, renewable. Note: See Elementary VI, D.
       Additional course work not required for renewal.

Administration

I. Authorization
    A. A School Administrator endorsement is required for the following: superintendent, associate superintendent, assistant superintendent, principal, vice principal, supervisor, administrative assistant, and program administrator.
    B. A Program Administrator endorsement is required for an individual who supervises or coordinates a program of: nursing, school psychology, speech therapy, physical therapy, and occupational therapy.

II. Limited School Administrator Endorsement
    A. Requirements
       1. Master's degree.
       2. Valid special license in the program for which an endorsement is requested.
       3. Three years of teaching experience at the K–12 level in state-approved schools.
       4. Completion of 18 semester hours of graduate courses in school administration including administration and organization of schools; supervision of instruction; evaluation and development of personnel; school finance; school law; curriculum development; educational research; internship or field experience in school administration; or other courses considered to be part of an administrative program for educators.
    B. Term—Five years, not renewable. Holder must complete requirements for Professional School Administrator during term of certificate.

III. Professional School Administrator Endorsement
    A. Requirements
       1. Meet the requirements for a limited endorsement (see II, A, 1-4 directly above).
       2. Complete an additional 12 semester hours of graduate courses, which must include any remaining course work not previously completed in II, A, 4 and which may include other courses considered to be part of an administrative degree program for educators;
         or
         Hold a qualifying valid teaching license with the appropriate teaching

experience and have a master's degree or higher in educational administration from an accredited institution.

B. An endorsement as a professional administrator of a school may be issued on the basis of a reciprocal agreement with another state if that state has been approved.

IV. Limited Program Administrator Endorsements
  A. Requirements
    1. Master's degree.
    2. Valid special license in the program for which an endorsement is requested.
    3. Three years of experience as a licensed employee at the K–12 level in state-approved schools.
    4. Completion of 12 semester hours of graduate courses in area in which endorsement is requested.
  B. Term—Five years, not renewable. Holder must complete requirements for the Professional Program Administrator Endorsement during term of certificate.

V. Professional Program Administrator Endorsement
  A. Requirements
    1. Meet the requirements for a limited endorsement as an administrator of a program (see IV, A, 1-4 directly above).
    2. Complete an additional 12 semester hours of graduate courses considered to be part of an educational administrative degree program.

School Counselor

I. Authorization
  A. Endorsements are issued to serve as either an elementary or secondary school counselor.

II. Requirements
  A. M. Ed., M.A., M.S., or more advanced degree from an accredited institution in counseling,
    or
    Master's or more advanced degree in a related field, plus two years of teaching or school counseling experience,
    or
    Certification as a National Certified Counselor by the Commission on Professional Standards in Education.
  B. Whatever option is met in II, A, all candidates must complete a program of graduate courses in school counseling, semester hours 36
    1. To include courses in the following areas:
      a. process of individual and group counseling; individual and group assessment; structuring and managing comprehensive programs for guidance; developmental group guidance; child and family guidance; counseling on abuse of controlled substances; developing careers and choosing occupations; and a practicum for individual counseling at the appropriate grade level.
      b. Also to include any two of the following areas: crisis intervention;

exceptional children; counseling persons from different cultures; advanced human growth and development; and education research.

Library

I. Endorsement to Teach Library Science (K–12)
  A. Valid elementary or secondary license.
  B. Completion of a program, which has been approved by the board, for teaching library science,
    or
    Twenty-one semester hours of course work in specified subjects in library science.
II. Endorsement as Library Specialist (K–12) (for individuals who are not licensed as teachers)
  A. Hold a bachelor's degree in library science or an equivalent degree,
    or
    Have completed all the special courses required for an endorsement authorizing a licensed teacher to serve as a library specialist, as well as an additional 8 semester hours of preparation in library science.
III. Endorsement as a Professional Librarian (K–12)
  A. Master's degree in library science or some other master's degree.
  B. Have completed 30 semester hours of preparation in library science in all the areas required for an endorsement authorizing a licensed teacher to serve as a library specialist.
  C. Three years of experience as a librarian or library specialist in a state-approved school.

New Hampshire

New Hampshire requires all applicants to pass the Pre-Professional Skills Test or the Computer Based Test. In addition, effective July 1, 1999, applicants seeking initial certification (see Alternatives 1–5 below) in English, social studies, general science, or mathematics must pass the appropriate PRAXIS II content-specific test. This new requirement also applies to those with expired credentials.

Criminal record checks are conducted at the district level upon employment.

Certified Educator

I. Alternative 1—Approved Programs in New Hampshire.
   A. New Hampshire State Board of Education approved programs of professional preparation in education.
   B. Certification for teachers, education specialists, and administrators.
      1. Successful completion of the approved program.
      2. Written recommendation by designated official of the institution.
      3. Application to New Hampshire Department of Education, Bureau of Teacher Education and Professional Standards.
II. Alternative 2—States Other Than New Hampshire (Covers states and territories participating in the Interstate Certification Compact).
   A. Graduate of an approved collegiate program with less than three years' teaching experience.
      1. Eligible for initial approval issued to graduates of programs approved by New Hampshire Board of Education.
   B. Experienced teacher with required type and length of service.
      1. At least three years of experience in past seven years, two of which must be under a valid credential.
      2. Meets educational requirement for a comparable certificate at initial regular level in any of the participating states.
   C. Competence in the basic skills of reading, writing and mathematics, as demonstrated by one of the following:
      1. Master's degree.
      2. Valid teaching credential from a state requiring a basic skills competence test for educational certification.
      3. Statement from candidate's undergraduate institution verifying basic skill competence.
III. Alternative 3—Demonstrated Competence and Equivalent Experiences.
   A. Candidates for certification who have gained the competencies, skills, and knowledge through means other than Alternatives 1 and 2 may request teaching, administrative or education specialist certification on basis of demonstrated competencies and equivalent experiences.

      1. Must submit description of background, with three to five references from persons in area in which certification is being sought.

      2. Will be reviewed by a Board of Examiners whose recommendation may be based on preliminary materials presented, written examinations, personal interviews, or on-site observations.

  B. See II, C.

  C. Candidates from states not party to the interstate compact will be handled on an individual basis.

IV. Alternative 4—Individualized Professional Development Plan (Critical Staffing Clause–Restricted).

  A. Secondary teachers recommended under Critical Staffing Clause.

    1. Bachelor's degree from an approved institution with a collegiate major compatible with prospective teaching assignment.

  B. Vocational Specialties candidates recommended under Critical Staffing Clause.

    1. Demonstrated vocational competence.

    2. Four years of recent, successful, full-time work experience in the appropriate area, *or*

    3. Completion of 2-year vocational technical program plus 2 years of full-time work experience.

  C. Business Administrator candidates (who have not completed an approved program in business administration) recommended under the Critical Staffing Clause.

    1. Demonstrated equivalent competence through experience in comparable business management positions.

  D. All candidates for Alternative 4 must demonstrate basic skills competence as outlined in II, C and meet entry level requirements.

V. Alternative 5—Provisional Certification Plan

  A. Available in elementary and secondary teaching areas, excluding vocational and special education.

  B. Qualifications.

    1. Bachelor's degree from an approved institution.

    2. Candidates who have graduated within 5 years preceding application shall possess

      a. (for secondary level) The equivalent of a 30 credit major in the subject to be taught and an overall grade point average of 2.5.

      b. (for elementary level) A 4 year liberal arts background, including a major and an overall grade point average of 2.5.

    3. Candidates who have graduated more than 5 years preceding application may complete any of the programs of academic study outlined in V, B, but 5 years of documented, successful experience in an area related to the subject to be taught may be substituted for the overall grade point average of 2.5.

  C. Candidates must complete a specially designed education plan, containing both pre-service and in-service components, normally during the first year of service.

Levels of Professional Certification

I. Beginning Educator Certificate (Valid 3 years).

  A. Successful completion of an approved program of professional preparation in education.

    B. Recommendation by designated official of preparatory institution.

    C. Upon recommendation of Superintendent of Schools, a beginning educator may be eligible for Experienced Educator Certificate at the close of the three-year period.

II. Experienced Educator Certificate (Valid 3 years).

    A. Has met all requirements for previous levels of certification.

       or

    B. Successful completion of approved graduate program that extends clinical experience to a full year under supervision.

New Jersey

Instructional Certificates

I. Requirements for Traditional Route to Certification
   A. Bachelor's degree from an accredited college or university.
      1. Completion of an academic major in liberal arts, science or technology.
   B. Passing score on the appropriate Praxis II Subject Assessment test(s) or on specialization area test of the National Teacher Examinations for secondary teachers and in the general knowledge test for elementary teachers.
   C. Completion of an approved teacher preparation program or the Provisional Teacher Program (alternative route to certification).
      1. Novice teachers completing an approved teacher preparation program are issued a certificate of eligibility with advanced standing. Once candidates receive an offer of employment, they are assigned a support-mentor and must complete one year of full-time, successful teaching experience under a provisional New Jersey certificate.
   D. Applicants from out of state under any form of reciprocity in accordance with the Interstate Certification Compact will have met the study requirements but must pass the required test for issuance of a regular instructional certificate in a specific field.
      1. Out of state applicants not entitled to reciprocity shall meet requirements in I, A–C.
   E. No instructional certificates are issued in instructional fields based on course by course evaluation. Applicants must complete either a college approved teacher preparation program or a district training program through the alternative route to certification. Exceptions are bilingual/ESL education and special education in which emergency certificates are issued.
   F. There are different requirements for vocational teaching areas and certain other areas. Those interested in the areas listed immediately below should write the Office of Licensing and Credentials (address in Appendix 1) for details.
      1. Agricultural occupations; practical nursing; production, personal, or service occupations; skilled trades; technical occupations; bilingual/bicultural education; and English as a second language.

II. Requirements for Alternative Route to Certification
   A. Bachelor's degree from an accredited college or university.
   B. Completion of an academic major in the subject teaching field for secondary candidates or in the liberal arts or sciences for elementary candidates.
   C. See I, B.
   D. Candidates completing II, A–C receive a certificate of eligibility and may then seek employment through the Provisional Teacher Program.
      1. Once candidates receive an offer of employment, they must apply for provisional certification.

2. Provisional teachers attend a program of approximately 200 hours of formal instruction in essential professional knowledge concurrently with employment during the first year.
3. Provisional teachers are also subject to guidance and evaluation requirements during the first year (write the Office of Licensing and Credentials for details).
4. Those successfully completing the one year Provisional Teacher Program are eligible for regular certification in the teaching area(s) listed on the certificate of eligibility.

Administrative Certificates

I. Supervisor
    A. Requirements.
        1. Regular New Jersey instructional certificate or equivalent.
        2. Three years of successful teaching experience.
        3. Master's degree from accredited or approved institution.
        4. Successful completion of one of the following:
            a. An approved program,
                or
            b. Graduate semester hours 12
                1) To include supervision and curriculum development in addition to requirements for instructional certificate, and to include:
                    a) At least 1 course in general principles of educational supervision for grades K–12.
                    b) At least 1 course in general principles of curriculum development and evaluation for grades K–12.
                    c) Additional study may be oriented directly toward supervision or curriculum development in particular grade levels or in special subject fields.
        5. When candidates have completed their preparation for this endorsement in an out-of-state college or university, a master's degree in educational administration or supervision from a program accredited by the National Council for Accreditation of Teacher Education (NCATE) will be accepted as meeting the college study requirements indicated above.
II. Principal
    A. Requirements for the Provisional Certificate (one year term; leads to the Standard Certificate)
        1. Master's degree in administration, leadership, or management.
        2. Passing score on the NTE Educational Leadership test.
        3. Formal assessment of performance by state-approved assessors.
        4. Offer of employment in a position requiring the principal endorsement by a school or district which has reviewed the candidate's assessment and has agreed to sponsor the candidate in a principal residency program (one to two years in length).
    B. The Standard Certificate will be issued upon a comprehensive evaluation report by

the mentor on the resident's performance which carries a recommendation of "approved."

III. School Administrator (includes superintendent, assistant superintendent, executive superintendent, and director)
   A. Same as Principal II, A and B, except that the assessment, employment, and residency program is for administrators.
   B. The Standard Certificate will be issued upon a comprehensive evaluation report by the mentor on the resident's performance which carries a recommendation of "approved."

IV. School Business Administrator
   A. Contact the Office of Licensing and Credentials for details.

Educational Services Certificates

I. Director of Student Personnel Services
   A. Authorization.
      1. This endorsement is required for any person who is assigned as a director, administrator, or supervisor of guidance and personnel services of a school system, including the supervision of the various special services in a given school district.
   B. Requirements.
      1. Bachelor's degree from an accredited or approved institution.
      2. Regular New Jersey student personnel services endorsement or its equivalent, and 3 years of successful experience in school student personnel work.
      3. Post-baccalaureate course work, semester hours 40
         a. Guidance, semester hours 18
            To include principles of guidance; individual analysis; organization and administration of guidance programs; job analysis; research; seminar in guidance; counseling; group methods in guidance; student personnel work; occupational and educational information; placement; vocational education; practicum.
         b. Psychology, semester hours... 10
            (Exclusive of introductory courses in general and educational psychology) To include psychology of physical and mental growth; child and adolescent psychology; tests and measurements; psychology of parent and child relationships; mental hygiene; statistics; mental abnormalities and defects.
         c. At least 1 course in each of the following, semester hours 12
            Sociology, administration and curriculum; supervision of instruction.

II. Student Personnel Services
   A. Authorization.
      1. This endorsement is required for any person assigned to perform student personnel services such as study and assessment of individual pupils; counseling with teachers, students, and parents; and developing cooperative relationships with community agencies in assisting children and families.

B. Requirements.
1. Bachelor's or higher degree.
2. Regular New Jersey instructional certificate or its equivalent, and one year of successful teaching experience.
3. Post-baccalaureate course work, in addition to the teacher's certificate, semester hours 33
   To include study in each of the 5 areas listed below. Starred areas are required.
   a. Guidance and counseling, semester hours 9
      To include *theory and procedures in individual group guidance; *counseling and interviewing techniques; *vocational guidance; occupational and educational information; placement.
   b. Testing and evaluation, semester hours... 3
   c. Psychology semester hours 6
      To include child and adolescent development; psychology of exceptional children; psychology of learning; child and youth study.
   d. Sociological foundations, semester hours.. 6
      To include *community agencies, organizations, and resources; educational sociology; social problems, juvenile delinquency, law, the family; urban sociology.
   e. Electives in the field, semester hours.. 9

III. Educational Media Specialist
A. Authorization.
1. This endorsement is required for any person who is assigned to develop and coordinate educational media services in the public schools. Educational media are defined as all print and nonprint resources and equipment needed for their use.
B. Requirements.
1. Master's degree.
2. Regular New Jersey instructional certificate or associate educational media specialist endorsement.
3. One year of successful teaching or one year of successful experience as associate educational media specialist.
4. Post-baccalaureate studies, semester hours 30
   a. To include organization and coordination of school media services and materials; application of learning theory in reading, listening, and viewing educational media materials; design and development of educational media programs; design and development of educational media materials; integration of educational media through the school curriculum; evaluation, selection, and utilization of educational media; development of individual and group processes in the media program; field experience in a school media program.

IV. Associate Educational Media Specialist
A. Authorization.
1. This endorsement is required for any person assigned to perform educational media services in the public schools under the supervision of a qualified

supervisor. Educational media are defined as all print and nonprint resources and the equipment needed for their use.

B.   Requirements.
1.   Bachelor's degree.
2.   Regular New Jersey instructional certificate.
3.   Undergraduate or graduate credits, semester hours 18
a.   To include organization and retrieval of information and media resources; production of educational media; evaluation, selection and utilization of educational media; integration of educational media through the school curriculum; field experience in a school media program.

New Mexico

The NTE Core Battery will be required of all individuals applying for licensure prior to July 1, 1999. All individuals applying for licensure after July 1, 1999 who have not passed the NTE Core Battery after July 1, 1996 will be required to pass the New Mexico Teacher Assessments. These are comprised of the New Mexico Assessment of Teacher Basic Skills; New Mexico Assessment of Teacher General Knowledge, and New Mexico Assessment of Teacher Competency. Contact the New Mexico Department of Education (address in Appendix 1) for further details.

Licensure Levels

I. Initial Licensure—Level 1 (classroom instruction)
    A. Valid for 3 years; nonrenewable.
    B. 54 semester hours in general education (see Elementary Education below for details).
    C. Professional education courses which incorporate the State Board's prescribed pedagogical competencies.
    D. Teaching field in at least one content area which incorporates the State Board's teaching field competencies.
II. Continuing Licensure—Level 2 (classroom instruction)
    A. Valid for 9 years; renewable.
    B. Fulfillment of Level 1 requirements.
    C. Verification by local superintendent or private school official that applicant has met State Board's prescribed teaching competencies.
III. Initial Licensure—Level 3-A (instructional leadership)
    A. Valid for 9 years; renewable.
    B. Fulfillment of Level 2 requirements.
    C. Master's degree.
    D. Verification by local superintendent or private school official that applicant has met the State Board's prescribed Level 3-A competencies.
IV. Initial Licensure—Level 3-B (educational administration/management)
    A. Valid for 9 years; renewable.
    B. Fulfillment of Level 2 requirements.
    C. Master's degree.
    D. Completion of an administrative internship or apprenticeship.
    E. 18 semester hours of graduate credit in educational administration which incorporates the State Board's prescribed Level 3-B competencies.

Note: Detailed competencies for each level of certification are available from the New Mexico State Board of Education (see Appendix 1 for address).

Out-of-State Application for Licensure

I.   There are three options for those seeking New Mexico teacher or administrator licensure.
    A.   Option One (valid for one year)
        1.   Bachelor's and/or master's degree from a regionally accredited college or university.
        2.   Completion of an educator preparation program accepted by the New Mexico Board of Education.
        3.   Core Battery of the NTE must be passed during the one year license period.
    B.   Option Two (valid for one year)
        1.   See I, A, 1.
        2.   Valid standard certificate or license issued by another state.
        3.   Three years of satisfactory experience at the grade level, developmental area, and/or license/endorsement being sought.
        4.   See I, A, 3.
    C.   Option Three (period variable depending on licensure being sought)
        1.   Valid certificate issued by the National Board for the Professional Teaching Standards for the appropriate grade level and type.
    D.   Administrative Licensure
        1.   Master's degree from a regionally accredited college or university.
        2.   Valid teaching license accepted by the New Mexico State Board of Education.

Elementary Education (K–8)

I.   Requirements for Level 1 Licensure
    A.   Bachelor's degree from an accredited institution.
    B.   General education, total semester hours.. 54
        1.   English, semester hours 12
        2.   History (including American history and Western civilization), semester hours 12
        3.   Mathematics, semester hours... 6
        4.   Government, economics, or sociology, semester hours 6
        5.   Science (including biology, chemistry, physics, geology, zoology, or botany), semester hours 12
    C.   Professional education, semester hours 30–36
        1.   Completion of the State Board's approved functional areas and related competencies in professional education.
        2.   Completion of a student teaching component.
    D.   Teaching field, semester hours...24–36
    (such as mathematics, science(s), language arts, reading, social studies, or other content related areas)
        1.   Completion of State Board's approved functional areas and related competencies in the teaching field.

Secondary Education (7–12)

I. Requirements for Level 1 Licensure
    A. See Elementary Education I, A and B.
    B. Professional education, semester hours 24–30
        1. See Elementary Education I, C, 1 and 2.
    C. Teaching field, semester hours 24–36
        1. 12 semester hours must be in upper division courses as defined by the institution.
        2. See Elementary Education I, D, 1.

Educational Administration (K–12)

I. Requirements for Level 3–B Licensure
    A. Valid New Mexico teaching license, level 2.
    B. Bachelor's degree and master's degree from an accredited institution. For students first entering a college or university in Fall 1986 and thereafter, an apprenticeship is required.
        1. The apprenticeship may be completed at an institution with an approved program in educational administration and must consist of at least 180 clock hours. (One-half of the 180 clock hours must be at the beginning of the school year and one-half at the end of the school year.)
            or
            The apprenticeship may be completed under the supervision of a local school superintendent or a private school official at the school and consist of at least 180 clock hours.
    C. Eighteen semester hours of graduate credit in an approved educational administration program which incorporates the State Board's approved functional areas and related competencies in educational administration.

School Counseling (K–12)

I. Requirements
    A. Bachelor's degree and master's degree from accredited institutions.
        1. Master's degree in school counseling from a New Mexico institution which must incorporate the State Board's prescribed competencies in the area of school counseling;
            or
        2. Master's degree from an out-of-state institution in a school counseling program approved by the State Board;
            or
        3. If master's degree is in a discipline other than school counseling, 36–42 semester hours of graduate credit from a New Mexico institution which incorporates the State Board's prescribed competencies in school counseling and includes a practicum in a school setting;
            or

4. If master's degree is in a discipline other than school counseling, 36–42 semester hours of graduate credit from an out-of-state institution in school counseling which is approved by the State Board and includes a practicum in a school setting.

B. Background experience.
1. Holding a valid New Mexico teaching license, level 2 or above;
    or
2. Three years of verified, satisfactory experience in one or more of the following areas: teaching, educational administration, or school counseling; clinical practice; or mental health work.

New York

All persons applying for their initial (provisional) New York State elementary, secondary, special subjects, or school media certificates are required to have successfully completed the New York State Teacher Certification Examination's liberal arts and sciences test (LAST) and its written assessment of teaching skills test (ATS-W). Applicants for *all* initial New York State certificates are required to have completed two clock hours of course work or training regarding the identification and reporting of suspected child abuse or maltreatment. Those outside New York State should contact the State Education Department for information on long-distance training courses.

Elementary (PreK–6)

I. Provisional Certificate (Valid 5 years)
    A. Completion of an approved program registered by the State Education Department specifically for service as a teacher of lower and elementary grades (PreK–6), which includes
        1. Bachelor's degree with a concentration in one of the liberal arts and sciences and college-level work in English, mathematics, science, social studies, and a language other than English.
        2. Special training in the teaching of reading.
        3. College-supervised student teaching in both the lower (PreK–3) and upper (4–6) elementary levels.
    or
    B. Completion of alternative requirements which include
        1. Bachelor's degree from a regionally accredited or approved institution.
        2. Successful completion of at least 6 semester hours of college-level credit in each of the following subjects: English, mathematics, science, and social studies.
        3. Concentration (satisfactory to the commissioner) in professional education, semester hours 30
            a. Teaching of reading, semester hours 6
        4. Satisfactory concentration in one of the liberal arts and sciences, semester hours 36
        5. One year of college-level study, or its equivalent, of a language other than English.
        6. College-supervised student teaching in both the lower (PreK–3) and upper (4–6) elementary levels (with recommendation, one year of paid, full-time teaching experience at the appropriate level may be substituted).
    or
    C. Meet conditions of the Interstate Agreement.
    D. All applicants must achieve a satisfactory level of performance on the liberal arts and sciences portion and on the written assessment of teaching skills portion of the New York State Teacher Certification Examinations.

II.   Permanent Certificate
    A.   Satisfy requirements for provisional certificate.
    B.   Satisfactory completion of a supervised internship of one academic year or two years of experience in a public or nonpublic school.
    C.   Master's degree in, or functionally related to, the field of teaching service.
    D.   Satisfactory level of performance on an examination for permanent certification in the area of the teaching certificate and on an assessment of teaching skills.

III. Extension of Elementary Certificate for Individual Subjects in the Early Secondary Grades (7–9)
    A.   Available for English, languages other than English, mathematics, a science, or social studies.
    B.   Academic concentration for each subject, semester hours.................................... 36
    C.   College-level study in middle-level education, semester hours 6
    D.   For a permanent extension, the applicant must achieve a satisfactory level of performance on an examination in the area of the certificate extension.

IV.   Annotation of Special Preparation in Early Childhood Education on a Provisional Elementary Certificate
    A.   Completion of an approved program registered by the State Education Department specifically for teachers of early childhood years (PreK–3).
       or
    B.   Completion of alternative requirements which include
       1.   College-level study, or the equivalent, in the arts, semester hours 6
       2.   College-level study in child development and the family, semester hours 6
       3.   College-level study in early childhood education theory and techniques, semester hours 12
       4.   Successful completion of a supervised practicum with preschool-age children or a minimum of one year of successful teaching of young children in a public or nonpublic school.
    C.   A permanent elementary certificate may be annotated for early childhood education upon meeting all requirements for the annotations of a provisional certificate and achieving a satisfactory level of performance on an examination in early childhood education.

Secondary Academic Subjects (7–12)

I.   Provisional Certificate (Valid 5 years)
    A.   Completion of an approved program registered by the State Education Department specifically for service as a teacher of English, languages other than English, mathematics, a science, or social studies in grades 7–12, which includes
       1.   Bachelor's degree with a concentration in one of the liberal arts or sciences appropriate to the area of the certificate and college-level study in a language other than English
       2.   College-supervised student teaching in both the middle level and high school grades, except for certificates in which instruction is provided exclusively at one or the other level, in which case student teaching shall be at the appropriate level.
       or

B. Completion of alternative requirements which include
   1. Bachelor's degree from a regionally accredited or approved institution.
   2. Concentration (satisfactory to the commissioner) in professional education, semester hours 18
   3. Concentration in area of certification, semester hours 36
      a. For certification in a specific area of science, at least 18 semester hours of the concentration must be in that area (biology, chemistry, physics, or earth science); for extension of the certificate to teach general science, 18 semester hours in one science and study in at least two others are required.
   4. One year of college-level study in a language other than English.
   5. Same as I, A, 2 directly above, except one year of paid, full-time teaching experience at the appropriate level may be substituted.
   or
C. Meet conditions of the Interstate Agreement.
D. All applicants must achieve a satisfactory level of performance on the liberal arts and sciences portion and on the written assessment of teaching skills portion of the New York State Teacher Certification Examinations.

II. Permanent Certificate
A. Same as Elementary II, A–D, except at the secondary level.

Special Subjects

I. Subjects Valid for Certification
A. Art, business and distributive education (general), dance, home economics (general), health, music, physical education, recreation, speech, and technology education.

II. Provisional Certificate (Valid 5 years)
A. Bachelor's degree from a regionally accredited or approved institution, to include
   1. Professional education, semester hours 12
   2. Technical courses in subject of certificate, semester hours 36

III. Permanent Certificate
A. Satisfy requirements for Provisional Certificate.
   1. With recommendation, one year of full-time teaching experience on the appropriate level may be substituted for student teaching.
B. Master's degree in, or functionally related to, field of teaching service.
C. Two years of Special Subject(s) teaching experience.

Administration and Supervision

I. School District Administrator (includes superintendent of schools as well as district, deputy, associate, or assistant superintendent)
A. Permanent Certificate
   1. Bachelor's degree from a regionally accredited or approved institution.
   2. Graduate study, semester hours 60
      a. To include 24 semester hours in the field of administration and supervision.
   3. Approved administrative-supervisory internship (carrying graduate credit), or one year of full-time experience in a school administrative or supervisory position.

4. Master's degree.
5. Three years of teaching and/or administrative and/or supervisory and/or pupil personnel experience in elementary or secondary public schools.

    B. The Commissioner of Education, at the request of a board of education, may approve the issuance of a certificate to exceptionally qualified persons who do not meet all the graduate course or public school teaching requirements noted in I, A, 2 and 5.

II. School Administrator and Supervisor
    A. Provisional Certificate
        1. See I, A, 1.
        2. Graduate study, semester hours 30
            a. To include 18 semester hours in field of school administration and supervision.
        3. See I, A, 3.
        4. See I, A, 5.
    B. Permanent Certificate
        1. Completion of requirements for Provisional Certificate.
        2. Two years in an administrative/supervisory position.
        3. Master's degree.

III. School Business Administrator (includes deputy, associate, or assistant superintendent of schools for business)
    A. Permanent Certificate
        1. See I, A, 1 and 2.
        2. Same as I, A, 3, except that the one year of full-time experience must be as the chief business official of a school district.
        3. See I, A, 4.

Pupil Personnel Service—School Counselor

I. Provisional Certificate (Valid 5 years)
    A. Bachelor's degree from a regionally accredited or approved institution.
    B. Approved graduate study in the field of school counseling, including supervised practice in guidance, semester hours 30

II. Permanent Certificate
    A. Graduate study in the field of school counseling, in addition to requirements for provisional certificate, semester hours 30
    B. Master's degree.
    C. Two years of pupil personnel service in the elementary and/or secondary schools.

School Media Specialist, School Media Specialist (Library) and School Media Specialist (Educational Communications)

I. Provisional Certificate (Valid 5 years)
    A. Bachelor's degree.
    B. Program of preparation.
        1. School media, school media (library), or school media (educational communications), semester hours 36

      2.   Professional education, semester hours 12

      3.   College-supervised practicum in areas listed in B, 1.

  C.   Substitutions and exceptions

      1.   One year of paid, full-time experience in school media shown above may be accepted in lieu of a practicum, with recommendation of employing school district administrator.

  D.   Distribution

      1.   The school media specialist certificate is granted to applicants whose preparation includes 18 semester hours in school media (library) and 18 semester hours in school media (educational communications); the school media specialist (library) certificate is granted to applicants when preparation includes at least 24 semester hours in school media (library); and the school media specialist (educational communications) certificate is granted to applicants when preparation includes at least 24 semester hours in school media (educational communications).

II. Permanent Certificate

  A.   Master's degree in the field of media.

  B.   Two years of experience as a school media specialist.

  C.   Program of preparation.

      1.   Professional education, semester hours 12

      2.   School media, semester hours 36

      3.   A college-supervised practicum.

North Carolina

Professional Licenses

I. Initial Licenses
   A. Granted upon completion of an approved teacher education program
   B. Required testing
      1. Passing scores on the NTE/PRAXIS Principles of Learning and Teaching test (effective July 1, 1998), and at least one NTE specialty area test or the set of PRAXIS subject assessments (requirement to be met prior to initial licensing by all graduates of teacher education programs in North Carolina institutions of higher education; to be met during first school year of employment by other qualified individuals)

II. Continuing Licenses
   A. Granted upon successful completion of an Initial Licensure Program (ILP) through employment with a North Carolina school system having an approved ILP plan
   B. Valid for five-year cycles

III. Renewal and Reinstatement of Licenses
   A. Awarded for 10 semester hours or 15 units (1 unit = 10 contact hours) of credit earned within the current five-year period (credit earned must be directly related to license areas and/or professional responsibilities)
   B. Acceptable means for earning renewal credit
      1. Courses at accredited colleges or universities (1 semester hour is equivalent to 1.5 units of credit; 1 quarter hour is equivalent to 1 unit of credit)
      2. Courses or workshops offered by a school administrative unit or local governing board
      3. Full-time teaching experience (1 unit of credit for each full-time year of teaching within the renewal cycle)
   C. Renewal credit must be approved by the employer.

Licensing Areas

I. Teaching Areas
   A. Birth through kindergarten
   B. Elementary (K–6)
   C. Elementary second language endorsement
   D. Middle grades (6–9; subject specific)
   E. Secondary (9–12)
   F. Endorsements (valid for less than half-time assignments in grades 9–12)
   G. Special subjects (K–12)
   H. Exceptional children (K–12)
   I. Workforce development (middle grades and secondary)

II. Special Service Personnel
   A. Superintendent
   B. Principal
   C. Curriculum-Instructional Specialist
   D. Counselor
   E. School Social Worker
   F. School Psychologist
   G. Mentor
   H. Speech-Language Pathologist
   I. Audiologist
   J. Media Coordinator

Special Licensing Requirements

I. Administration
   A. Superintendent or Principal
      1. Completion of an approved program in school administration at sixth-year or doctoral level
      2. Satisfactory score on the ISSLLC Administrators Test
      3. Recommendation by the North Carolina Administrative Standards Board
   B. Curriculum-instructional specialist: completion of an approved program in curriculum and instruction (including competencies in administration, supervision, curriculum methods, and educational research) at the master's level
II. Student Service Personnel
   A. School psychologist: sixth-year degree in school psychology from an accredited institution
   B. School counselor: master's degree in school counseling from an accredited institution
   C. Speech-Language pathologist: master's degree in speech-language pathology in an approved program at an accredited institution, *or* master's degree in speech pathology and a North Carolina license to practice as a speech pathologist.
   D. Audiologist: master's degree in audiology from an approved program at an accredited institution, *or* master's degree in audiology and a North Carolina Board of Examiners license to practice as an audiologist.
   E. Media coordinator: completion of a master's level program in school media
III. Teachers
   A. Secondary endorsements: 18 semester hours in a specific subject area (must be attached to full licensing in another subject)

North Dakota

Effective July 1, 1997, North Dakota adopted new standards for its superintendent, elementary principal, and secondary principal credentials. Through June 30, 1999, these credentials may be issued based on either the previous or new standards. After that date, all credentials (and credential renewals) will be based on the new standards. Those wishing information on the previous standards may either consult the 1997–98 edition of *Requirements for Certification* or contact the Department of Public Instruction (address in Appendix 1).

Elementary School

I. North Dakota Educator's Professional Certificate
    A. Bachelor's degree from an accredited college approved to offer teacher education
    B. Professional requirements, credits in professional education including student teaching, overall GPA 2.5, semester hours 34
    C. Valid for two years for teaching in the level of preparation
    D. A five-year renewal may be issued with two years of successful full-time teaching experience in the state. Each renewal of the five-year certificate requires 4 semester hours of work.

Secondary School

I. North Dakota Educator's Professional Certificate
    A. Same as Elementary School, I, A–D
    B. Semester hours 26

Administration

I. Superintendent Provisional Credential
    A. Valid ND teaching certificate and at least 3 years of successful teaching experience
    B. At least 2 years of administrative experience with at least half-time as an elementary or secondary principal in an approved school, a central office director in an approved school (district enrollment of 3,000 or more), or an administrator of an approved school with a 12-year program
    C. Master's degree in educational administration from a state-approved program; *or* master's degree in a content field with at least 20 semester hours of credit aligned with a master's degree in educational administration from a state-approved program
    D. Credential is valid for 1 year and is nonrenewable except under special circumstances of appeal
II. Superintendent Professional Credential
    A. Same as I, A–C

   B. Evidence of successful service in the last employing school/district
   C. Credential is valid for 5 years with a current ND teaching certificate and is renewable

III. Elementary or Secondary Principal: Provisional Credentials
   A. Valid ND teaching certificate based on a bachelor's degree with a major, minor, or endorsement in elementary education
   B. At least 3 years (full-time equivalency, employed under contract) of successful teaching and/or administrative experience
     and
   C. (Level II) Completion of 20 semester hours of graduate credit aligned with a master's degree in educational administration from a state approved program
     or
   D. (Level I) Master's degree in educational administration from a state approved program; *or* master's degree in a content field with at least 20 semester hours of credit aligned with a master's degree in educational administration from a state approved program
   E. Credential is valid for 2 years and is nonrenewable except under special circumstances of appeal

IV. Level II Elementary or Secondary Principal Professional Credentials
   A. Same as III, A–C
   B. Evidence of successful service in the last employing school/district
   C. Credential is valid for 5 years and is nonrenewable for principals serving elementary schools with enrollments of 100 or more students (renewable when less than 100 students)

V. Level I Elementary or Secondary Principal Professional Credentials
   A. Same as III, A, B, and D
   B. Evidence of successful service in the last employing school/district
   C. Credential is valid for 5 years

VI. Renewal for Superintendent and Level I Principal Professional Credentials
   A. Evidence of satisfactory completion of at least 8 semester hours of graduate credit in education, of which 4 semester hours are in administration
     or
   B. Evidence of satisfactory completion of at least 4 semester hours of graduate credit in education and evidence (certified statements from conference sponsors) of attendance/participation in at least 6 approved conferences or workshops
     and
   C. Evidence of successful service in the last employing school/district

School Counselor

I. Professional Credential—Elementary, Secondary, or K–12
   A. Master's degree with specified core guidance courses and practicum
   B. Experience: Two years of teaching experience or related human services experience
   C. First year on a provisional basis
   D. Valid North Dakota Educator's Professional Certificate

Library Media

I.   Librarian Designate (LM04)
   A.   Bachelor's degree
   B.   Valid North Dakota Educator's Professional Certificate
   C.   Course work in library media from Section I of the "Guide for Course Preparation" (write Department of Public Instruction for details), semester hours 8
   D.   This credential is valid for five years and is not renewable although it may be upgraded to one of the credentials below.

II. Librarian (LM03)
   A.   See I, A and B
   B.   Same as I, C, except hours are doubled, semester hours 16

III. Library Media Specialist (LM02)
   A.   See I, A and B
   B.   See II, B
   C.   Course work in library media from Section II of the "Guide for Course Preparation," semester hours 10

IV. Library Media Director (LM01)
   A.   Master's degree in library science, media education, or other
   B.   See I, B
   C.   See II, B and III, C
   D.   Course work in library media from Section III of the "Guide for Course Preparation," semester hours 12

V.   Renewal (LM03, LM02, LM01)
   A.   Librarians with North Dakota First and Second Grade Professional Life Certificates.
      1.   Credentials are valid for five years.
      2.   Completion of four semester hours of undergraduate or graduate credit in the areas of library, media, education, curriculum, and communications
      3.   Recommendation from last employing school
   B.   Librarians with North Dakota Educator's Professional Certificate.
      1.   Librarians with an initial two- or five-year Educator's Professional Certificate will have the library media credential automatically renewed each time the teaching certificate is renewed.

Speech Therapist

I.   Speech Clinician Preparation
   A.   A valid North Dakota Educator's Professional Certificate
   B.   A special education credential in speech correction awarded on completion of the following 30 semester hours of specialized course work issued by the Department of Public Instruction
      1.   A total of 6 semester hours of credit distributed in phonetics, anatomy and physiology of the speech mechanism, psychology of speech, voice, science, semantics
      2.   A total of 12 semester hours credit in professional speech correction and speech pathology courses

3. Three semester credits in audiology
4. At least 200 clock hours of supervised clinical practicum, representing actual work with major types of speech defects at varying age levels in addition to observation periods, assistance with scheduling routine and other noncorrective activities
5. At least 9 semester hours of electives in allied fields which must include courses in child psychology and mental hygiene
6. Personal speech habits in both voice and diction which meet an acceptable standard, as well as personal characteristics acceptable in a teacher of children
7. Adherence to the Professional Code of Ethics of the American Speech and Hearing Association; the completion of these courses and requirements entitles the applicant to the Speech Clinician I Credential.

Ohio

Ohio's new standards are performance-based and lead to licensing based on assessments (administered under the authority of the state board of education) of the performance of teachers and principals during their participation in an entry year program.

Provisional Licenses

I. Provisional Teacher License (valid two years)
   A. Holds a degree required by the license
   B. Deemed to be of good moral character
   C. Successfully completed an approved program of preparation
   D. Recommended by the dean or head of teacher education at an institution approved to prepare teachers
   E. Successfully completed an examination prescribed by the state board of education
   F. Demonstrated skill in integrating educational technology in the instruction of children
   G. Completed course work in the teaching of reading, semester hours........................ 6
      1. For the early childhood and middle childhood license, this must include at least one separate 3 semester hour course in the teaching of phonics
II. Provisional Principal License
   A. Holds a master's degree
   B. Deemed to be of good moral character
   C. Successfully completed an approved principal preparation program
   D. Recommended by the dean or head of teacher education at an institution approved to prepare principals
   D. Successfully completed an examination prescribed by the state board of education
   E. Successfully completed two years of teaching under a professional teacher license at the age levels for which the principal license is sought

Entry Year Program

I. Requirements
   A. Candidate holds a provisional license
   B. Candidate's success in the classroom will be evaluated throughout the year on the basis of student success in different areas (write the Department of Education for details; address in Appendix 1)
   C. Upon successful completion of the entry year program and assessment, the individual will be deemed to have met the requirements for professional licensure

Professional Licenses

I.   Professional Teacher License (valid for 5 years)
   A.   Holds a Provisional License
   B.   Holds a baccalaureate degree
   C.   See Provisional Licenses I, B, C, and E

II.   Professional Teacher License Areas
   A.   Early childhood license (PreK–3)
      1.   Minimum course work in teaching of reading, semester hours 12
   B.   Middle childhood license (4–9)
      1.   The middle childhood teacher preparation program shall include preparation in the humanities (including the arts) and areas of concentration in at least two of the following: reading and language arts, mathematics, science, and social studies
      2.   See A, 1 directly above
   C.   Adolescence to young adult license (7–12)
      1.   Preparation in the teaching field shall constitute at least an academic major or its equivalent with sufficient advanced course work in all areas to be taught
      2.   Licenses are issued in the following teaching fields:
         a.   Earth sciences, integrated language arts, integrated mathematics, integrated science, integrated social studies, life sciences, and physical sciences
   D.   Multiage license (PreK–12)
      1.   See C, 1
      2.   Licenses are issued in the following teaching fields:
         a.   Dance, drama/theater, foreign language, health, library/media, music, physical education, and visual arts
   E.   Other professional teacher license areas include intervention specialist, early childhood intervention specialist, and a variety of vocational areas. Please write the Department of Education (address in Appendix 1) for details.

Professional Pupil Services Licenses

I.   Professional Pupil Services License (valid for 5 years)
   A.   Deemed to be of good moral character
   B.   Completed an approved program of preparation
   C.   Recommended by the dean or head of teacher education
   D.   Completed an examination prescribed by the state board of education

II.   License Areas
   A.   School audiologist
      1.   Master's degree and current license to practice audiology
   B.   School counselor
      1.   Master's degree and 2 years of successful teaching experience under a provisional or professional teacher license; *or* five years experience as a licensed school counselor in another state
   C.   School psychologist

1. Master's degree and successful completion of a 9 month, full-time internship in an approved school setting
    D. Other professional pupil personnel license areas include school social worker; school speech-language pathologist; school nurse; and orientation and mobility specialist. Please write the Department of Education (address in Appendix 1) for details.

Professional Administrator Licenses

I. Professional Administrator License
    A. Deemed to be of good moral character
    B. Holds a master's degree
    C. Recommended by the dean or head of teacher education at an institution approved to prepare teachers
    D. Successfully completed an examination prescribed by the state board of education
II. License Areas
    A. Principal License
        1. Added to a valid professional teaching license after successful completion of the entry year program for principals
        2. Valid for working with:
            a. Grades PreK–6 with an early childhood, middle childhood, multiage, or intervention specialist license
            b. Grades 4–9 with a middle childhood, multiage, adolescence to young adult, or intervention specialist license
            c. Grades 5–12 with a middle childhood, multiage, intervention specialist, adolescence to young adult, or vocational license.
    B. Administrative Specialist License
        1. Added to a valid professional teacher license or professional pupil services license and valid for working in a central office or supervisory capacity
        2. Prior to issuance, applicant must have completed 2 years of successful teaching experience under a professional teacher's license and must have successfully completed an approved program of preparation
    C. Superintendent License
        1. Added to a valid professional teacher license of an individual who holds a principal or administrative specialist license
        2. Prior to issuance, applicant must have completed 3 years of successful experience in a position requiring a principal or administrative specialist license and must have successfully completed an approved preparation program for superintendents

Oklahoma

Oklahoma is in the process of converting to a competency-based system of certification. Applicants should write to the State Department of Education for the latest information.

Teaching Certificate Subject Areas

I. Teaching Certificates
    A. Early Childhood Education (Grades PreK–3)
    B. Elementary (Grades 1–8)
    C. PreK–Grade 12
        1. Subject matter may be in art, foreign languages (French, German, Latin, Russian, and Spanish), music, physical education/health/safety, reading specialist, special education (blind/visual impairment, deaf/hard of hearing, mild/moderate disabilities, and severe-profound/multiple disabilities).
    D. Middle-Level Specialist (Grades 5–9)
        1. Subject matter may be in art, English, foreign languages (French, German, Latin, Russian, and Spanish), mathematics, music, physical education/health/safety, science, social studies, and technology education.
    E. Grades 6–12
        1. Subject matter may be in business education, driver/safety education, English, family and consumer sciences, journalism, mathematics, science, social studies, speech/drama/debate, vocational technical (agricultural education, marketing education, technology education, vocational business, and vocational family and consumer sciences).
II. Support Services Certificates
    A. School Counselor
    B. Library Media Specialist
    C. School Psychologist
    D. School Psychometrist/Education Diagnostician
    E. School Nurse
    F. Speech-Language Pathologist
    G. Junior Reserve Officers' Training Corps (ROTC)
III. Administrative/Supervisory Certificates
    A. Elementary Principal (Grades PreK–12)
    B. Middle Level Principal (Grades 5–9) (optional)
    C. Secondary Principal (Grades 6–12)

General Certificate Requirements

I. License (one year validity)
    A. To be eligible the applicant shall have

1. Completed an approved, competency-based certificate program at an accredited college or university.
2. A baccalaureate degree.
3. Passed the state teacher certification tests in general education, professional education, and subject matter.

B. A license also may be issued to applicants falling in the following categories:
1. Out-of-state applicant holding a valid out-of-state certificate with credentials in the area sought;
2. Out-of-state applicant who has held a certificate in the area sought, holds a master's degree, and has earned an additional fifteen or more semester hours in a teaching field; or
3. Applicant who has an expired Oklahoma license, which was issued with course requirements completed for the Standard Certificate.

C. Conditions leading to certification for licenses issued under B, 1–3
1. Successful completion of the Residency Program,
2. Successful employment for one year in an Oklahoma-accredited school under the supervision of an administrator and with the assistance of an appropriate colleague,
3. Completion of a two semester hour course in education of the exceptional child, and
4. Passing results on the state teacher certification tests.

II. A Provisional Level II Certificate may be issued to applicants falling in the following categories:
A. See Licenses I, B, 1–3.
B. Conditions leading to certification for licenses issued under B, 1–3
1. See Licenses I, C, 2–4.

III. Standard Certificate (five year term)
A. Standard Certificate (undergraduate)—To be eligible an applicant shall have:
1. Completed an approved, competency-based certificate program at an accredited college or university.
2. A baccalaureate degree,
3. Passed the state certification tests.
4. Successfully completed the Residency Program as a licensed teacher.
B. Standard Certificate (graduate)–To be eligible for a Standard Certificate for School Counselor, Library Media Specialist, Elementary School Principal, Middle Level Principal, Secondary School Principal, School Superintendent, School Psychometrist, School Psychologist, Speech-Language Pathologist or Reading Specialist, the applicant shall have
1. Completed an approved certificate program at the baccalaureate level which includes the requirements detailed in IV, A, 1–3, directly above, as well as earned a Master's degree.
2. Passed the state certification tests.

IV. Alternative Placement Program
A. Alternative Placement Program I (License or Provisional)–To be eligible an applicant shall have

1. Earned a baccalaureate degree;
2. Completed a major in a field of study corresponding to an area of Oklahoma certification for an Elementary-Secondary Certificate, Secondary Certificate, or Vocational-Technical Certificate;
3. Passed the Teacher Certification Test(s) in the subject(s) for which certification is sought;
4. Declared the intention to earn a Standard Certificate in three years or less;
5. Declared the intention to seek employment as a teacher at an accredited public district in the state;
6. Never been denied admission to an approved teacher education program nor have enrolled in and subsequently failed courses necessary to meet the minimum requirements of such a program;
7. Filed the appropriate application and fee with the Professional Standards Section of the State Department of Education;
8. Documented at least two years of teaching experience or subject matter work experience that is related to the subject area of specialization if the person has only a baccalaureate degree with no postbaccalaureate work in a related area.

B. Alternative Placement Program II (Standard)—To be eligible an applicant shall have:
1. Completed A, 1–8 directly above;
2. Successfully completed the Residency program;
3. Completed a professional education component consisting of a maximum of eighteen semester hours or two hundred seventy clock hours (a two semester hour course in education of the exceptional child is required).

Reciprocity

Oklahoma has signed an exchange certification agreement with Missouri, Iowa, Nebraska, Kansas, South Dakota, and Arkansas (MINKSOA) which allows individuals certified in one of the member states to be eligible for a two-year exchange certificate in any of the participating states.

Oregon

All applicants must demonstrate knowledge of the laws prohibiting discrimination, including Title VI of the Civil Rights Act of 1964 and Title IX of the Education Amendments of 1972.

Teaching Licenses

I. Transitional License (valid 3 years, by which time the individual must qualify for the Initial Teaching License; not renewable)
   A. Baccalaureate degree.
   B. Completion of an approved teacher education program in the endorsement area(s) requested.
   C. Recommendation by the teacher education institution or possession of a current license issued by another state.
   D. Affidavit indicating knowledge of civil rights laws.

Note: The Transitional License replaces the Reciprocal License and is usually the initial license issued to out-of-state applicants.

II. Initial Teaching License (valid 3 years and renewable for one 3-year term, by which time the individual must qualify for the Continuing Teaching License)
   A. Baccalaureate degree which must be conferred by an approved teacher education institution unless verification of *five* years of successful public school teaching experience is provided.
   B. Completion of an approved teacher education program in the endorsement area(s) requested
      or
      Current license which is not limited due to course work, issued by another state and valid for the endorsement(s) requested on the Oregon license.
   C. Completion of TSPC-approved civil rights workshop.
   D. Recent experience.
      1. One year of successful public school teaching experience within the three-year period immediately preceding application
         or
         Nine quarter hours of additional preparation in an approved teacher education institution within the past three years.
   E. Professional knowledge.
      1. Completion of five years of public school teaching
         or
         Passing score of 661 on the Professional Knowledge test of the NTE Core Battery.

2. Completion of academic preparation for one or more of the initial endorsements established by Oregon's Teacher Standards and Practices Commission (TSPC) *and* five years of public school teaching in the endorsement on the license valid for the assignment

   or

   Acceptable scores as set by TSPC on one or more of the National Teacher Examination Specialty Area Test(s) in the subject areas requested on the Oregon license. (For all subject matter endorsements for which TSPC has not adopted tests, a transcript evaluation is required; see Subject Matter Endorsements Section.)

3. Passing scores on one of the Praxis I Series: PPST Mathematics (175); PPST Reading (174); and PPST Writing (171)

   or

   on the CBT Series: Mathematics (320); Reading (321); and Writing (317)

   or

   on the California Basic Educational Skills Test (CBEST) (123)

   or

   Verification of five years of full-time successful public school experience (if initial Oregon license).

III. Continuing Teaching License (valid 5 years; renewable)

   A. Completion of a fifth-year teacher education program consisting of 45 quarter hours of upper-division and graduate preparation beyond the bachelor's degree

   or

   Completion of a master's degree from an approved teacher education institution in another state.

   B. Three years of one-half time or more experience on an Initial Teaching License in the Oregon schools.

   C. Completion of a standard endorsement in one of the endorsements held on the license. Holders of special education endorsements must complete a continuing endorsement program in one special education endorsement. (See Subject Matter Endorsements.)

Administrative Licenses

I. Initial Administrative License (valid 2 years and renewable once, by which time the individual must qualify for the Continuing Administrative License)

   A. Master's degree from an approved teacher education institution.

   B. Completion of an approved administrative program in the endorsement area(s) requested

   or

   Current license which is not limited due to course work, issued by another state, and valid for the endorsement areas requested in Oregon.

   C. Completion of TSPC-approved civil rights workshop.

   D. Recent experience.

1. One year of successful public school administrative experience within the three-year period immediately preceding application

    or

    Nine quarter hours of additional preparation in an approved teacher education institution within the past three years.

E. Professional knowledge.

1. Completion of academic preparation for one or both initial endorsements *and* five years of public school administrative experience in the endorsement area being requested

    or

    Completion of academic preparation for one or more of the initial endorsements *and* acceptable score as set by TSPC on the National Teacher Exam (NTE) Specialty Area Test for administration and supervision.

    a. Initial administrator endorsement requires 12 quarter hours of graduate credit in school administration, to include preparation in Oregon school law and a 5 quarter hour supervised practicum. (One year of full-time successful administrative experience in the public schools on a valid license may be substituted for the practicum.)

    b. The initial administrator endorsement requires verification of three years of full-time successful public school teaching experience.

    c. Initial superintendent endorsement requires 18 quarter hours of graduate credit in school administration, to include preparation in Oregon school law and a 6 quarter hour supervised practicum. (One year of full-time successful administrative experience in the public schools on a valid license may be substituted for the practicum.)

F. Passing scores on the Praxis I Series: PPST Mathematics (175); PPST Reading (174); and PPST Writing (171)

    or

    on the CBT Series: Mathematics (320); Reading (321); and Writing (317)

    or

    on the California Basic Educational Skills Test (CBEST) (123)

    or

    Verification of five years of full-time successful public school experience (if initial Oregon license).

II. Continuing Administrative License (valid 5 years)

A. Completion of three years of successful administrative experience in the Oregon schools on an Initial Administrative License.

B. Completion of an approved Continuing Administrative License Program.

C. Completion of academic preparation for one or both continuing endorsements.

1. Continuing Administrator endorsement requires 18 quarter hours of graduate administrative credit completed in addition to those required for the initial endorsement.

2. Continuing Superintendent endorsement requires 24 quarter hours of graduate administrative credit in addition to those required for the initial endorsement.

Personnel Service Licenses

I. Initial Personnel Service License (valid 3 years and renewable once, by which time the individual must qualify for the Continuing Personnel License)

    A. Completion of an approved program in the endorsement area(s) requested

       or

       Current License which is not limited due to course work, issued by another state, and valid for the endorsement in which Oregon licensure is requested.

    B. Recent experience.

       1. One year of successful personnel service experience in the past three years

          or

          Nine quarter hours of personnel service course work completed within the past three years.

    C. Completion of TSPC-approved civil rights workshop.

    D. Completion of the academic preparation for one or more of the basic endorsements and five years of public school personnel service experience in the endorsement area on a license valid for the assignment

       or

       Acceptable score(s) as set by TSPC on one or more of the NTE Specialty Area Tests for the endorsements being requested:

       1. Basic counselor—630 on the NTE School Counseling Test 42

       2. Basic school psychologist—620 on the NTE School Psychologist Test 40

       3. Basic supervisor—630 on the NTE Administration and Supervision Test 41

    E. Passing scores on the Praxis I Series: PPST Mathematics (175); PPST Reading (174); and PPST Writing (171)

       or

       on the CBT Series: Mathematics (320); Reading (321); and Writing (317)

       or

       on the California Basic Educational Skills Test (CBEST) (123)

       or

       Verification of five years of full-time successful public school experience (if initial Oregon license).

    F. Initial personnel service endorsements.

       1. Initial counselor.

          a. Hold or be eligible for an Oregon teaching license or a comparable teaching license issued by another state.

          b. Two years of successful teaching experience in the public schools, or one year of successful teaching experience plus one year of public school intern counseling experience.

          c. Completion of 24 quarter hours of graduate counseling preparation in an approved program including a 6 quarter hour practicum or internship, or one year of successful counseling experience in the public schools on a valid license.

       2. Initial supervisor.

          a. Hold or be eligible for an Oregon teaching license or a comparable teaching license issued by another state.

        b.   Hold or be eligible for an Oregon standard subject matter, special education, or personnel service endorsement.

        c.   Three years of successful teaching experience in public schools.

        d.   Completion of 12 quarter hours of graduate preparation in an approved program in school supervision, plus a supervised practicum or internship of 5 quarter hours or one year of full-time successful supervisory experience in the public schools on a valid license.

   3.   School psychologist.

        a.   Completion of a *master's degree* from an approved teacher education institution.

        b.   Completion of 75 quarter hours of graduate credit in an approved program including a clinical practicum.

        c.   Completion of full-time public school practicum for 9 weeks under the supervision of a licensed school psychologist.

        d.   Demonstrate knowledge of school psychology theory and practice by a passing score on the NTE specialty area test for school psychologist and by holding a current National School Psychology Certificate awarded by the National Association of School Psychologists.

II.   Continuing Personnel Service License (valid 5 years; renewable)

   A.   Two years of successful personnel service experience in Oregon schools while holding an initial Personnel Service License.

   B.   Completion of an approved Continuing Personnel Service License program
or
Completion of a master's degree from an approved teacher education institution in another state.

      1.   Continuing Counselor endorsement requires 24 quarter hours of graduate credit in guidance and counseling (in addition to those required for the initial counselor endorsement).

      2.   Continuing Supervisor endorsement requires 18 quarter hours of graduate credit in school supervision (in addition to those required for the initial endorsement).

Subject Matter Endorsements

Effective October 1, 1995 the Oregon TSPC implemented the new NTE PRAXIS Series examinations for the following endorsements: basic skills, biology, chemistry, elementary education, integrated science, language arts, basic mathematics, advanced mathematics, physical education, physics, social studies, Spanish, and early intervention/special education. Nonetheless, Oregon will continue to honor NTE examinations in these fields if taken prior to October 1, 1995. The Specialty Area Tests in the other fields remain unchanged. For information on specific tests and passing scores, please write the Oregon TSPC (address in Appendix 1). Program requirements for endorsements for the Initial and Continuing Teaching Licenses (in quarter hours of credit) may be found below. Please note that subject matter preparation in the endorsement area for the Continuing Teaching License must be on the graduate level.

	Initial	Continuing
Agriculture	60	15
Art	45	15
Biology	45	15
Business education	48	15
Chemistry	27	15
Chemistry/Physics	27 each	15 each
Drama	24	15
Early childhood	21	none
With PP–12, elementary, or special education endorsements.		
Educational media	24	15
French	45	15
German	45	15
Health	42	15
Home economics	48	15
Integrated science	45	15
Japanese	45	15
Language arts	45	15
Latin	45	15
Marketing	48	15
Mathematics (basic)	21	none
Mathematics (advanced)	42	15
Music	60	15
Physical education	48	15
Adapted PE (with physical education only)	24	none
Physics	27	15
Reading	21	15
Russian	45	15
Social studies	54	15
Spanish	45	15
Speech	24	15
Technology education	60	15

Special Education Endorsements

	Initial	Continuing
Handicapped learner I	33	15
May only be obtained by the holder of a Teaching License with subject matter endorsement.		
Handicapped learner II	48	15
Severely handicapped learner	45	15
Speech impaired*	42	15
Visually impaired	30	15
Hearing impaired	45	15
Elementary	60	15

Pennsylvania

I. Instructional (Classroom Teaching) Certificates
   A. Intern Certificate
      1. Earned baccalaureate degree (not in education).
      2. Completed appropriate professional education courses in an approved intern program.
      3. Recommendation by preparing institution.
      4. Successful completion of the required communication skills, general knowledge and subject matter tests.
      5. Valid for no more than 3 years.
      6. Applicant will be issued an Instructional Certificate I upon completion of the approved intern program and the passing of the appropriate Principles of Learning and Teaching test.
   B. Instructional Level I Certificate (Provisional)
      1. Completion of approved program of studies.
      2. Bachelor's degree.
      3. Recommendation by preparing institution.
      4. Valid for 6 service years.
      5. Successful completion of Pennsylvania Teacher Certification Testing Program.* (See end of Pennsylvania requirements section for details.)
   C. Instructional Level II Certificate (Permanent)
      1. Completion of a Department-approved induction program.
      2. Three years of satisfactory teaching on Pennsylvania Instructional Certificate I.
      3. Completion of 24 semester hours of post-baccalaureate study.
      4. The 24 semester hours may be satisfied in whole or in part through PDE approved in-service programs.
II. Educational Specialist (Nonteaching Professional) Certificates
   A. Educational Specialist I (Provisional)
      1. See I, B, 1, 2, 3, and 4 above.
   B. Educational Specialist II (Permanent)
      1. Three years of satisfactory service in single area of Educational Specialist I Certificate.
      2. See I, C, 3 and 4 above.
   C. Areas of authorization (all are for K–12, unless otherwise noted)
      1. Dental hygienist, elementary school counselor (K–6), home and school visitor, instructional technology specialist, nutrition service specialist, school nurse, school psychologist, secondary school counselor (7–12), and social restoration (7–12).
III. Supervisory Certificates

* Contact the Teacher Standards and Practices Commission for alternative requirements for the speech impaired endorsement.

   A. Supervisory I (Provisional)
     1. Five years of satisfactory professional experience in the area in which certification is sought.
     2. Completion of approved program of graduate study preparing for supervision and direction of professional and nonprofessional employees.
   B. Supervisory I (for Curriculum and Instruction or Pupil Personnel Services)
     1. Five years of satisfactory service in the program area.
     2. Completion of graduate program in the endorsement area.
     3. Recommendation of preparing institution.
   C. Supervisory II (Permanent)
     1. Three years of satisfactory service on the Pennsylvania Supervisory I Certificate.
IV. Administrative Certificates
   A. Administrative I (Provisional)
     1. Five years of professional school experience.
     2. Recommendation of preparing institution.
     3. Valid for 3 service years.
   B. Administrative II (Permanent)—Principal, Vocational School Director
     1. Three years of satisfactory service on the Pennsylvania Administrative I Certificate.
   C. Letters of Eligibility—Superintendent, Assistant Superintendent
     1. Completion of a Pennsylvania-approved graduate level program of educational administrative study equal to 2 full academic years of study; *or* have been prepared through an out-of-state equivalent program.
     2. Six years of professional (certificated) school service including three years of supervisory or administrative experience.
     3. Recommendation of preparing institution.
   D. Letter of Eligibility—Intermediate Unit Executive Director
     1. See IV, C, 1.
     2. Six years professional experience, three of which were supervisory.
V. Vocational Certificates
   A. Vocational Instructional Intern Certificate
     1. High school graduation or equivalent.
     2. Satisfactory passing of occupational competency examination of the Department; *or* acceptance of credentials and adequate work experience by the Department for those competency areas where examinations do not exist; *or* State licensure or occupational accreditation by a Board of Examiners recognized by Pennsylvania; *or* certification from another state with criteria similar to those of Pennsylvania.
     3. Acceptance for enrollment in an approved vocational teacher preparation program.
     4. Recommendation of preparing institution.
     5. Valid for 3 *calendar* years during which period the holder must complete 18 semester hours within the "vocational teacher" approved program.
   B. Vocational Instructional I (Provisional)
     1. Valid only in the areas for which occupational competency credential is held.

2. Two years of wage-earning experience.
3. Successful completion of basic skills test and occupational competency test.
4. Completion of 18 credit hours in an approved program of vocational teacher education and recommendation of preparing institution.
5. Valid for 7 years, during which time candidate must complete requirements for Vocational Instructional II Certificate.

C. Vocational Instructional II (Permanent)
1. Evidence of 3 years of satisfactory service on the Vocational Instructional I Certificate.
2. Completion of 60 semester hours in an approved program in the appropriate vocational field.
3. Satisfactory completion of the general knowledge and professional knowledge tests.
4. Completion of a Department-approved induction program.

D. Supervisor of Comprehensive Vocational Education I (Provisional)
1. Have 3 years of satisfactory service in a vocational field.
2. Have completed an approved preparation/certification program for supervision in *all* fields of vocational education, and have received the recommendation of the preparing institution.

E. Supervisor of Comprehensive Vocational Education II (Permanent)
1. Have three years of satisfactory service on a Supervisor of Comprehensive Vocational Education I (Provisional) Certificate.

VI. Certification for graduates of out-of-state institutions
A. Recommending institution has a state-approved preparation/certification program in the area of certification requested.
B. Competency recommendation from the dean or the department of education chairperson of the preparing institution or possession of a teaching certificate comparable to the Pennsylvania Level I certificate.
C. Completed preparation program is comparable to approved programs offered by Pennsylvania institutions (certification issued for major subject areas only).
D. For initial Pennsylvania Instructional Certificate, successful completion of Pennsylvania Teacher Certification Testing Program.* (See below)

VII. Other Conditions (once a certificate is issued)
A. Candidates for employment are required by the local school entity to produce a background clearance as required by Act 34 and a child abuse clearance as required by Act 151; Pennsylvania state police background check for Pennsylvania residents plus an F.B.I. background check for out-of-state applicants. Applicants may not teach without these clearances.
B. New teachers will participate in a district-developed, PDE-approved plan for continuing professional development.

* Pennsylvania Teacher Certification Testing Program consists of
  — PRAXIS II Communications Skills Test; passing score: 646
  — PRAXIS II General Knowledge Test; passing score: 644
  — PRAXIS II Principles of Learning and Teaching, K–6; passing score: 162
  — PRAXIS II Principles of Learning and Teaching, 7–12; passing score: 159
  — Area of Specialization Test (NTE or Pennsylvania tests, as determined)

Rhode Island

All applicants who have not been certified previously in Rhode Island must successfully take the Core Battery of the National Teachers Examination. Cut-off scores are as follows: communication skills, 657; general knowledge, 649; professional knowledge, 648. Individuals who take the Core Battery of the NTE and do not achieve the cut-off scores are granted a special one-year provisional certificate.

Early Childhood (Preschool–2)

I. Provisional Certificate (valid for 3 years; nonrenewable)
   A. Bachelor's degree from an approved institution.
   B. (Option 1) Completion of an approved program for the certified area of teaching,
      or
      (Option 2) Six semester hours of student teaching in the area, and
      Course work, semester hours.. 24
      In each of the following content areas: child growth and development; curriculum and methods in early childhood education; reading readiness and developmental reading; health and nutrition for the young child; child, family, and community relationships; and identification and service to special needs children.
II. Professional Certificate (valid for 5 years; renewable)
   A. Completion of 6 credits while on provisional certification in Rhode Island. Three of the 6 credits may be approved in-service course work. Three of the 6 credits must be college credits from an accredited or an approved institution of higher education as defined in these regulations.
   B. Three years of documented teaching experience in an approved educational setting in Rhode Island while on provisional certification.
   C. Renewal.
      1. This certificate may be renewed every 5 years upon the completion of 9 credits and verification of continued teaching experience as an early childhood teacher. Six of the 9 credits must be graduate level course work either in early childhood education or in an area directly related to early childhood education. Three of the 9 credits may be approved in-service course work.

Elementary (Grades 1–8, except where grades 7 and 8 are organized on the middle school or secondary school plan.)

I. Provisional Certificate (valid for 3 years; nonrenewable)
   A. Bachelor's degree from an approved institution.
   B. (Option 1) Completion of an approved program for the certified area of teaching,
      or

177

(Option 2) Six semester hours of student teaching in the area, and

Course work, semester hours... 24

To include work in each of the following content areas: child growth and development; methods and materials of teaching reading, math, language arts, science, social studies in the elementary schools; the arts; identification and service to special needs children; and foundations of education.

II. Professional Certificate (valid for 5 years)
  A. See Early Childhood II, A, B, and C.

Secondary (7–12)

I. Provisional Certificate (valid for 3 years; nonrenewable)
  A. Bachelor's degree from an approved institution.
  B. (Option 1) Completion of an approved program for the certified area of teaching,
      or
      (Option 2) Six semester hours of student teaching, and

      Course work, semester hours... 18

      To include work in each of the following content areas: adolescent psychology, secondary methods, measurements and evaluation, identification of and service to special needs students, teaching of reading in the content area, and foundations of education.
  C. Academic requirements, semester hours
      1. Agriculture... 36
      2. Business Education (Secretarial and Social) 36
      3. English... 30
      4. History (may include 6 hours in Social Studies) 30
      5. Language, classical and foreign.. 30
          A statement showing competency in language to be certified may be presented to waive a portion of academic requirement.
      6. Mathematics... 30
      7. Science
          a. General Science must include 6 hours in Biology, Physics, and
              Chemistry.. 30
          b. Biology.. 30
          c. Chemistry.. 30
          d. Physics.. 30
      8. Social Studies 36
      9. Academic areas not listed above.. 18

II. Professional Certificate (valid for 5 years; renewable)
  A. See Early Childhood II, A.
  B. Three years of documented teaching experience on the secondary level in Rhode Island while on provisional certification.
  C. Renewal.
      1. This certificate may be renewed every 5 years upon completion of 9 credits and verification of continued teaching experience as a secondary teacher. Six of the 9

credits must be on the graduate level, and 3 of the 6 graduate credits must be in the academic area in which secondary certification is held. Three of the 9 credits may be in approved in-service course work.

Administration

I. Elementary School
    A. Provisional Elementary School Principal (valid for 3 years; nonrenewable)
        1. Master's degree from an approved institution.
        2. Eligibility for a Rhode Island elementary school teacher's certificate.
        3. Three years of teaching experience at the elementary level.
        4. (Option 1) Completion of an approved program for the preparation of elementary school principals,
            or

            (Option 2) Course work, graduate semester hours 24
            To include work in each of the following content areas: school/community relations; elementary curriculum development; organization/administration of the elementary school; supervision of instruction; supervision and evaluation of professional staff; educational research; program evaluation; fiscal planning; and school law.
    B. Professional Elementary School Principal Certificate (valid for 5 years; renewable)
        1. Completion of 6 graduate credits in educational administration, curriculum, or supervision while on provisional certification.
        2. Three years of documented service as an elementary principal in Rhode Island.
        3. Renewal. Same as Secondary Professional Certificate II, C, 1, except that service must be as elementary principal and courses must be in educational administration and related areas.
II. Secondary School
    A. Provisional Secondary School Principal (valid for 3 years; nonrenewable)
        1. See Provisional Elementary School Principal I, A, 1–4, except that courses shall be for secondary school service.
    B. Professional Secondary School Principal Certificate (valid for 5 years; renewable)
        1. See Professional Elementary School Principal I, B, 1–3, except that courses and experiences shall be for secondary school service.
III. Superintendent
    A. Provisional Superintendent Certificate (valid for 3 years; nonrenewable)
        1. Doctorate, certificate of advanced graduate study, or master's degree.
        2. Completion of at least 36 semester hours of graduate credit including work in each of the following areas: school/community relations; curriculum construction; school administration; supervision of instruction; supervision and evaluation of professional staff; educational research; program evaluation; school plant planning; and school finance.
        3. Eligibility for a Rhode Island teacher's certificate.
        4. Eight years of educational experience, to include both teaching and administration.

B.   Professional Superintendent Certificate (valid for 5 years; renewable)
1.   Completion of 6 graduate credits in educational administration while on provisional certification.
2.   Three years of service as a superintendent of schools in Rhode Island while on provisional certification.

School Counselor and Supervisor (PreK–12)

I.   Provisional School Counselor's Certificate (valid 3 years; nonrenewable)*
A.   Bachelor's degree from an approved institution.
B.   Advanced degree in an approved program in school counseling or a master's degree from an approved institution and completion of 24 semester hours of graduate level course work in school counseling, including course work in the following:
1.   Introduction to pupil personnel services, techniques of counseling, psychological and educational assessment, vocational and educational placement, and a minimum of a 3 semester hour internship in school counseling.
C.   Eligibility for Rhode Island teacher's certificate, plus two years of successful teaching experience at the elementary or secondary level.
II.   Professional School Counselor's Certificate (valid for 5 years; renewable)
A.   Completion of 6 graduate credits in school counseling.
B.   Three years of service as a school counselor in Rhode Island while on provisional certification.
III.   Provisional School Counselor Supervisor Certificate (valid 3 years; nonrenewable)*
A.   Master's degree from an approved institution.
B.   Eligibility for a Rhode Island school counselor's certificate.
C.   Three years of experience as a school counselor.
D.   Approved graduate courses, semester hours 9
To include courses in educational administration in the areas of administration and organization of counseling programs, supervision of personnel, and curriculum development and evaluation.
IV.   Professional School Counselor Supervisor Certificate (valid for 5 years; renewable)
A.   Completion of 6 graduate credits (while on provisional certification) in the supervision of counseling programs, curriculum, or educational administration.
B.   Three years of service as a school counselor supervisor while on provisional certification.

*   Individuals who have served as a school counselor/school counselor supervisor in Rhode Island's public Schools for 3 years may not renew the provisional certificate. Those who have not served as a school counselor/school counselor supervisor for either all or part of the term of the provisional certificate are entitled to an extension, provided they have completed the requirements listed under II, A or IV, A above.

Special Subjects (All grades)

I.   Provisional Certificate (valid 3 years)
A.   Bachelor's degree from an accredited or an approved institution of higher education.

B. Completion of an approved program designed for the preparation of special subjects teachers.

C. Those applicants who have not completed an approved program shall present evidence of at least 6 semester hours of student teaching in the special subjects field. This student teaching must include placement at both the elementary and secondary levels. The applicant must also present evidence of at least 18 semester hours of course work to include work in each of the following content areas:

> Human Growth and Development; Foundations of Education; Methodology (must include at least one course in the special subject field); Measurement and Evaluation; Identification of and Service to Special Needs Students; and the Teaching of Reading in the Content Area.

D. The student teaching requirement may be waived for an applicant who has had 2 or more documented years of successful teaching experience in the special subjects field prior to applying for certification in Rhode Island. Certified teachers who have had 2 or more years of teaching experience and who seek a special subjects certificate may fulfill the student teaching requirement by completing a one-year supervised internship in the special subjects field. After completing the necessary course work for the special subjects certificate, and arranging through the local community for a one-year internship, the individual may request the issuance of a one-year temporary provisional certificate. The Department of Education must approve the internship in advance, and the supervisor must have at least 3 years of teaching experience. The internship must include placement at both the elementary and secondary levels. Upon successful completion of the internship, the individual will be issued a three-year provisional certificate.

E. Academic Requirements, semester hours (see footnote)
   1. Art 36
   2. Dance 24
   3. Health 24
   4. Physical Education 24
   5. Health and Physical Education (24 semester hours in each) 48
   6. Home Economics 36
   7. Industrial Arts 36
   8. Library/Media 36
   9. Music 36
   10. Theater 24
   11. Special Subject Areas not listed above 18*
       a. A teaching certificate will be issued in any special subject area not listed above provided the candidate has met all requirements listed under Parts A and C of Section I and has 18 semester hours of credit in the special subject area for which certification is sought.

F. The provisional certificate is not renewable for individuals who have taught in the public schools of Rhode Island for 3 years. Holder must qualify for professional certification. Individuals who have not taught for either all or part of the term of the provisional certificate are entitled to an extension of the provisional certificate provided they have completed the requirement under II, A.

II. Professional Certificate (valid 5 years)

A. Completion of 6 credits while on provisional certification in Rhode Island. Three of the 6 credits may be approved in-service course work. Three of the 6 credits must be college credits from an approved institution.

B. Three years of documented teaching experience in the special subjects field in Rhode Island while on provisional certification.

C. This certificate may be renewed every 5 years upon the completion of 9 credits and verification of continued successful experience as a special subject teacher. Six of the 9 credits must be on the graduate level, and 3 of the 6 graduate credits must be in the special subject area in which special subject certification is held. Three of the 9 credits may be approved in-service course work.

* Individuals who desire to secure certification in a special subjects field by means of transcript evaluation will be required to submit evidence that they have completed appropriate special subjects course work. The Certification Office will publish an updated list annually of special subjects course work required for each special subjects field. This list of courses will take into consideration the desired distribution and appropriate level of special subjects course work which must be completed by individuals desiring to teach in the special subjects field(s).

South Carolina

Beginning September 1, 1999, all applicants must take the PRAXIS Examinations.

General

The following requirements apply to all teachers in South Carolina (early childhood, elementary, middle school, and secondary education).

I.   Requirements for initial certification
    A. Completion of a state board of education approved teacher training program (from any state).
    B. Qualifying scores on the National Teacher Examination (N.T.E.) Core Battery Professional Knowledge Examination or the Principles of Learning and Teaching Examination.
    C. Qualifying scores on the respective N.T.E. Specialty Area Examination, PRAXIS II Subject Examination, or South Carolina Area Examination (in German or Latin only).
    D. FBI fingerprint review and fee of $49.

II.   Types and levels of credentials
    A. Class I—Advanced Professional.
        1. Doctorate from an approved program.
        2. Fulfillment of requirements for an initial area of certification as adopted by the State Board.
    B. Class I—Specialist Professional.
        1. Master's or specialist's degree, consisting of at least 60 semester hours, of which 30 semester hours of graduate credit must be in a planned program approved by the State Board.
        2. See A, 2.
    C. Class I—Professional.
        1. Master's degree.
        2. See A, 2.
    D. Class II—Professional.
        1. Bachelor's degree, plus 18 semester hours of graduate credit.
        2. See A, 2.
    E. Class III—Professional.
        1. Bachelor's degree.
        2. See A, 2.

III. Additional areas of certification
    A. Areas of certification (regular subjects, special subjects, exceptional children, etc.)

may be added to professional South Carolina teaching credentials. Approved programs of specific course requirements are available from the Department of Education (see Appendix 1 for address).

Administration

I. Elementary School Principal and Supervisor
    A. Valid Professional Certificate at the elementary level.
    B. 590 on NTE in Administration/Supervision.
    C. Three years of teaching experience, including at least one year in elementary school.
    D. Completion of an advanced program approved for the training of elementary principals and supervisors.

II. Secondary School Principal and Supervisor
    A. Valid Professional Certificate at the secondary level.
    B. 590 on NTE in Administration/Supervision.
    C. Three years of teaching experience, including at least one year at secondary level.
    D. See I, D, only at secondary level.

III. School Superintendent
    A. Valid Principal's or Teacher's Professional Certificate.
    B. 590 on NTE in Administration/Supervision.
    C. Seven years of experience as teacher and administrator, at least two years as a school or district administrator.
    D. See I, D, only at superintendent level.

Guidance Counselor

I. Elementary or Secondary School Guidance Counselor
    A. Requirements for initial certification.
        1. Master's degree.
        2. 550 on NTE in Guidance Counselor.
        3. Completion of a state board of education approved program in counseling and guidance.

School Media

I. Media Specialist
    A. Bachelor's degree.
    B. Score of 590 on the NTE Teaching Area Examination for Librarian-Media Specialist.
    C. Completion of a state board of education approved program in media.

II. Media Communication Specialist
    A. See I, A, B, and C (only program must be in media communication).

III. Media Supervisor
    A. Master's degree.
    B. Certification as elementary or secondary supervisor.
    C. Valid South Carolina teaching credential with endorsement as a Media Specialist or

Media Communication Specialist.

D. Three years of successful experience as a Media Specialist or Media Communication Specialist in a school media center.

E. Graduate credit, semester hours 6

  1. To be in supervision of school media programs and in research and evaluation of school media programs.

South Dakota

South Dakota has planned a number of changes in its requirements effective September 1, 2000. Please write the Office of Policy and Accountability for additional details (address in Appendix 1).

In addition to the standard certificates listed below, South Dakota also has a number of limited and alternative certificates. A one-year teacher certificate may be issued to certifiable persons who do not meet recent credit requirements and a two-year teacher certificate to those who have completed a teacher education program in another state but have not met the requirements unique to South Dakota. Requirements for the five-year teacher certificate, which may be issued to persons who have met all certification requirements upon submitting their initial application, are given below.

Elementary School

I. Elementary Certificate Endorsement
  A. An elementary endorsement shall be issued for a period of 5 years upon completion of an approved bachelor's degree program in elementary education. If the applicant graduated from college more than 5 years prior to the time application is made for a certificate of endorsement, the applicant must have earned 6 semester or 9 quarter hours of credit within the five-year period immediately preceding the issuance of the certificate endorsement. The credits must have been earned at an approved college or university in courses designated by the college as resident courses. The holder of an advanced degree may have a certificate endorsement issued without the earning of additional credits, provided the advanced degree was obtained within the ten-year period immediately preceding issuance.
  B. An elementary certificate endorsement shall be issued for a period of 5 years upon completion of an approved bachelor's degree program in elementary education at an accredited 4-year college or university. The course work shall include the following:
    1. Student teaching at the elementary level: 10 weeks
    2. Education courses: 21 semester hours, including
      a. Methods: 11 semester hours, including language arts, social studies, computers in education, science, arithmetic, and 3 semester hours in reading
      b. Professional studies: 7 semester hours, including psychology of teaching, learning, child development, and the exceptional child (including learning disabilities)
      c. Human relations: 3 semester hours
    3. Subject areas: 34 semester hours, including
      a. Composition and grammar: 5 semester hours
      b. Speech: 2 semester hours
      c. Music: 2 semester hours

    d.   Art: 2 semester hours
    e.   First Aid & Health: 2 semester hours
    f.   United States government: 2 semester hours
    g.   South Dakota Indian studies: 3 semester hours;
    h.   Geography: 2 semester hours
    i.   Mathematics, including arithmetic for elementary teachers: 6 semester hours
    j.   Physical science and earth science: 2 semester hours
    k.   Biological science: 2 semester hours
    l.   American history: 2 semester hours
    m.   Reading: 2 semester hours

Reading Specialist

I.   Reading Specialist Certificate Endorsement (K–12)
    A.   Valid South Dakota elementary or secondary certificate.
    B.   Completion of 3 years of classroom teaching in which the teaching of reading was an important responsibility of the position.
    C.   Undergraduate or graduate credits in the following:
        1.   Measurement or evaluation, or both; child or adolescent psychology, or both; literature for children or adolescents, or both; and language development in children
    D.   Completion of a minimum of 12 semester hours in graduate-level reading courses with at least one course each in foundations or survey of reading; diagnosis and correction of reading disabilities; and clinical or laboratory practicum in reading.

Secondary School

I.   Secondary Certificate Endorsement
    A.   A secondary endorsement shall be issued for a period of 5 years upon completion of an approved bachelor's degree in secondary education. The degree must contain a major in an academic or special field. If the applicant graduated from college more than 5 years prior to the time application for a certificate endorsement is made, the applicant must have earned 6 semester or 9 quarter hours of credit within the five-year period immediately preceding issuance of the certificate endorsement. The credits must have been earned at an approved college or university in courses designated by the college as resident courses. The holder of an advanced degree may have a certificate endorsement issued without the earning of additional credits, provided the advanced degree was obtained within the 10-year period immediately preceding the issuance.
II.   Approved secondary degree program must include the following:
    A.   Student teaching at the secondary level or grades 7 through 12, except for the area of trades and industries, which may be at either the secondary level or at post-secondary vocational-technical schools under the office of vocational education: 10 weeks.
    B.   Education courses: 16 semester hours, including

1. Secondary school methods: 6 semester hours, including 3 semester hours of teaching reading in the content area
2. Professional studies: 7 semester hours, including the psychology of teaching, learning, the adolescent, and the exceptional child (including learning disabilities)
3. Human relations: 3 semester hours
C. Subject areas
1. South Dakota Indian studies: 3 semester hours
2. A major in an academic or special field approved for endorsement

Middle School/Junior High School

I.   Middle School/Junior High Certificate Endorsement
A. A middle school/junior high endorsement valid for teaching grades 5 through 8 shall be issued for a period of 5 years upon completion of an approved bachelor's degree program in middle school/junior high education.
II. Approved program must include the following:
A. Student teaching at the middle school/junior high level, including grades 5 through 8: 10 weeks.
B. Education courses: 19 semester hours, including
1. Middle school/junior high methods: 9 semester hours, including 3 semester hours of teaching reading and 3 semester hours in two of the areas of concentration specified in II, C, 3, a
2. Professional studies: 7 semester hours, including psychology of teaching, learning, the adolescent, and the exceptional child (including learning disabilities)
3. Human relations: 3 semester hours
C. Subject areas
1. South Dakota Indian studies: 3 semester hours
2. Middle school/junior high teacher endorsement for middle school/junior high language arts
3. Middle school/junior high teacher endorsement for two of the following:
a. middle school/junior high social science, science, or mathematics
III. Requirements for adding the Middle School/Junior High Endorsement to an elementary or secondary teacher certificate.
A. Education courses: 8 semester hours, including middle school/junior high teaching methods, adolescent psychology, interdisciplinary planning, advisee-advisor relationships, cooperative learning, and other topics relevant to middle level education.
B. Subject areas: the minimum semester hours for middle school/junior high teachers in each academic subject area taught (write the State Department of Education for details)

Note: Persons who have 50% or more of their assignment in middle or junior high schools must have the middle school/junior high school endorsement.

Administration

I. Elementary Principal Certificate Endorsement
   A. Master's degree from a college or university approved for teacher education.
   B. Four years' of teaching experience at the elementary level on an elementary teacher endorsement or another endorsement which includes the elementary grades.
   C. Completion of an approved program for elementary principals at a college or university.

II. Secondary Principal Certificate Endorsement
   A. See I, A.
   B. Four years' of teaching experience at the secondary level on a secondary teacher endorsement or another endorsement which includes the secondary grades.
   C. Completion of an approved program for secondary principals at a college or university.

III. Superintendent Certificate Endorsement
   A. Master's degree, as well as 15 additional semester hours, from a college or university approved for teacher education.
   B. Four years of experience at the elementary or secondary school level or both on a valid certificate, two years of which were classroom teaching.
   C. Completion of an approved program for superintendents at a college or university.
   D. This endorsement is valid for 5 years only; certificate renewal must meet the requirements of the advanced superintendent certificate endorsement.

IV. Advanced Superintendent Certificate Endorsement
   A. Completion of an approved six-year specialist degree or doctoral degree program for superintendents at a college or university.
   B. Four years of teaching experience and one year of administrative experience at the elementary or secondary level, or both, on a valid teacher certificate.

School Counselor

I. School Counselor Certificate Endorsement
   A. Bachelor's degree from an accredited college or university.
   B. Either one of the following:
      1. Elementary or secondary teacher endorsement and completion of an approved master's degree in school guidance and counseling
         or
      2. An approved master's degree in school guidance and counseling including 500 clock hours of internship in a school under the supervision of a certified counselor and a counselor educator

Renewals and Fees

I. Renewal of certificates with an elementary or a secondary endorsement.
   A. The elementary or the secondary endorsement may be renewed for a period of five years upon proper application and presenting an official transcript of credits from an

approved institution or from an accredited four-year college or university showing the applicant has earned 6 semester hours of credit within the five-year period immediately preceding renewal. Credits may be either graduate or undergraduate, and may include workshops, telecourses, or independent studies sponsored by a college or university in addition to on-campus and extension classes. Credits must be related to areas in which the applicant is qualified to teach or must be a part of the school district's staff development plan. A maximum of 3 semester hours of division of education renewal credit earned at workshops which have received advance approval will be accepted toward meeting the certificate renewal requirement. The holder of an advanced degree may have the certificate endorsement renewed without the earning of additional credits, provided the advanced degree was obtained within the ten-year period immediately preceding issuance or renewal.

II. Renewal of certificates with a limited endorsement.
   A. See I above.
   B. Specific course work identified at issuance or in the candidate's professional development plan may also be required.

III. Fees to be charged for certificates.
   A. One-year validity—$10.00.
   B. Two-year validity—$15.00.
   C. Five-year validity—$20.00.
   D. Duplicate—$10.00.
   E. Additional Endorsements—$10.00 (if not added to certificate at original issuance or at renewal).

Reciprocity

South Dakota does not have a reciprocity system that allows educators to serve in S.D. schools using certification or licensure from other states. However, completion of a recent approved program in another state or foreign country is accepted for issuance of the 2-year nonrenewable certificate. South Dakota has also signed an exchange certification agreement with Missouri, Iowa, Nebraska, Kansas, Oklahoma, and Arkansas (MINKSOA) which allows individuals certified in one of the member states to be eligible for a two-year exchange certificate in any of the participating states.

Tennessee

Applicants for all initial teaching licenses are required to pass the Principles of Learning and Teaching (PLT) exam of the PRAXIS series and the specialty area test(s) required in the area(s) of certification. Effective September 1, 1998, passing scores for the PLT are as follows: for PLT K–6 (test number 0522)—155 and for PLT 7–12 (test number 0524)—159. If a specialty area test is specified for the major area on the applicant's transcript, passing scores on that specialty area test must be submitted. In the case of a double major where a specialty area test is available for both majors, each test is required. If a test is unavailable for an area, no specialty area test is required. Exemption from taking the PRAXIS tests is granted to individuals who can provide documentation that they were fully certified or licensed in any state prior to July 1, 1984.

Tennessee has adopted detailed knowledge and skills requirements instead of specific course work and credit hours requirements for all teaching areas, school counseling, and school social workers. Each state institution develops its own programs which must be approved by the State Board of Education. Please contact the Office of Teacher Education and Accreditation (address in Appendix 1) for further information.

Types of Certificates

I. Apprentice License
    Initial five-year license issued to a teacher who completes an approved teacher preparation program. After teaching on the Apprentice License for three years in a Tennessee public school system and receiving a positive local evaluation, the license holder will advance to the Professional License

II. Professional License
    A ten-year license issued to a teacher who has completed a minimum of three years experience in an approved school and who has received a positive local evaluation in a Tennessee public school system. (The three years of experience can be a combination of in-state/out-of-state experience but the last year must be served in a Tennessee public school to participate in the local evaluation process.) Renewable.

III. Out-of-State Teacher's License
    Initial five-year license (equivalent to an Apprentice License) issued to an applicant who meets Tennessee licensure requirements and has at least one year of acceptable teaching experience in another state. Upon completion of a minimum of three years of teaching (a combination of in-state/out-of-state experience, with at least one year in Tennessee) and receipt of a positive local evaluation, the license holder will advance to the Professional License.

IV. Interim "A" Teacher's License
    A one-year license requiring a minimum of a bachelor's degree in the teaching field from a regionally accredited institution and completion of at least 6 semester hours of professional education. A Tennessee superintendent of schools also must state intent to employ. This license may be issued only for secondary education endorsement areas

191

(7–12), fine arts endorsement areas (K–12), health (K–12), physical education (K–12), and speech/language (PreK–12). Renewable twice under certain conditions.

V. Interim "B" Teacher's License

A one-year license issued to applicants who meet all certification requirements but lack minimum qualifying scores on required PRAXIS tests. Requires intention of employment by a Tennessee education agency. Renewable one time.

VI. Occupational Education License

A ten-year license issued upon a minimum of a high school diploma or equivalency examination (GED), a minimum of five years of appropriate employment experience, and successful completion of the apprentice teacher period. Renewable.

VII. Apprentice Special Group Licenses

Initial five-year licenses issued for the following areas: school guidance counselor (grades PreK–12), school psychologist, and school social worker. After serving in an endorsement area for a minimum of three years, (with at least the last year being in a Tennessee public school system with receipt of a positive local evaluation), the individual will then advance to the Professional School Service Personnel License. The Professional School Service Personnel License is issued for a ten-year period and may be renewed by meeting renewal requirements for a Professional Teacher License (See II, directly above).

Administrator (K–12)

I. Principal—Beginning Administrator Endorsement
   A. Graduate degree.
   B. Completion of an approved graduate level program of studies in school administration and supervision. (Standards for preparation and professional development programs will be based on the knowledge and skills needed by a principal for effective leadership and management.)
   C. Recommendation for endorsement by an approved institution of higher education.
   D. Passing grades on the state required test/assessment.
   E. Within three years of employment as a principal, a beginning principal will be required to attain a professional administrator endorsement.

II. Principal—Professional Administrator Endorsement
   A. Completion of a customized professional development program, including
      1. Mentoring by an experienced principal assigned by the school system, and
      2. Recommendation for the professional administrator endorsement by the superintendent within three years of employment as a principal.

Librarian
(Effective September 1, 2000)

I. Librarian must complete a graduate level program leading to a master's degree with a major in library information which must be an area of initial or additional endorsement.
   A. Upon completion of the program, the candidate must be recommended by a college or university and must receive passing scores on the appropriate parts of the PRAXIS series examination.

Texas

I. Applicability of certificates
   A. Provisional and professional certificates qualify holders to teach in one or more of the following areas, in which the applicant has completed the college or university teacher education program approved for said area or areas.
      1. Elementary, grades 1–8 inclusive.
         a. The following are the approved academic specializations and delivery systems for elementary certification: art, bilingual education (delivery system), biology, early childhood education (d.s.), earth science, English, generic special education (d.s.), geography, health education, history, life/earth science, mathematics, music, other languages (French, German, Spanish, and others as approved), physical education, physical science, reading, social studies, speech communications, and theater arts.
      2. Secondary, grades 6–12 inclusive.
         a. The following are the approved academic specializations and delivery systems for secondary certification: art, biology, business administration, business (basic, composite, and secretarial programs), chemistry, computer information systems, dance, earth science, economics, English, English language arts, generic special education (d.s.), geography, government, health education, history, industrial arts, journalism, life/earth science, mathematics, music, other languages (French, German, Spanish, Latin, and others as approved), physical education, physical science, physics, psychology, reading, science, social studies, sociology, speech communications, and theater arts.
      3. All-level, grades PreK–12 inclusive.
         a. The following are the approved specializations for all-level certification: art, music, physical education, and speech communication/theater arts.
      4. Hearing impaired, grades PreK–12 inclusive.
II. Provisional certificate
   A. Bachelor's degree from a college or university approved for teacher education by the State Board of Education.
   B. General education, total semester hours (minimum) 60
      1. English (six semester hours in mechanics and composition), semester hours 12
      2. Speech (with emphasis on oral language), semester hours............................ 3
      3. American history, semester hours.. 6
      4. Political Science (U.S. and Texas constitutions), semester hours 3–6
      5. Natural science (laboratory), semester hours 3
      6. Mathematics (college algebra or above), semester hours 3
      7. Computing and information technology, semester hours 3
         (Demonstration of competency also accepted)

8. Fine arts, semester hours.. 3
9. Electives, semester hours 9
C. Academic specialization, semester hours 36–48
D. Professional development sequence—18 semester hours of upper-division courses. The following three components must be included:
1. Core requirements—common to all grade level options, which include studies of:
    a. teaching-learning processes, including measurement and evaluation of student achievement.
    b. human growth and development.
    c. knowledge and skills concerning the unique needs of special learners.
    d. legal and ethical aspects of teaching to include the recognition of and response to signs of abuse and neglect in children.
    e. structure, organization, and management of the American school system, with emphasis upon the state and local structure in Texas.
    f. education computing, media, and other technologies.
2. Methodology—specifically designed for the grade level option selected, to include studies of the following:
    a. instructional methods and strategies that emphasize practical applications of the teaching-learning processes.
    b. curriculum organization, planning, and evaluation.
    c. basic principles and procedures of classroom management with emphasis on classroom discipline, utilizing group and individual processes, as well as different techniques and procedures adapted to the personality of the teacher.
    d. the scope and sequence of the essential elements for all subjects required in the elementary course of study that are not included in the academic specializations when elementary options are selected.
3. Field experience
    a. pre-student teaching—not fewer than 45 clock hours, at least one-half of which shall include observation and experience at the level for which a student teaching assignment is anticipated.
    b. student teaching—a minimum of six semester hours completed in a school or schools accredited or recognized by the Texas Education Agency. (Student teaching may be waived if the student has served successfully for two years in an accredited or recognized school as a regular classroom teacher of record in the area and at the level for which certification is sought.)
III. Professional certificate
   A. Bachelor's degree from an accredited college or university.
   B. Valid Texas provisional teacher certificate.
   C. Completion of 30 semester hours in approved graduate program in area of specialization.
   D. Three years of teaching experience.

Note: A basic skills test is required for admission to teacher education programs. Upon completion of an approved teacher education program, an Examination for the Certification of Educators in Texas (ExCet) test must be completed successfully at the appropriate level of professional development and for each content specialization area to be indicated on the certificate. Teachers seeking initial Texas certification based on out-of-state credentials are required to complete an ExCet test at the appropriate level of professional development *and* an ExCet test for each content specialization area to be indicated on the certificate.

Utah

Early Childhood Education (K–3)

I. Basic Certificate (valid for 4 years)
    A. Bachelor's degree in an approved program for early childhood education.
    B. Recommendation by an institution whose program of preparation has been approved by the State Board of Education.
    C. Applicants holding an Elementary Teaching Certificate and with 2 years of successful teaching in a full kindergarten program may be issued a concurrent Early Childhood Education Certificate.
    D. Authorization: required for teaching kindergarten and permits assignment in grades K–3; recommended for teaching in formal programs below kindergarten level.
II. Standard Certificate
    A. See Elementary Teaching Standard Certificate.

Elementary Certificate (1–8)

I. Basic Certificate (valid for 4 years)
    A. Bachelor's degree in an approved program for elementary school teachers.
    B. Recommendation by an institution whose program of preparation has been approved by the State Board of Education.
    C. Must be subject-specific endorsed to teach assigned subjects at the 7–8 grade level.
II. Standard Certificate
    A. Completion of at least 2 years of successful teaching experience under a Basic Teaching Certificate or its equivalent.
    B. Recommendation by the employing school district.
    C. Valid indefinitely providing holder verifies appropriate employment in education of at least 3 years during each succeeding 5 year interval.
        1. Three years of appropriate education employment *or* 6 semester hours of approved credit earned within the 5 year period prior to date of application if more than 5 years have elapsed since applicant received bachelor's or higher degree.

Secondary Teaching Certificate (6–12)*

I. Basic Certificate (valid for 4 years)
    A. Bachelor's degree in an approved program for secondary school teachers.
    B. Completed an approved teaching major and minor, or composite major.
        1. Teaching major, semester hours.. 30
            a. At least half must be in upper division work.
        2. Teaching minor, semester hours 16

        3. Composite major, semester hours.. 46
    C. Completed an approved program in professional education. Shall include student teaching, education of the exceptional child, teaching of reading in content area, and introduction to computers.
    D. Recommendation of institution approved by State Board of Education.
    E. See Elementary I, C.
II. Standard Certificate
    A. See Elementary Teaching Standard Certificate.

* One cannot teach in an elementary, self-contained class under this certificate.

Special Education (Birth–Age 5)

I. Requirements
    A. Bachelor's degree from an accredited institution.
    B. Completion of an approved program for teaching preschool children with handicaps which addresses newly adopted early childhood handicaps and special education endorsement competencies.
    C. Recommendation by the institution.

Special Education (K–12)

I. Requirements
    A. Bachelor's degree from an accredited institution.
    B. Completion of an approved program in the specific area of endorsement:
        1. Mild/moderate learning and behavior problems.
        2. Severe learning and behavior problems.
        3. Hearing handicaps.
        4. Visual handicaps.
    C. Recommendation by the institution.

Communications Disorders (K–12)

I. Requirements
    A. Completion of an approved program for teaching pupils with communications disorders, which included a master's degree or 33 semester hours earned after meeting requirements for the bachelor's degree.
    B. Recommendation by the institution.
    C. Provisional Communications Disorders Certificate also available (write to Utah Board of Education for details).

Administrative/Supervisory

I. General
    A. The Administrative/Supervisory Certificate permits the holder to teach on levels

where previously certificated, and to administer or supervise on elementary, middle, or secondary levels.

B. Individual must hold either a Basic or Standard Administrative/Supervisory Certificate in order to assume duties and responsibilities of any of the following positions: superintendent; assistant superintendent; administrative assistant; director, all levels; specialist, subject matter; supervisor, all levels; curriculum coordinator; principal, all levels; assistant principal, all levels.

C. A principal of an elementary or middle school with fewer than six teachers may perform duties appropriate to the position while holding a Basic or Standard Elementary Teaching Certificate.

II. Basic Certificate

A. Hold a Basic or a Standard Teaching Certificate.

B. Complete a fifth year of training in a teacher education program including a master's degree *or* 33 semester hours of appropriate credit beyond the bachelor's degree.

C. Complete sufficient additional study in an approved program for school administrators/supervisors to have acquired the following competencies:
1. Administrative/supervisory processes such as discovering, diagnosing, goal setting, planning, decision-making, organizing, delegating, communicating and evaluating.
2. Administration/supervision of education programs, administration of funds and facilities, personnel administration, and continuing self-development.
3. Understanding the crucial and dynamic role of the school.
4. Human relations skills to select and develop school personnel.
5. Knowledge and skills in relation to the following: the learner and the learning process; curriculum development; school organization and operation; supervision of professional and nonprofessional personnel; school board relationships; school law; professional personnel responsibilities; negotiations, school finance, and public relations; relevant concepts from social and behavioral sciences; performance and interpretation of research and development; school-community needs.

D. Complete course work or experience to assure administrative/supervisory competence at level on which the applicant was not previously certificated.

E. Two years of acceptable professional experience.

F. Recommendation of an institution whose program of preparation has been approved by the State Board of Education.

III. Standard Certificate

A. Complete an approved program for the preparation of administrators/supervisors, which provides for the acquisition of the professional competencies listed in II, C, above.

B. See II, D, above.

C. Three years of successful professional administrative/supervisory experience under a Basic Administrative/Supervisory Certificate or its equivalent.

D. Recommendation of employing school district.

School Counselor

I.   Provisional Endorsement (Level I) (valid for 3 years only)
  A.   Be formally admitted into a state-approved counselor training program.
  B.   Completion of all requirements in the "Standards for Approval of Programs for the Preparation of School Counselors" as adopted by the Utah State Board of Education.
  C.   Completion of a practicum experience which must include: test administration and interpretation, guidance curriculum planning, individual and group counseling, individual education and career planning, and use of career information delivery systems.
  D.   Recommendation for Level I certification by an institution with an approved program for preparation of school counselors.
II. Basic Certificate (Level II)
  A.   See I, A and B.
  B.   Completion of an approved 600 hour field experience under the supervision of a school counselor holding a Level III school counselor certificate in a school setting and demonstration of specified competencies.
    1.   Only 400 hours of field experience are required if the applicant has 2 or more years of successful teaching or counseling experience.
III. Standard Certificate (Level III)
  A.   Meets all Level II requirements from an institution with an approved program for preparation of school counselors.
  B.   Completion of at least 2 years of successful experience as a school counselor under a Basic School Counselor Certificate or its equivalent.
  C.   Recommendation by the superintendent of the employing school district.

Library Media

The Library Media Certificate is required of all new personnel entering the library media field. The certificate permits service at the elementary or secondary level (K–12). A person assigned to serve as a district or regional media coordinator, supervisor, or director must hold an Administrative/Supervisory Certificate. A Standard Library Media Certificate is also required.

I.   Basic Certificate (valid for 4 years)
  A.   Hold, or be eligible to hold, a Basic or Standard Early Childhood, Elementary, Secondary, or Special Education Certificate.
  B.   Complete an approved program for the preparation of library media professionals which meets the competency standards set by the State Board of Education.
  C.   Demonstrate competence in computer applications for library media programs.
  D.   Have been recommended by an institution whose program of preparation in library media or library science has been approved by the State Board of Education.
II. Standard Certificate (valid for 5 years)
  An applicant for a Standard Library Media Certificate must have:
  A.   At least two years of successful experience under a Basic Library Media Certificate (as determined by the State Board of Education).

B. Recommendation of the employing school district.
C. Master's degree with a school library media specialty or 33 semester hours (55 quarter hours) of approved library media or library science graduate hours which meet the State Board's competency standards.
D. Recommendation by an institution with a State Board approved program of preparation in library media.

Vermont

In addition to the requirements listed below, the Professional Standards Board has drawn up specific and detailed qualitative competencies for each of its educator positions. Individuals should contact the Licensing Office (see Appendix 1 for address) for further information.

Eligibility for Initial Licensure

I. Eligibility Requirements
    A. Graduation from a Vermont Professional Standards Board approved preparation program and recommendation for licensure from the institution.
    B. Graduation from an approved teacher preparation program from a state with which Vermont has signed a reciprocal agreement. Persons certified in a state with which Vermont does not have an Interstate Reciprocity Contract, as well as all educators seeking vocational, administrative, and support services licensure, will be evaluated on an individual basis.
    C. A person presenting evidence of competence, preparation, and experience equivalent to approved program graduation in the endorsement area being sought may be licensed through an evaluation process. Evaluators are chosen by the Standards Board and must be qualified in the field of endorsement specialty.
    D. A Superintendent of Schools can present a formal, written request for a waiver to the Standards Board when there is a severe shortage of licensed teachers in the field and when a local district is unable to find applicants because of this shortage. The Standards Board may waive one or more requirements for licensure if the waiver criteria are met. Such a waiver shall expire at the end of the contract year.

II. General requirements for all licensure candidates
    A. The applicant must hold a baccalaureate degree from a regionally accredited or state-approved institution and must have successfully completed a major, or its equivalent, in the liberal arts and sciences.
        1. Candidates for a trades and industry position are not subject to this requirement.
        2. Candidates for school nurse must have graduated from a nationally accredited four year nursing program.
    B. Demonstrated ability to communicate effectively in speaking, writing, and other forms of creative expressions and ability to apply basic mathematical skills, critical thinking skills, and creative thinking skills.
    C. Documentation of the specified competencies and prerequisites for the endorsement(s) being sought.
    D. Evidence of at least 12 consecutive weeks of student teaching or an equivalent learning experience as determined by the Vermont State Board of Education or by the requirements of the endorsement.
        1. Candidates for school nurse must provide evidence of a minimum of two years

of clinical or community nursing experience, 200 days of which must have been within the last four years; and have completed an approved educational orientation program.

E. Competency in teaching as specified in the following requirements:

1. Ability to identify the processes by which students learn and ability to select appropriate methods and materials to meet students' learning needs.

2. Ability to select, use, and interpret assessment processes and instruments to identify the strengths and weaknesses of individual students.

3. Ability to teach reading skills as they relate to the subject matter being taught.

4. Ability to recognize the individual learners' physical, intellectual, and psychological developmental needs.

5. Ability to apply the knowledge of child development, and of early and late adolescence development, to learning.

6. Ability to integrate special education students into appropriate learning situations.

7. Ability to develop students' awareness of and responsibility for personal health.

8. Ability to select and use appropriate technology within the endorsement area(s).

9. Ability to apply current state and federal laws and regulations as they apply to all children.

10. Ability to identify conditions and actions which would tend to discriminate against students on the basis of sex, race, color, creed, age, handicap, or national origin; and to develop teaching strategies to overcome those conditions and actions.

Levels of Licensure and Renewal Requirements

I. Level One: Beginning Educator's License
   A. Valid for two years and renewable.
   B. Renewal requires recommendation from the appropriate Local or Regional Standards Board, if employed in a public school district. All other renewals are handled through the Licensing Office.

II. Level Two: Professional Educator's (or Administrator's) License
   A. Valid for seven years and renewable.
   B. At least two years of experience under a Level One License.
   C. Recommendation of a local or regional standards board.
   D. Possession of an approved Individual Professional Development Plan (IPDP) for the ensuing licensure period.
   E. Demonstration of the following characteristics:
      1. Ability to plan instruction.
      2. Ability to maintain a positive learning environment.
      3. Ability to conduct learning experiences for individuals as well as groups.
      4. Knowledge of content area.
      5. Interest and motivation in continuing professional development.

III. Renewal Requirements for the Level II License

A. Recommendation for renewal of the license and endorsement(s) from the local or regional standards board.
B. Presentation of a professional portfolio approved by that board which includes at a minimum:
    1. Current IPDP with evidence of satisfactory professional growth pursuant to IPDP goals
    2. Documentation of a minimum of 9 relicensing credits in subject areas related to each endorsement and to the IPDP goals.
    3. Evidence of professional growth in each of the five standards specified in "Standards for Vermont Educators."
    4. Evidence of any required additional licenses, credentials, or reports specific to a particular endorsement.
    5. Approved IPDP for the ensuring licensure period.

Elementary Education

I. Requirements
    A. The elementary education license authorizes an individual to teach in K–6. The holder can teach any other subject(s) in grades 7 and 8, provided the holder has at least a minor in the subject field.
    B. Candidate must meet the competencies for elementary educators as specified by the Standards Board.

Subject Area Endorsements

I. Guidelines for determining competence for all subject area endorsements have been drawn up by and are available from the Standards Board (address in Appendix 1). These give the qualifications for competence necessary for teaching in each of the following subjects:
    A. Art, bilingual-multicultural, computer science teacher, dance, driver education, early childhood, elementary education, English, English as a second language, guidance, health education, library/media, mathematics, middle grades, modern and classical languages, music, physical education, reading coordinator, reading teacher, school nurse, school psychologist, science, social studies, support services counselor, and theater arts.

Administration

I. Superintendent
    A. Initial License
        1. Master's degree or equivalent with a concentration in educational administration.
        2. At least five years of educational experience:
            a. A minimum of three years of teaching experience.
            b. A minimum of two years of successful school management experience.
        3. Candidate must meet the competencies for the position of superintendent as specified by the Standards Board.

II. Principal
  A. Initial license
     1. See I, A, 1.
     2. At least three years of successful teaching experience.
     3. Same as I, Λ, 3, except for the position of principal.

Guidance Counselor

I. Requirements
  A. Initial license
     1. Master's degree with a concentration in school guidance or its equivalent.
     2. Completion of 180 clock hours of field experiences which provide for an awareness of the application of guidance services at the elementary (60 hours), middle/junior high (60 hours), and senior high (60 hours) school levels.
     3. Supervised internship (300 clock hours) in school guidance.
     4. Candidate must meet the competencies for the position of guidance counselor as specified by the Standards Board.

Library Media

I. Requirements
  A. Initial License
     1. Knowledge of a wide array of subject areas traditionally attained in a liberal arts education.
     2. Meet the practical educational experience requirements
     3. Candidate must meet competencies, through graduate level course work, for a library media position.
     4. Holder of this license is authorized to professionally manage, administer, and supervise the combined print, audio-visual, and networking services, resources, and staff at the building, district, or supervisory level, and to instruct students.

Special Education

I. Teacher of the Handicapped encompasses four endorsements: Essential Early Education Classroom or Home Programs; Intensive Special Education Classrooms or Multi-Handicapped; Special Education Class Programs/Resource Teacher Programs; and Secondary Diversified Occupations Programs
  A. Candidate must meet specific competencies for each endorsement as specified by the Standards Board.
II. Speech Language Pathologist
  A. Master's degree or its equivalent in speech/language pathology.
  B. Supervised clinical experience of 300 clock hours.
  C. Meet specific competencies (see I, A).
  D. Holder is authorized to diagnose speech/language disorders and to assist regular and special education personnel in designing, implementing, and evaluating individual

education programs for the areas of language, hearing, articulation, fluency, and voice.

III. Audiologist
    A. Master's degree or its equivalent in audiology.
    B. Supervised clinical experience of 300 clock hours.
    C. Meet specific competencies (see I, A).

IV. Consulting Teacher/Learning Specialist
    A. Master's degree or its equivalent in special education.
    B. Supervised advanced clinical practicum with handicapped students.
    C. Two years of educational work experience with handicapped and nonhandicapped students.
    D. Meet specific competencies (see I, A).
    E. Holder is authorized to assist and share responsibility with regular and special education personnel in designing, implementing, and evaluating Individual Education Programs for handicapped students.

Trades and Industry

I. Initial License
    A. High School diploma or the equivalent.
    B. One of the following options must be met:
        1. Completion of an approved program in industrial education and two years of trade experience.
        or
        2. Two years of recent trade experience beyond the recognized training or apprenticeship period.
        or
        3. A total of six or more years of recent trade experience.
    C. Expertise in one or more vocational skill areas and the specific competencies outlined for them
        1. Agriculture education, business and office occupations, consumer and family sciences, cooperative vocational education, distribution and marketing, health occupations, occupational home economics education, technology education, trades and industry education, vocational guidance coordinator, and vocational special needs teacher.
        2. Note that specializations within some of the areas above also have specific competencies that must be met.

Virginia

Effective July 1, 1998, Virginia implemented new licensure regulations primarily based on meeting specific and detailed competencies to qualify for endorsements. The requirements below list semester-hour requirements for each endorsement area. Institutions of higher education with approved programs in Virginia will incorporate the competencies in their programs and are not subject to the specific semester-hour requirements. The endorsement requirements found below will be applied to individuals seeking licensure outside of state-approved programs and individuals seeking licensure through the alternative route.

Types of Licenses

I. Provisional Certificate is a three-year, nonrenewable certificate granted to an applicant who is employed by a Virginia educational agency and
   A. Enters the teaching field through the alternate route to licensure upon recommendation of the employing educational agency
   or
   B. Fails to meet an allowable portion of general, professional, or specific endorsement requirements
   or
   C. Seeks the Technical Professional License
   or
   D. Is eligible for licensure but needs to successfully complete the professional teacher's assessment prescribed by the Board of Education
II. Collegiate Professional Certificate is a five-year renewable certificate granted to an applicant who has satisfied the professional teacher's assessment requirement prescribed by the Board of Education
   and
   A. Has satisfied all other requirements for licensure
   or
   B. Holds a current, valid license from another state
   or
   C. Has completed an approved teacher preparation program in another state in a comparable endorsement area
III. Postgraduate Professional License is a five-year, renewable certificate granted to an applicant who:
   A. Has qualified for the Collegiate Professional License
   B. Holds an appropriate graduate degree from an accredited institution
IV. Pupil Personnel Services License is a five-year, renewable certificate which is applicable to the areas of counselor education, school psychology, school social work, and visiting teachers.

V.   Technical Professional License is a five-year, renewable license in the areas of vocational education, educational technology, and military science issued to an applicant who:
   A.   Has graduated from an accredited high school (or possesses a General Education Development Certificate)
   B.   Meets Virginia's standards of academic proficiency, technical competency, and occupational experience and has completed 9 semester hours of specialized professional studies credit from an accredited college or university

Alternate Route to Licensure

I.   This route to a Provisional License is available to an individual employed by an educational agency seeking teaching endorsements (K–12) who:
   A.   Holds a baccalaureate degree in the arts and sciences from an accredited institution
      1.   Those with an undergraduate degree other than in arts and sciences wishing to teach at the PreK–8 levels must meet the equivalent requirements for courses in the arts and sciences prior to employment.
   B.   Has completed course work, or its equivalent, in general studies
   C.   Has met endorsement requirements for subject areas
   D.   Completed a professional teacher's assessment
II.   During the validity period of the Provisional License the following requirements must be met:
   A.   Professional studies, semester hours 18
      1.   Human growth and development (3); curriculum and instructional procedures (6); foundations of education (3); and reading at the appropriate level (6)
   B.   Completion of one year of successful, full-time experience in the appropriate teaching area (a fully licensed, experienced teacher must be available in the school building to assist the beginning teacher employed through the alternate route)
III.   A Virginia educational agency may submit an alternative program for licensure for approval.

Professional Studies

I.   Requirements for the Early/Primary Education, Elementary Education, and Middle Education Endorsements
   A.   Professional studies, semester hours 18
      1.   See Alternative Route to Licensure II, A, 1.
   B.   Supervised classroom experience
      1.   Student teaching experience must provide for the prospective teacher to be in classrooms full-time for a minimum of 300 clock hours, with at least half of that time spent supervised in direct teaching activities (providing direct instruction) at the level of endorsement
      2.   One year of successful, full-time teaching experience in the endorsement area in any accredited public or nonpublic school may be accepted in lieu of the supervised teaching experience.

Early/Primary Education (PreK–3)

I. Requirements
    A. Completion of an approved teacher preparation program in early/ primary education PreK–3
        or
    B. Degree in the liberal arts and sciences (or equivalent) and completed course work which covers the early/primary education preK–3 competencies and fulfills the following 51-semester-hour requirements:
        1. English (12), mathematics (9), science (9), history (6), social science (6), arts and humanities (6), and computer/technology (3).

Elementary Education (PreK–6)

I. Requirements
    A. Completion of an approved teacher preparation program in elementary education PreK–6
        or
    B. Degree in the liberal arts and sciences (or equivalent) and completion of course work which covers the elementary education PreK–3 competencies and fulfills the following 60-semester-hour requirements:
        1. English (12), mathematics (12), science (12), history (9), social science (6), arts and humanities (6), and computer/technology (3).

Middle Education (6–8)

I. Requirements
    A. Completion of an approved teacher preparation, discipline-specific, program in middle education 6–8 with two areas of concentration from the areas of English, mathematics, science, and history/social science
        or
    B. Degree in the liberal arts and sciences (or equivalent) and completion of a minimum of 21 semester hours in two areas of concentration to be listed on the license (There are also minimum requirements for those two areas in which the individual is not seeking an area of concentration.)

Teaching Endorsement Areas

I. Applicants should note that endorsements in a specific subject field may be inclusive of requirements specified in that field under the General Studies section. There are usually three ways of meeting endorsement requirements: graduating from an approved program in the endorsement subject area, completion of a major in the subject, or completion of a certain number of semester hours in the subject. In all cases, the applicant must meet the stipulated competencies required for the endorsement. For further details on specific subject competencies and course distributions in each subject field, as well as for additional teaching endorsement areas, please contact the Virginia Department of Education (see Appendix 1 for address).

A. Art, semester hours 36
B. Biology, semester hours 32
C. Chemistry, semester hours 32
D. Earth Science, semester hours... 32
E. English, semester hours... 36
F. English as a second language, semester hours 24
G. Foreign language (6–12), semester hours.. 30
H. History and social science, semester hours 51
I. Library media (PreK–12), semester hours 24
J. Mathematics, semester hours 36
K. Music (choral/instrumental), semester hours 42
L. Physical education (PreK–12), semester hours 33
M. Physics, semester hours... 32

School Counselor (PreK–12)

I. Requirements (Option 1)
   A. Master's degree from an approved counselor education program which shall include at least 100 clock hours of clinical experiences in the preK–6 setting and 100 clock hours of clinical experiences in the grades 7–12 setting
   B. Two years of successful, full-time teaching experience or two years of successful, full-time experience in guidance and counseling (Two years of successful, full-time experience in guidance and counseling under a provisional license may be accepted to meet this requirement)

II. Requirements (Option 2)
   A. Master's degree from an accredited college or university and certification by an approved counselor education program that the candidate has completed sufficient course work and clinical experience to acquire the stipulated competencies in school counseling
   B. See I, B directly above.

Support Personnel

I. School principal (elementary, middle, and secondary)
   A. Requirements for Option One—Virginia approved program
      1. Master's degree from an accredited institution
      2. Three years of successful, full-time teaching experience in an accredited nonpublic or public school
      3. Completion of an approved administration and supervision program in Virginia which shall ensure that the candidate has demonstrated meeting the stipulated competencies
   B. Requirements for Option Two—Out-of-state approved program
      1. See I, A, 1–2 directly above.

2. Completion of an out-of-state approved program in administration and supervision
3. Completion of a beginning administration and supervision assessment (when prescribed by the Board of Education) reflecting the knowledge and understanding of the stipulated competencies or completion of a full-time internship as a school principal
    a. One year of successful, full-time experience as a principal or assistant principal may be substituted for the internship.

C. Requirements for Option Three—Out-of-state administration license
1. Master's degree from an accredited institution
2. Current, valid out-of-state license with endorsements in administration and supervision
3. See I, B, 3 directly above.

II. Division superintendent
A. Requirements for Option One
1. Doctoral degree in educational administration or educational leadership from an accredited institution
2. Five years of educational experience in a public and/or accredited nonpublic school, two of which must be teaching experience at the PreK–12 level and two of which must be in administration/supervision at the PreK–12 level

B. Requirements for Option Two
1. Master's degree from an accredited institution, plus 30 graduate hours beyond the master's degree
2. Completion of requirements for administration and supervision PreK–12 endorsement which includes the demonstration of the stipulated competencies
3. See II, A, 2 directly above.

C. Requirements for Option Three
1. Master's degree from an accredited institution
2. Current, valid out-of-state license with an endorsement as a division/district superintendent
3. See II, A, 2 directly above

Washington

Types of Certificates

I. The teacher certificate authorizes service in the primary role of teacher.
II. The administrator certificate authorizes service in the primary role of district-wide general administration (superintendent), building level administration (principal), and program administration (program administrator).
III. The educational staff associate certificate authorizes service as school psychologist, counselor, communication disorders specialist, school nurse, social worker, physical therapist, occupational therapist, or reading resource specialist.
IV. Levels of Certificates
    A. Emergency certificate—valid only for the school year in which it is issued
    B. Initial certificate
    C. Continuing certificate
    D. Certificate endorsements
        1. Initial and continuing certificates are endorsed to indicate grade level(s), content area(s), and/or specialization(s) for which the professional is or has been prepared.

Teaching Certificates
P–3, K–8, 4–12, and K–12

I. Initial Teacher Certificate
    A. Baccalaureate degree from a regionally accredited institution and completion of a state-approved teacher education program.
    B. Completion of a major (45 quarter hours or 30 semester hours) in one endorsement area.
    C. Valid for 4 years; renewable for an additional 3 years while the holder meets requirements for a continuing certificate.
II. Continuing Teacher Certificate
    A. See Initial Certificate I, A.
    B. Master's degree from a regionally accredited institution
        or
        45 quarter hours of study at the upper division or graduate level.
    C. Experience—180 days of full-time teaching experience, of which 30 days must be in one district. Substitute teaching, out-of-state teaching, and teaching in more than one district are acceptable.
    D. Completion of a course or course work relating to issues of abuse. The course must be 1 quarter hour or 10 clock hours and must include information related to identification of physical, emotional, sexual, and substance abuse.
    E. Must have at least 2 endorsements on certificate.
    F. Validity maintained by the completion of 150 clock hours every 5 years.

III. Library Media Specialist (Learning Resources Endorsement)
   A. Regular teaching certificate.
   B. Courses in media, selection, cataloging, reference, media utilization and production, curriculum and administration, with minimum of 16 semester hours.

Administrative Certification

I. Initial Principal Certificate
   A. Must hold a valid teaching certificate.
   B. Master's degree.
   C. Completion of an approved graduate level program for preparation of principals.
   D. Verification of 3 years of teaching experience.
   E. Valid for 7 years.
II. Continuing Principal Certificate
   A. See Initial Principal Certificate I, A–C.
   B. Completion of 15 quarter hours and/or 150 clock hours of graduate course work based on principal performance domains.
   C. Verification of 180 days of experience as a principal, vice principal, or assistant principal.
   D. Completion of a course or course work relating to issues of abuse. The course must be 1 quarter hour of 10 clock hours and must include information related to identification of physical, emotional, sexual, and substance abuse.
   E. Valid for life upon completion of 150 clock hours every five years.
III. Initial Program Administrator Certificate
   A. Master's degree.
   B. Completion of approved program of preparation for the program administrator.
   C. Completion of 24 quarter hours of graduate work in education.
   D. Valid for 7 years.
IV. Continuing Program Administrator Certificate
   A. See III, A and C.
   B. Completion of 30 quarter hours of graduate work subsequent to the bachelor's degree in education or a doctorate in education.
   C. Verification of 180 days of experience as a program administrator.
   D. See I, D.
   E. Valid for life upon completion of 150 clock hours every five years.
V. Initial Superintendent Certificate
   A. Most hold a valid teacher, educational staff associate, or program administrator certificate.
   B. Master's degree.
   C. Completion of approved preparation program for the superintendency.
   D. Completion of 45 quarter hours of graduate study beyond the bachelor's degree in education or a doctorate in education.
   E. Valid for 7 years.
VI. Continuing Superintendent Certificate
   A. See V, A–C.

B.   Completion of 60 quarter hours of graduate work beyond the bachelor's degree in education or a doctorate in education.

C.   Verification of 180 days of experience as a superintendent, assistant superintendent, or deputy superintendent.

D.   See I, D.

E.   Valid for life upon completion of 150 clock hours every five years.

Educational Staff Associate Certification

I.   Initial E. S. A. Certificate for communication disorders specialist, school counselor, school psychologist, and school social worker

A.   Completion of all course work (except special projects or thesis) for a master's degree with a major in the appropriate specialization.

B.   Completion of a state-approved preparation for certification in the E. S. A. role.

C.   Valid for 7 years.

II. Initial E. S. A. Certificate for school occupational therapist, school physical therapist, school nurse, and school speech-language pathologist or audiologist

A.   Baccalaureate degree in specialization, except master's degree for school speech-language pathologist or audiologist.

B.   Thirty clock hours or 3 quarter hours of course work orienting candidate to the school environment.

C.   Valid Washington State license in specialization, when required.

D.   Valid for 7 years.

III. Continuing E. S. A. Certificate for school counselor, school psychologist, and school social worker

A.   See I, A–C.

B.   Master's degree in appropriate specialization.

C.   Verification of 180 days of experience in the role.

D.   Completion of a college level course which includes peer review while employed in the role.

E.   Completion of a comprehensive, written examination (unless already taken as part of a master's degree) is required for out-of-state applicants.

F.   Valid for life upon completion of 150 clock hours every five years.

IV. Continuing E. S. A. Certificate for school occupational therapist, school physical therapist, school nurse, and school speech-language pathologist or audiologist.

A.   See II, A–C.

B.   Completion of 15 quarter hours (45 quarter hours for school nurse) subsequent to the bachelor's degree in the appropriate area, other health sciences, or education. (No additional course work required for school speech-language pathologist or audiologist.)

C.   Verification of 180 days of experience.

D.   For school speech-language pathologist or audiologist, completion of a comprehensive, written examination (unless already taken as part of a master's degree) is required of out-of-state applicants.

West Virginia

I. Candidates for certification must complete a state-approved preparation program through an accredited institution of higher education consisting of:
   A. Preprofessional skills component, to include:
      1. Basic educational skills of reading, writing, mathematics, speaking, listening, and computer literacy
      2. The PRAXIS I Pre-Professional Skills Tests at a state-established proficiency level; *or* acceptable scores on the ACT or SAT tests; *or* a doctorate
   B. Content specialization component, to include PRAXIS II content tests and attainment of an established proficiency level for each endorsed area
      1. Distribution of credit hours is determined by the institution
      2. Endorsements (other than teaching areas) such as principals and counselors shall be validated against a task analysis of their roles and functions in the public schools.
   C. Professional education component, to include performance assessment measurement
      1. Courses to include, but not be limited to, theory, skills, strategies and methods of designing, implementing, and evaluating education at the early childhood, middle childhood, adolescent, and adult levels
      2. Assessment through the administration of a performance instrument by college and public school personnel
      3. Passing score on the Principles of Learning and Teaching Test
II. Professional certification for out-of-state applicants
   A. Qualifications for eligibility
      1. U.S. citizenship
      2. Bachelor's degree from an accredited institution of higher education with a minimum GPA of 2.5
   B. Professional Component
      1. Evidence or verification of completion of a state-approved educational preparation program in a specialization comparable to one offered in West Virginia, unless the applicant holds a valid out-of-state certificate and has had three years of experience within the last seven years in a specialization offered in West Virginia
   C. Passing scores on required examinations
      1. PRAXIS I Pre-Professional Skills Test
      2. Principles of Learning and Teaching Test
      3. PRAXIS II content specialization test for each endorsement requested
III. Alternative Program for the Education of Teachers (APET)
   A. To qualify for eligibility individuals must:
      1. Be a U.S. citizen, of good moral character, and 18 years of age
      2. Hold a bachelor's degree from an accredited institution of higher education in a discipline taught in the public schools and in a teaching specialization approved by the state board for APET

    3.   Have an overall grade point average of 2.5 or better

    4.   Satisfy the appropriate state board approved basic skills and subject matter test requirements, *or* have completed three years of successful teaching experience within the last seven years in the area for which licensure is being sought

    5.   Have not previously completed a state-approved teacher preparation program

B.   Components of the APET

    1.   The program includes approximately 200 hours of formal instruction including a full-time seminar practicum of twenty to thirty days duration and continuing on-the-job supervision and evaluation.

    2.   The APET certificate expires on June 30 of the school year in which it is issued. The final evaluation will recommend the issuance of the professional certificate; re-entry to an alternative program; or disapproval of further participation in the alternative program.

Note: There are no state-mandated minimum semester hours required within any particular content specialization. The institutions of higher education have developed programs which incorporate West Virginia Board of Education–approved goals, objectives, and standards for each specialization in which they offer approved programs. West Virginia certifies only on the basis of completion of state-approved programs from accredited institutions as defined by the West Virginia Board of Education, except for the experienced educator option described in II above. There is no provision for certification by credit count.

Wisconsin

General Requirements

I. Completion of a college/university approved program with a minimum grade point average of 2.75 on a 4.00 scale (in major, minor, and professional courses) or a standing in the top 50% of the class (as determined by the policy of the granting institution)

II. Recommendation for licensure from the certifying officer at the preparing institution

III. Passing scores on the Pre-Professional Skills Test in the areas of mathematics, reading, and writing

IV. Completion of course work in the following:
   A. Special education (3 semester credits)
   B. Human relations
   C. Children at risk
   D. Historical, philosophical, and social foundations of education
   E. Legal, political, economic, and governmental foundations of education
   F. Gifted and talented children
   G. Environmental education (for early childhood, elementary, social studies, science, and agriculture licenses only)
   H. Education for employment
   I. Conflict resolution
   J. Reading and language arts (those with initial teacher training completed prior to July 1, 1992, need only a discrete reading course)
   K. Student teaching (applicable to those completing their initial professional education training on or after August 31, 1990; others should write to the Teacher Education Licensing and Placement Office for information)
      1. Within Wisconsin—completion of a student teaching experience consisting of full days for a full semester at the cooperating school
      2. Outside Wisconsin—if a student teaching experience of less than full days for a full semester is completed, then two consecutive semesters of successful regular classroom teaching experience under the supervision of the employing school district will be considered equivalent

Early Childhood (PreK–3)

I. Completion of all general license requirements

II. Completion of a minimum of 22 semester credits of professional education including:
   A. Growth and development of children from birth through age 8; educational psychology; methods and curriculum in early childhood education; assessment of children from birth through age 8; language development; parent involvement in

early childhood education; function and guidance of play; and models of early childhood education programs.
    B.   Student teaching in prekindergarten, kindergarten and in at least one of grades 1 through 3 (see General Requirements V, J)
III. Other required courses
    A.   Reading and language arts (12 semester credits), including a clinical experience in teaching reading (this latter requirement may be waived in light of one year of successful teaching experience)
    B.   At least 12 semester credits in content, curriculum, and methods in each of the following areas: mathematics, science, and social studies

Elementary (1–6)

  I. Completion of all general license requirements
 II. Completion of a minimum of 26 semester credits of professional education including:
    A.   Development of elementary school aged children; methods of teaching; and student teaching in at least one of grades 1 through 6 (see General Requirements V, J)
    B.   An approved program minor
III. Same as Early Childhood III, except courses should be related to elementary level.

Elementary/Middle (1–9)

  I. Completion of all general license requirements
 II. Completion of a minimum of 26 semester credits of professional education including:
    A.   Development of elementary school-aged children and of the young adolescent; methods of teaching at the elementary and the middle levels; an approved program minor; and student teaching in at least one of grades 1–6 and in another of grades 6–9 (see General Requirements V, J)
III. Other required courses
    A.   Same as Early Childhood III, A–B, except reading and language arts courses should relate to the elementary and young adolescent level

Middle (5–9)

  I. Completion of all general license requirements
 II. Completion of an approved program which includes 2 minors and the following:
    A.   Development of the young adolescent; methods of teaching in both of the minor subjects; and student teaching in at least one of grades 5 through 9 including student teaching in at least one of the subject areas in which licensure is being sought (see General Requirements V, J)
III. Other required courses
    A.   Reading and language arts (6 semester credits), including a clinical experience in teaching reading (this latter requirement may be waived in light of one year of successful teaching experience)
    B.   See Early Childhood III, B

Middle/Secondary (6–12)

I.   Completion of all general license requirements
II. Completion of an approved program with at least 18 semester credits of professional credits including:
   A. Development of the adolescent and the young adolescent; methods of teaching this level; methods of teaching at least in the major subject; and student teaching in at least one of grades 6–9 and 9–12 (see General Requirements V, J)
III. Other required courses
   A. See Middle III, A
IV. License may be issued in the subject area in which applicant completed a major; additional licenses may be acquired in subjects for which at least a minor has been completed (with some exceptions)

Secondary (9–12)

I.   Completion of all general license requirements
II. Completion of an approved program with at least 18 semester credits of professional credits including:
   A. Development of the adolescent; methods of teaching at least in the major subject; completion of at least a minor; and student teaching in at least one of grades 9–12 (see General Requirements V, J)
III. Other required courses
   A. See Middle III, A
IV. See Middle/Secondary IV

Special Subjects

I.   Completion of all general license requirements
II. A minimum of 18 semester credits of professional education including:
   A. Child or adolescent development, educational psychology or psychology of learning; curriculum; methods; and student teaching as specified in general requirements
III. Write the Superintendent of Public Instruction for details regarding requirements for specific areas (applicants must have a major or a master's degree in desired area): agriculture, art, business education, business education with shorthand, family and consumer education, technology education, instrumental music, choral music, general music, and physical education

School Administrators

I.   General Requirements
   A. Completion of an approved master's degree program or the equivalent at the appropriate level of school administration
       or

A master's degree (or the equivalent) and an approved program for the level of the license being sought

B.   Graduate or undergraduate course work in each of the following—child psychology, early adolescent psychology, and adolescent psychology—or in human growth and development

C.   Completion of 21 graduate semester credits in the following areas:

1.   Human relations; oral and written communication; educational leadership; organization and operation of public schools; governance of education; supervision of instruction; evaluation of personnel; school law; school business administration and budgeting; and politics of education

D.   Completion of 18 semester credits of professional education course work which are not included as part of an approved program leading to an administrative license

E.   Hold or be eligible to hold a license to teach at the elementary, elementary/middle, middle, middle/secondary, secondary, or K–12 levels

or

Hold or be eligible to hold a license as a school counselor, school psychologist, or a school social worker

or

Have completed an approved program leading to any of these licenses

F.   Completion of 3 years of successful experience at the elementary, elementary/middle, middle, middle/secondary, secondary, or K–12 levels

or

Completion of 3 years as a school counselor, school psychologist, or a school social worker which includes at least 540 hours of successful classroom teaching experiences

II.   Superintendent (valid 5 years)

A.   See I, A–F

B.   Hold or be eligible to hold a principal license

C.   Completion of an approved program or the equivalent, including 12 graduate semester credits in all the following areas:

1.   Superintendency; advanced program planning and evaluation; economics of education; advanced politics of education; personnel administration; collective bargaining and contract administration; practicum or internship

D.   Renewal—For each subsequent five-year license, 6 semesters of professional credits or an approved equivalent must be completed

III.   K–12 Principal (valid 5 years)

A.   See I, A–F

B.   Completion of an approved program or the equivalent, leading to licensure as a principal, including 12 graduate semester credits in all the following areas:

1.   Principalship; coordination of special school programs; curriculum development; practicum or internship

C.   Renewal—See II, D

School Counselor

I. Complete or possess the following:
    A. A master's degree with a major in school counseling and guidance or a master's degree with at least 30 semester credits in an approved school counseling and guidance program and the institutional endorsement
    B. One of the following:
        1. Eligibility for a Wisconsin license to teach in the elementary or secondary schools, or completion of an approved elementary or secondary teacher education program and 2 years of successful teaching experience at the elementary or secondary school level,
            or
        2. An approved one-year, full-time internship in school counseling at the elementary or secondary level,
            or
        3. A minimum of 2 years of successful experience as a licensed school counselor in an assigned position of one-half time or more

Instructional Library Media Specialist

I. Initial license (valid 5 years)
    A. Complete all of the following:
        1. The general requirements in the Approved Program and institutional endorsement
        2. Eligibility to hold a Wisconsin license to teach in the elementary or secondary schools or completion of an approved elementary or secondary classroom teacher preparation program
        3. Student teaching in library media services
        4. A minimum of 24 semester credits in an approved library media services program covering specific competency areas (write to Wisconsin's Department of Teacher Education, Licensing, and Placement for further details)
II. Regular license
    A. Complete all of the following:
        1. Eligibility to hold the initial instructional library media specialist license
        2. A master's degree in an approved library media services program or a total of 39 semester credits in an approved library media services program, 15 of which must be completed after the bachelor's degree and must cover specific competency areas (write to Wisconsin's Department of Teacher Education, Licensing, and Placement for further details)

License Renewal

Renewal of the regular license for all professional school employees requires the completion of a continuing professional education requirement of 6 semester credits at an accredited college or university or the equivalent. The equivalent must be pre-approved by the state superintendent. The continuing professional education requirement shall be completed in the area directly and substantively related to one or more of the licenses held or to professional competency.

Wyoming

Wyoming's system of certification, Program Approval, is based on student-demonstrated skills, competencies, and knowledge rather than simply completing course work. College and university teacher education programs will be assessed, either through on-site visits or reciprocity with other states, to determine whether their programs meet Wyoming's standards. Graduates of these approved programs will qualify for Wyoming certification. Detailed standards for each program may be obtained from the Professional Teaching Standards Board (address in Appendix 1).

General Requirements

I. The applicant shall hold a bachelor's degree and have an institutional recommendation from an approved institution of higher learning.
    A. The general education program, embracing those studies commonly known as the liberal arts, shall include such broad areas as the humanities, mathematics, the biological and physical sciences, the social and behavioral sciences, and oral and written communication skills.
    B. The professional education program is based on those studies which include foundations of education, methods and materials of teaching, and supervised experiences designed to provide different kinds of knowledge and competencies in guiding student learning.
        1. The program shall require a student teaching (or internship) experience in a recognized K–12 setting of sufficient length and concentration to experience the full range of teacher activities.
    C. The teaching field or field of study shall consist of a carefully planned pattern of courses and on-campus or off-campus experiences designed to produce a strong academic background and competencies necessary for successful teaching at the particular grade levels for which each program is designed.

Grade Levels of the Standard Teaching Certificate

I.   Pre-school years (birth to age 5)
II.   Elementary grades (K–8)
      A. The elementary level also satisfies the elementary endorsement.
III. Middle school grades (5–8)
IV.   Secondary grades (7–12)
      A. The applicant must also satisfy the requirements for one or more of the teaching endorsements at this level.
V.   Grades K–12
      A. The applicant must also satisfy the requirements for one or more of the teaching endorsements at this level.

Endorsements

Endorsement(s) for which an applicant qualifies will appear on the standard certificate. As determined by the program approval standards, the endorsement(s) will allow the teacher to provide instruction in the classroom, or the administrator or pupil personnel person to provide services in the areas identified on the certificate. Teaching endorsements are valid at the level for which they are issued.

I. Pre-school years (birth to age 5)
    A. Endorsements are for early childhood and early childhood special education.
II. Elementary grades (K–8)
    A. Endorsements are in art, bilingual, English as a second language, exceptional children generalist, music, physical education, early childhood (K–3), and elementary education.
III. Middle grades (5–8)
    A. Endorsements are in art, bilingual, English as a second language, exceptional children generalist, music, and physical education.
    B. Endorsements for subjects listed in IV, A may be added to this level.
IV. Secondary grades (7–12)
    A. Endorsements are in agriculture, art, bilingual, business education, classical language, computer science, drama (theater), driver education, English, English as a second language, exceptional children generalist, home economics, industrial technology, journalism, marketing education, mathematics, modern foreign language, music, physical education, psychology, science, social studies, and speech.
V. Grades K–12
    A. Endorsements are in art, exceptional children generalist, behaviorally disordered/emotionally disturbed, athletic coaching, learning disabled, mentally retarded, hearing impaired, vision impaired, health education, library media, music, reading, physical education, and school nurse.
    B. Upon completion of an advanced program, the following endorsements may be added to the grades K–12 level: director/coordinator/supervisor, educational diagnostician, school audiologist, school counselor, school principal, school psychologist, school social worker, school superintendent, and speech/language pathologist.
VI. Additional Endorsements
    A. Native language endorsement (Arapahoe or Shoshoni) and a transitional (one year) endorsement for those meeting at least two-thirds of the competencies, skills, and knowledge of the approved program.

Advanced Programs

I. Advanced programs for teachers holding initial, standard certificates may be taken in the following areas: director/coordinator/supervisor, educational diagnostician, school counselor, school principal, or school superintendent.
    A. General standards and requirements for advanced programs.
        1. Program stipulates prior completion of a state-approved teacher preparation

        program or a regionally or NCATE accredited teacher preparation program.

    2.   Mastery of advanced content in both specialty and appropriate cognate support areas, demonstrated competence in the application of skills at an advanced level, and familiarity with appropriate research and its implementation.

    3.   Knowledge of the philosophy, ethics, organization, practice, and activities of the education profession, and its relationship to the area of specialty.

    4.   Successful experience in a recognized K–12 setting.

    5.   A supervised internship or practicum.

II.   Advanced programs for individuals *not* holding initial, standard certificates but holding bachelor's degrees may be taken in the following areas: school audiologist, school psychologist, school social worker, and speech/language pathologist.

  A.   General standards and requirements for advanced programs.

    1.   Completion of a state-approved program or a regionally or NCATE accredited program.

    2.   See I, A, 3 and 5 directly above.

Appendix 1

Addresses for State Offices of Certification

Alabama
Teacher Education and Certification
State Department of Education
P.O. Box 302101
Montgomery, AL 36130-2101
334-242-9560
334-242-0498 (fax)

Alaska
Department of Education
Teacher Education & Certification
801 West 10th Street, Suite 200
Juneau, AK 99801–1894
907-465-2831 or 2026

Arizona
Arizona Dept. of Education
Certification Unit
P.O. Box 6490
Phoenix, AZ 85005-6490
602-542-4367
www.ade.state.az.us

Arkansas
Teacher Education & Licensure
State Dept. of Education
4 State Capitol Mall
Little Rock, AR 72201-1071
501-682-4342
501-682-4898 (fax)

California
Commission on Teacher
  Credentialing
Box 944270
Sacramento, CA 94244-2700
916-445-7254
916-327-3166 (fax)
credentials@ctc.ca.gov (e-mail)
www.ctc.ca.gov

Colorado
Educator Licensing
State Dept. of Education
201 E. Colfax Avenue
Denver, CO 80203
303-866-6628

Connecticut
Bureau of Certification and
  Teacher Preparation
State Dept. of Education
P.O. Box 150471
Hartford, CT 06115-0471
860-566-5201
860-566-8929 (fax)
www.state.ct.us/sde

Delaware
Teacher Certification
Dept. of Public Instruction
P.O. Box 1402
Dover, DE 19903
302-739-4686

District of Columbia
Educational Credentialing &
  Standards
825 N. Capitol Street, N.E.
6th Floor
Washington, DC 20002
202-442-5377
202-442-5311 (fax)

Florida
Bureau of Teacher Certification
Florida Education Center
325 W. Gaines, Rm. 201
Tallahassee, FL 32399-0400
850-488-2317 (out of state)
800-445-6739 (in state)

Georgia
Professional Standards Commission
Certification Section
1454 Twin Towers East
Atlanta, GA 30334
404-657-9000
mail@gapsc.com (e-mail)

Hawaii
Office of Personnel Services
Teacher Recruitment Unit
P.O. Box 2360
Honolulu, HI 96804
808-586-3420
800-305-5104
808-586-3419 (fax)

Idaho
Teacher Certification
State Dept. of Education
P.O. Box 83720
Boise, ID 83720-0027
208-332-6880
www.sde.state.id.us/certification

Illinois
Illinois State Board of Education
Certification & Placement Section
100 N. First Street
Springfield, IL 62777-0001
217-782-4321

Indiana
Indiana Professional Standards
  Board
Teacher Licensing
251 East Ohio Street, Suite 201
Indianapolis, IN 46204-2133
317-232-9010
317-232-9023 (fax)

Iowa
Board of Educational Examiners
Grimes State Office Building
Des Moines, IA 50319-0147
515-281-3245

Kansas
Certification Section
Kansas State Dept. of Education
Kansas State Education Building
120 SE 10th Ave.
Topeka, KS 66612-1182
785-296-2288

Kentucky
Kentucky Dept. of Education
Division of Certification
1024 Capital Center Drive
Frankfort, KY 40601-1972
502-573-4606

Louisiana
Louisiana Dept. of Education
Teacher Certification, Room 700
P.O. Box 94064
Baton Rouge, LA 70804-9064
225-342-3490
225-342-3499

Maine
Division of Certification
Department of Education
State House Station 23
Augusta, ME 04333
207-287-5944

Maryland
Division of Certification 18100
State Dept. of Education
200 West Baltimore St.
Baltimore, MD 21201
410-767-0412
www.msde.md.us

Massachusetts
Massachusetts Dept. of Education
Office of Teacher Certification
   and Credentialling
350 Main Street
Malden, MA 02148
781-388-3300, x665
781-388-3475 (fax)
www.doe.mass.edu

Michigan
Office of Professional Preparation
   & Certification
Michigan Dept. of Education
P.O. Box 30008
Lansing, MI 48909
517-373-3310

Minnesota
Teacher Licensing
State Dept. of Children, Families
   and Learning
1500 Highway 36 West
Roseville MN 55113
651-582-8691

Mississippi
Teacher Certification
State Dept. of Education
Box 771
Jackson, MS 39205-0771
601-359-3483
601-359-2778 (fax)

Missouri
Teacher Certification
Dept. of Elementary and
   Secondary Education
P.O. Box 480
Jefferson City, MO 65102
573-751-3486

Montana
Teacher Certification
Office of Public Instruction
P.O. Box 202501
Helena, MT 59620-2501
406-444-3150

Nebraska
Teacher Certification
State Dept. of Education
301 Centennial Mall South
Box 94987
Lincoln, NE 68509-4987
800-371-4642

Nevada
Licensure and Certification
Nevada Dept. of Education
700 East 5th St.
Carson City, NV 89701
702-687-3115

New Hampshire
Bureau of Credentialing
State Dept. of Education
101 Pleasant St.
Concord, NH 03301
603-271-2407
603-271-4134 (fax)

New Jersey
Office of Licensing and
   Credentials
P.O. Box 500
Trenton, NJ 08625-0500
609-292-2070

New Mexico
Director
Professional Licensure Unit
Education Building
300 Don Gaspar
Santa Fe, NM 87501-2786
505-827-6587

New York
Office of Teaching
State Education Department
Albany, NY 12234
518-474-3901/2/3/4

North Carolina
North Carolina Dept. of Public
   Instruction
Licensure Section
301 N. Wilmington Street
Raleigh, NC 27601-2825
919-733-4125
800-577-7994

North Dakota
Education Standards and Practice
   Board
Teacher Certification
600 E. Boulevard Ave.
Bismarck, ND 58505-0880
701-328-2264

Ohio
Professional Development and
  Licensure
State Dept. of Education
65 South Front St., Rm. 412
Columbus, OH 43215-4183
614-466-3593
614-466-1999 (fax)
www.ode.ohio.gov

Oklahoma
Professional Standards
State Dept. of Education
2500 N. Lincoln Blvd.
Rm. 211
Oklahoma City, OK 73105-4599
405-521-3301
405-521-6205 (fax)

Oregon
Teacher Standards and Practices
  Commission
Public Service Bldg.
255 Capitol Street, N. E.
Suite 105
Salem, OR 97310-1332
503-378-3586

Pennsylvania
Bureau of Teacher Certification &
  Preparation
Dept. of Education
333 Market Street
Harrisburg, PA 17126-0333
717-787-3356
00certifica@psupen.psu.edu (email)
www.cas.psu.edu/docs/pde/teachcert
  .html

Rhode Island
Office of Teacher Certification
State Dept. of Education
Shepard Building
255 Westminster St.
Providence, RI 02903-3400
401-222-4600

South Carolina
Office of Teacher Education,
  Certification, & Evaluation
1600 Gervais St.
Columbia, SC 29201
803-734-8466
803-734-2873 (fax)
licensure@sde.state.sc.us (email)

South Dakota
Teacher Certification
Office of Policy and Accountability
700 Governors Drive
Pierre, SD 57501-2291
605-773-3553
605-773-6139 (fax)
www.state.sd.us

Tennessee
Office of Teacher Licensing
State Dept. of Education
5th Floor, Andrew Johnson Tower
710 James Robertson Parkway
Nashville, TN 37243-0377
615-533-4885
615-532-7860 (fax)

Texas
State Board for Educator
  Certification
1001 Trinity
Austin, TX 78701
512-469-3001

Utah
Certification and Professional
  Development Section
State Board of Education
250 East 500 South Street
Salt Lake City, UT 84111
801-538-7740
801-538-7973 (fax)

Vermont
Licensing Office
Dept. of Education
120 State Street
Montpelier, VT 05620-2501
802-828-2445
802-828-3140 (fax)

Virginia
Office of Professional Licensure
Department of Education
P.O. Box 2120
Richmond, VA 23216-2120
804-225-2022

Washington
Office of Professional Education
Superintendent of Public Instruction
Old Capitol Building
P.O. Box 47200
Olympia, WA 98504-7200
360-753-6773

West Virginia
State Dept. of Education
Building 6, Room 337
1900 Kanawha Blvd., East
Charleston, WV 25305-0330
800-982-2378

Wisconsin
Teacher Education, Licensing and
  Placement
Box 7841
Madison, WI 53707-7841
608-266-1028 (direct line)
608-266-1027 (voice mail)
608-264-9558 (fax)
www.dpi.state.wi.us/dpi/dlsis/tel/ind
  ex.html

Wyoming
Professional Teaching Standards
  Board
2300 Capitol Avenue
Hathaway Building, 2nd Floor
Cheyenne, WY 82002
307-777-6234 (fax)
PTSB@www.k12.wy.us

Appendix 2

Addresses for Certification Information for U.S. Possessions and Territories

American Samoa
American Samoa Department of Education
Dr. LaAloulu Tagoilelagi, Director
Pago Pago, AS 96799
684-633-5237
684-633-4240 (fax)

Guam
Guam Department of Education
P.O. Box DE
Agana, GU 96932
671-475-0457/0462

Marshall Islands
Federated States of Micronesia
Republic of Palau
Secretary's Regional Office: Region IX
    San Francisco
Secretary's Regional Representative
Room 205
50 United Nations Plaza
San Francisco, CA 94102-4987

Northern Mariana Islands
Human Resources Officer
CNMI Public School System
P.O. Box 1370
Saipan, MP 96950
670-664-3700
670-664-3707 (fax)

Puerto Rico
Puerto Rico Department of Education
Victor R. Fajardo, Secretary of Education
P.O. Box 190759
San Juan, PR 00919-0759
787-753-2062
787-250-0275 (fax)

Virgin Islands
Virgin Islands Department of Education
Liston A. Davis, Commissioner of Education
44-46 Kongens Gade
St. Thomas, VI 00802
340-774-2810
340-774-4679 (fax)

Appendix 3

Parties to the Interstate Agreement
Through September 30, 2000

Many of the states are parties to the National Association of State Directors of Teacher Education and Certification Interstate Contract. This agreement allows educators who hold certificates or licenses in one of the participating states to obtain analogous certification or licensure in any of the other participating states. Applicants should note that individual states may have special conditions upon granting certification, for example demonstrated knowledge of state history. Such conditions and even whether there is reciprocity for all classes of educational personnel vary from state to state. Many of these conditions are noted in the individual state requirements found in this volume, but not all.

The listing below shows which states are parties to the agreement according to type of certification: teachers, administrators, support personnel, and vocational personnel. Applicants seeking reciprocal certification in another state should contact the certification office there for full information.

Alabama

Teacher: AZ, AR, CA, CO, CT, DE, DC, FL, GA, GU, HI, ID, IL, IN, KY, LA, ME, MD, MA, MI, MS, MT, NV, NH, NJ, NM, NY, NC, OH, OK, OR, PA, RI, SC, TN, TX, UT, VT, VA, WA, WV, WY

Support: AZ, CT, DC, FL, GA, GU, IN, MD, MA, MI, MS, NH, NY, NC, OK, OR, RI, SC, TN, TX, UT, VA, WA, WV, WY

Administrator: AZ, CO, DE, FL, GA, GU, IN, MD, MA, MS, NH, NM, NY, OK, OR, RI, SC, TN, TX, UT, VA, WA, WV, WY

Vocational: No contracts

Arizona

Teacher: AL, AR, CA, CO, CT, DE, DC, FL, GA, HI, ID, IL, IN, LA, MD, MA, MI, MS, MT, NV, NH, NM, NY, OH, OK, PA, RI, SC, TN, TX, UT, VT, VA, WA, WV, WY

Support: AL, DC, FL, GA, IN, MD, MA, MS, NH, NY, OK, OR, RI, SC, TN, TX, VA, WA, WV, WY

Administrator: AL, CO, GA, IL, IN, MA, MD, MS, NH, NM, NY, OK, OR, RI, SC, TN, TX, VA, WA, WV, WY

Vocational: AR, DC, GA, MD, MS, NH, NY, OK, RI, SC, TN, TX, VA, WV, WY

Arkansas

Teacher: AL, AZ, CA, CO, CT, DC, DE, FL, GA, HI, ID, IN, KY, LA, MA, MD, ME, MI, MS, MT, NC, NH, NJ, NM, NV, NY, OH, OK, OR, PA, RI, SC, TN, TX, UT, VA, VT, WA, WV

Support: No contracts

Administrator: No contracts

Vocational: AZ, DC, GA, MD, MS, NH, NY, OK, RI, SC, TN, TX, VA, WV

California

Teacher: AL, AR, AZ, CO, CT, DC, DE, FL, GA, HI, ID, IL, IN, KY, LA, MA, MD, ME, MI, MS, MT, NC, NH, NJ, NM, NV, NY, OH, OK, OR, PA, RI, SC, TN, TX, UT, VA, VT, WA, WV

Support	No contracts
Administrator	No contracts
Vocational	No contracts

Colorado

Teacher	AL, AR, AZ, CA, CT, DC, DE, FL, GA, HI, ID, IL, IN, MA, MD, ME, MI, MS, MT, NC, NH, NV, NY, OH, OK, OR, PA, RI, SC, TN, TX, UT, VA, VT, WA, WV
Support	No contracts
Administrator	AL, AZ, GA, IN, MA, MD, MS, NH, NV, NY, OK, OR, RI, SC, TN, TX, VA, WA, WV
Vocational	No contracts

Connecticut

Teacher	AL, AR, AZ, CA, CO, DC, DE, FL, GA, HI, ID, IL, IN, KY, MA, MD, ME, MI, MS, MT, NC, NH, NJ, NM, NV, NY, OH, OK, OR, PA, RI, SC, TN, TX, UT, VA, VT, WA, WV
Support	AL, MA, MD, NC, NH, NY, RI, SC, UT, WA, WV
Administrator	No contracts
Vocational	NH, NY, RI, SC, UT, WV

Delaware

Teacher	AL, AR, AZ, CA, CO, CT, DC, FL, GA, HI, ID, IN, KY, LA, MA, MD, ME, MI, MS, MT, NC, NH, NJ, NM, NY, OH, OK, OR, PA, RI, SC, TN, TX, UT, VA, VT, WA, WV
Support	No contracts
Administrator	AL, IN, MA, MD, RI
Vocational	No contracts

District of Columbia

Teacher	AL, AR, AZ, CA, CO, CT, DE, FL, GA, HI, ID, IL, IN, KY, LA, MA, MD, ME, MI, MS, MT, NC, NH, NJ, NM, NV, NY, OH, OK, OR, PA, RI, SC, TN, TX, UT, VA, VT, WA, WV, WY
Support	AL, AZ, FL, GA, IN, MA, MD, MI, MS, NH, NY, OK, OR, RI, SC, TN, TX, VA, WA, WV, WY
Administrator	No contracts
Vocational	AR, AZ, GA, MD, MS, NH, NY, OK, RI, SC, TN, TX, VA, WV, WY

Florida

Teacher	AL, AR, AZ, CA, CO, CT, DC, DE, GA, HI, ID, IN, KY, LA, MA, MD, ME, MI, MS, MT, NC, NH, NJ, NM, NV, NY, OH, OK, OR, PA, RI, SC, TN, TX, UT, VA, VT, WA, WV
Support	AL, AZ, DC, GA, IN, MA, MD, MI, MS, NC, NH, NY, OK, OR, RI, SC, TN, TX, UT, VA, WA, WV
Administrator	AL
Vocational	No contracts

Georgia

Teacher	AL, AR, AZ, CA, CO, CT, DC, DE, FL, GU, HI, ID, IL, IN, KY, LA, MA, MD, ME, MI, MS, MT, NC, NH, NM, NV, NY, OH, OK, OR, PA, RI, SC, TN, TX, UT, VA, VT, WA, WV, WY
Support	AL, AZ, DC, FL, GU, IN, MA, MD, MI, MS, NC, NH, NY, OK, OR, RI, SC, TN, TX, VA, WA, WV, WY
Administrator	AL, AZ, CO, GU, IN, MA, MD, MS, NH, NM, NY, OK, OR, RI, SC, TN, TX, VA, WA, WV, WY
Vocational	AR, AZ, DC, GU, MD, MS, NH, NY, OK, RI, SC, TN, TX, VA, WV, WY

Guam

Teacher	AL, GA, NM, NY, OK, RI, TX, UT
Support	AL, GA, NY, OK, RI, VA
Administrator	AL, GA, NM, NY, OK, RI, TX
Vocational	GA, NY, OK, RI, TX

Hawaii

Teacher	AL, AR, AZ, CA, CO, CT, DC, DE, FL, GA, ID, IN, KY, LA, MA, MD, ME, MI, MS, MT, NC, NH, NJ, NM, NV, NY, OH, OK, OR, PA, RI, SC, TN, TX, UT, VA, VT, WA, WV, WY
Support	No contracts
Administrator	No contracts
Vocational	No contracts

Idaho

Teacher	AL, AR, AZ, CA, CO, CT, DC, DE, FL, GA, HI, IN, KY, LA, MA, MD, MI, MS, MT, NC, NH, NJ, NM, NV, NY, OH, OK, OR, PA, RI, SC, TN, TX, UT, VA, VT, WA, WV, WY
Support	No contracts
Administrator	No contracts
Vocational	No contracts

Illinois

Teacher	AL, AZ, CA, CO, CT, DC, GA, IN, KY, MA, MD, ME, MI, NC, NH, NM, NY, OH, OK, OR, PA, RI, SC, TN, TX, UT, VA, VT, WA, WV
Support	No contracts
Administrator	AZ, VA
Vocational	No contracts

Indiana

Teacher	AL, AR, AZ, CA, CO, CT, DC, DE, FL, GA, HI, ID, IL, KY, LA, MA, MD, ME, MI, MS, MT, NC, NH, NJ, NM, NV, NY, OH, OK, OR, PA, RI, SC, TN, TX, UT, VA, VT, WA, WV, WY
Support	AL, AZ, DC, FL, GA, MA, MD, MI, MS, NH, NY, OK, OR, RI, SC, TN, TX, VA, WA, WV, WY
Administrator	AL, AZ, CO, DE, GA, MA, MD, MS, NH, NM, NY, OK, OR, RI, SC, TN, TX, VA, WA, WV, WY
Vocational	No contracts

Kentucky

Teacher	AL, AR, CA, CT, DC, DE, FL, GA, HI, ID, IL, IN, MA, MD, ME, MI, MT, NC, NH, NJ, NV, NY, OH, OK, OR, PA, RI, SC, TN, TX, UT, VA, VT, WA, WV, WY
Support	No contracts
Administrator	No contracts
Vocational	No contracts

Louisiana

Teacher	AL, AR, AZ, CA, DC, DE, FL, GA, HI, ID, IN, MA, MD, MS, MT, NC, NH, NM, NV, NY, OH, OK, OR, PA, RI, SC, TX, VA, WA, WV, WY
Support	No contracts
Administrator	No contracts
Vocational	No contracts

Maine

Teacher	AL, AR, CA, CO, CT, DC, DE, FL, GA, HI, IL, IN, KY, MA, MD, MI, NC, NH, NJ, NM, NV, NY, OH, OR, PA, RI, SC, TN, TX, UT, VA, VT, WA, WV
Support	No contracts

Administrator	No contracts	Administrator	No contracts
Vocational	No contracts	Vocational	No contracts

Maryland

Teacher — AL, AR, AZ, CA, CO, CT, DC, DE, FL, GA, HI, ID, IL, IN, KY, LA, MA, ME, MI, MS, MT, NC, NH, NJ, NM, NV, NY, OH, OK, OR, PA, RI, SC, TN, TX, UT, VA, VT, WA, WV, WY

Support — AL, AZ, CT, DC, FL, GA, IN, MA, MI, MS, NC, NH, NY, OK, OR, RI, SC, TN, TX, VA, WA, WV, WY

Administrator — AL, AZ, CO, DE, GA, IN, MA, MS, NH, NM, NY, OK, OR, RI, SC, TN, TX, VA, WA, WV, WY

Vocational — AR, AZ, DC, GA, MS, NH, NY, OK, RI, SC, TN, TX, VA, WV, WY

Massachusetts

Teacher — AL, AR, AZ, CA, CO, CT, DC, DE, FL, GA, HI, ID, IL, IN, KY, LA, MD, ME, MI, MS, MT, NC, NH, NJ, NM, NV, NY, OH, OK, OR, PA, RI, SC, TN, TX, UT, VA, VT, WA, WV, WY

Support — AL, AZ, CT, DC, FL, GA, IN, MD, MI, MS, NC, NH, NY, OK, OR, RI, SC, TN, TX, UT, VA, WA, WV, WY

Administrator — AL, AZ, CO, DE, GA, IN, MD, MS, NH, NM, NY, OK, OR, RI, SC, TN, TX, UT, VA, WA, WV, WY

Vocational — No contracts

Michigan

Teacher — AL, AR, AZ, CA, CO, CT, DC, DE, FL, GA, HI, ID, IL, IN, KY, MA, MD, ME, MT, NC, NH, NJ, NV, NY, OH, OR, PA, RI, SC, TN, TX, UT, VA, VT, WA, WV

Support — AL, DC, FL, GA, IN, MA, MD, NC, NH, NY, OR, RI, SC, TN, TX, UT, VA, WA, WV

Mississippi

Teacher — AL, AR, AZ, CA, CO, CT, DC, DE, FL, GA, HI, ID, IN, LA, MA, MD, MT, NC, NH, NM, NV, NY, OH, OK, OR, PA, RI, SC, TN, TX, VA, VT, WA, WV

Support — AL, AZ, DC, FL, GA, GU, IN, MA, MD, NC, NH, NY, OK, OR, RI, SC, TX, VA, WA, WV

Administrator — AL, AZ, CO, GA, IN, MA, MD, NH, NM, NY, OK, OR, RI, SC, TN, TX, VA, WA, WV

Vocational — AR, AZ, DC, GA, MD, NH, NY, OK, RI, SC, TN, TX, VA, WV

Montana

Teacher — AL, AR, AZ, CA, CO, CT, DC, DE, FL, GA, HI, ID, IN, KY, LA, MA, MD, MI, MS, NH, NJ, NM, NV, NY, OH, OK, OR, PA, RI, SC, TN, TX, UT, VA, VT, WA, WV, WY

Support — No contracts

Administrator — No contracts

Vocational — No contracts

Nevada

Teacher — AL, AR, AZ, CA, CO, CT, DC, FL, GA, HI, ID, IN, KY, LA, MA, MD, ME, MI, MS, MT, NC, NH, NJ, NM, NY, OK, OR, PA, RI, SC, TN, TX, UT, VA, WA, WV, WY

Support — No contracts

Administrator — CO, NH, WA

Vocational — No contracts

New Hampshire

Teacher   AL, AR, AZ, CA, CO, CT, DC, DE,
FL, GA, HI, ID, IL, IN, KY, LA,
MA, MD, ME, MI, MS, MT, NC, NJ,
NM, NV, NY, OH, OK, OR, PA, RI,
SC, TN, TX, UT, VA, VT, WA, WV,
WY

Support   AL, AZ, CT, DC, FL, GA, IN, MA,
MD, MI, MS, NC, NY, OK, OR, RI,
SC, TN, TX, UT, VA, WA, WV, WY

Administrator   AL, AZ, CO, GA, IN, MA, MD, MS,
NM, NV, NY, OK, OR, RI, SC, TN,
TX, UT, VA, WA, WV, WY

Vocational   AR, AZ, CT, DC, GA, MD, MS, NY,
OK, RI, SC, TN, TX, UT, VA, WV,
WY

New Jersey

Teacher   AL, AR, CA, CT, DC, DE, FL, HI,
ID, IN, KY, MA, MD, ME, MI, MT,
NC, NH, NV, NY, OH, OR, PA, RI,
SC, TN, TX, UT, VA, VT, WA, WV

Support   No contracts

Administrator   No contracts

Vocational   No contracts

New Mexico

Teacher   AL, AR, AZ, CA, CT, DC, FL, GA,
GU, HI, ID, IL, IN, LA, MA, MD,
ME, MS, MT, NH, NV, NY, OK, OR,
PA, RI, SC, TN, TX, VA, VT, WA,
WV, WY

Support   No contracts

Administrator   AL, AZ, GA, GU, IN, MA, MD, MS,
NH, NY, OK, OR, RI, SC, TN, TX,
VA, WA, WV, WY

Vocational   No contracts

New York

Teacher   AL, AR, AZ, CA, CO, CT, DC, DE,
FL, GA, GU, HI, ID, IL, IN, KY, LA,
MA, MD, ME, MI, MS, MT, NC,
NH, NJ, NM, NV, OH, OK, OR, PA,
PR, RI, SC, TN, TX, UT, VA, VT,
WA, WV

Support   AL, AZ, CT, DC, FL, GA, GU, IN,
MA, MD, MI, MS, NC, NH, OK,
OR, PR, RI, SC, TN, TX, UT, VA,
WA, WV

Administrator   AL, AZ, CO, GA, GU, IN, MA, MD,
MS, NH, NM, OK, OR, PR, RI, SC,
TN, TX, UT, VA, WA, WV

Vocational   AR, AZ, CT, DC, GA, GU, MD, MS,
NH, OK, PR, RI, SC, TN, TX, UT,
VA, WV

North Carolina

Teacher   AL, AR, CA, CO, CT, DC, DE, FL,
GA, HI, ID, IL, IN, KY, LA, MA,
MD, ME, MI, MS, NH, NJ, NV, NY,
OH, OK, OR, PA, RI, SC, TN, TX,
UT, VA, VT, WA, WV

Support   AL, CT, FL, GA, MA, MD, MI, MS,
NH, NY, OK, RI, SC, TN, TX, UT,
VA, WA, WV

Administrator   No contracts

Vocational   No contracts

Ohio

Teacher   AL, AR, AZ, CA, CO, CT, DC, DE,
FL, GA, HI, ID, IL, IN, KY, MA,
MD, ME, MI, MS, MT, NC, NH, NJ,
NY, OK, OR, PA, RI, SC, TN, UT,
VA, VT, WA, WV, WY

Support   No contracts

Administrator   No contracts

Vocational   No contracts

Oklahoma

Teacher
AL, AR, AZ, CA, CO, CT, DC, DE, FL, GA, GU, HI, ID, IL, IN, KY, LA, MA, MD, MS, MT, NC, NH, NM, NV, NY, OH, OR, PA, RI, SC, TN, TX, UT, VA, VT, WA, WV

Support
AL, AZ, DC, FL, GA, GU, IN, MA, MD, MS, NC, NH, NY, OR, RI, SC, TN, TX, VA, WA, WV

Administrator
AL, AZ, CO, GA, GU, IN, MA, MD, MS, NH, NM, NY, OR, RI, SC, TN, TX, VA, WA, WV

Vocational
AR, AZ, DC, GA, GU, MD, MS, NH, NY, RI, SC, TN, TX, VA, WV

Oregon

Teacher
AL, AR, CA, CO, CT, DC, DE, FL, GA, HI, ID, IL, IN, KY, LA, MA, MD, ME, MI, MS, MT, NC, NH, NJ, NM, NV, NY, OH, OK, PA, RI, SC, TN, TX, UT, VA, VT, WA, WV

Support
AL, AZ, DC, FL, GA, IN, KY, MA, MD, MI, MS, NH, NY, OK, RI, SC, TN, TX, VA, WA, WV

Administrator
AL, *AZ*, CO, GA, IN, KY, MA, MD, MS, NH, NM, NY, OK, RI, SC, TN, TX, VA, WA, WV

Vocational
No contracts

Pennsylvania

Teacher
AL, AR, AZ, CA, CO, CT, DC, DE, FL, GA, HI, ID, IL, IN, KY, LA, MA, MD, ME, MI, MS, MT, NC, NH, NJ, NM, NV, NY, OH, OK, OR, PR, RI, SC, TN, TX, UT, VA, VT, WA, WV, WY

Support
No contracts

Administrator
No contracts

Vocational
No contracts

Puerto Rico

Teacher
NY, PA

Support
NY

Administrator
NY

Vocational
NY

Rhode Island

Teacher
AL, AR, AZ, CA, CO, CT, DC, DE, FL, GA, GU, HI, ID, IL, IN, KY, LA, MA, MD, ME, MI, MS, MT, NC, NH, NJ, NM, NV, NY, OH, OK, OR, PA, SC, TN, TX, UT, VA, VT, WA, WV, WY

Support
AL, AZ, CT, DC, FL, GA, GU, IN, MA, MD, MI, MS, NC, NH, NY, OK, OR, SC, TN, TX, UT, VA, WA, WV, WY

Administrator
AL, AZ, CO, DE, GA, GU, IN, MA, MD, MS, NH, NM, NY, OK, OR, SC, TN, TX, UT, VA, WA, WV, WY

Vocational
AR, AZ, CT, DC, GA, GU, MD, MS, NH, NY, OK, SC, TN, TX, UT, VA, WV, WY

South Carolina

Teacher
AL, AR, AZ, CA, CO, CT, DC, DE, FL, GA, HI, ID, IL, IN, KY, LA, MA, MD, ME, MI, MS, MT, NC, NH, NJ, NM, NV, NY, OH, OK, OR, PA, RI, TN, TX, UT, VA, VT, WA, WV, WY

Support
AL, AZ, CT, DC, FL, GA, IN, MA, MD, MI, MS, NC, NH, NY, OK, OR, RI, TN, TX, UT, VA, WA, WV, WY

Administrator
AL, AZ, CO, GA, IN, MA, MD, MS, NH, NM, NY, OK, OR, RI, TN, TX, UT, VA, WA, WV, WY

Vocational
AR, AZ, CT, DC, GA, MD, MS, NH, NY, OK, RI, TN, TX, UT, VA, WV, WY

Tennessee

Teacher
AL, AR, AZ, CA, CO, CT, DC, DE, FL, GA, HI, ID, IL, IN, KY, MA, MD, ME, MI, MS, MT, NC, NH, NJ, NM, NV, NY, OH, OK, OR, PA, RI, SC, TX, UT, VA, VT, WA, WV, WY

Support	AL, AZ, DC, FL, GA, IN, MA, MD, MI, NC, NH, NY, OK, OR, RI, SC, TX, VA, WA, WV, WY	Administrator	No contracts
		Vocational	No contracts
Administrator	AL, AZ, CO, GA, IN, MA, MD, MS, NH, NM, NY, OK, OR, RI, SC, TX, VA, WA, WV, WY	**Virginia**	
		Teacher	AL, AR, AZ, CA, CO, CT, DC, DE, FL, GA, HI, ID, IL, IN, KY, LA, MA, MD, ME, MI, MS, MT, NC, NH, NJ, NM, NV, NY, OH, OK, OR, PA, RI, SC, TN, TX, UT, VT, WA, WV
Vocational	AR, AZ, DC, GA, MD, MS, NH, NY, OK, RI, SC, TX, VA, WV, WY		
Texas			
Teacher	AL, AR, AZ, CA, CO, CT, DC, DE, FL, GA, GU, HI, ID, IL, IN, KY, LA, MA, MD, ME, MI, MS, MT, NC, NH, NJ, NM, NV, NY, OK, OR, PA, RI, SC, TN, VA, VT, WA, WV	Support	AL, AZ, DC, FL, GA, GU, IN, MA, MD, MI, MS, NC, NH, NY, OK, OR, RI, SC, TN, TX, WA, WV
		Administrator	AL, AZ, CO, GA, IL, IN, MA, MD, MS, NH, NM, NY, OK, OR, RI, SC, TN, TX, WA, WV
Support	AL, AZ, DC, FL, GA, IN, MA, MD, MI, MS, NC, NH, NY, OK, OR, RI, SC, TN, VA, WA, WV		
		Vocational	ARs, AZ, DC, GA, MD, MS, NH, NY, OK, RI, SC, TN, TX, WV
Administrator	AL, AZ, CO, GA, GU, IN, MA, MD, MS, NH, NM, NY, OK, OR, RI, SC, TN, VA, WA, WV	**Washington**	
		Teacher	AL, AR, AZ, CA, CO, CT, DC, DE, FL, GA, HI, ID, IL, IN, KY, LA, MA, MD, ME, MI, MS, MT, NC, NH, NJ, NM, NV, NY, OH, OK, OR, PA, RI, SC, TN, TX, UT, VA, VT, WV
Vocational	AR, AZ, DC, GA, GU, MD, MS, NH, NY, OK, RI, SC, TN, VA, WV		
Utah			
Teacher	AL, AR, AZ, CA, CO, CT, DC, DE, FL, GA, GU, HI, ID, IL, IN, KY, MA, MD, ME, MI, MT, NC, NH, NJ, NV, NY, OH, OK, OR, PA, RI, SC, TN, VA, VT, WA, WY	Support	AL, AZ, CT, DC, FL, GA, IN, MA, MD, MI, MS, NC, NH, NY, OK, OR, RI, SC, TN, TX, UT, VA, WV
		Administrator	AL, AZ, CO, GA, IN, MA, MD, MS, NH, NM, NV, NY, OK, OR, RI, SC, TN, TX, UT, VA, WV
Support	AL, CT, FL, MA, MI, NC, NH, NY, RI, SC, WA		
Administrator	AL, MA, NH, NY, RI, SC, WA	Vocational	No contracts
Vocational	CT, NH, NY, RI, SC	**West Virginia**	
Vermont		Teacher	AL, AR, AZ, CA, CO, CT, DC, DE, FL, GA, HI, ID, IL, IN, KY, LA, MA, MD, ME, MI, MS, MT, NC, NH, NJ, NV, NY, OH, OK, OR, PA, RI, SC, TN, TX, VA, VT, WA
Teacher	AL, AR, AZ, CA, CO, CT, DC, DE, FL, GA, HI, ID, IL, IN, KY, MA, MD, ME, MI, MS, MT, NC, NH, NJ, NM, NY, OH, OK, OR, PA, RI, SC, TN, TX, UT, VA, WA, WV		
		Support	AL, AZ, CT, DC, FL, GA, IN, MA, MD, MI, MS, NC, NH, NY, OK, OR, RI, SC, TN, TX, VA, WA
Support	No contracts		

Administrator	AL, AZ, CO, GA, IN, MA, MD, MS, NH, NM, NY, OK, OR, RI, SC, TN, TX, VA, WA
Vocational	AR, AZ, CT, DC, GA, MD, MS, NH, NY, OK, RI, SC, TN, TX, VA

Wyoming

Teacher	AL, AZ, DC, GA, HI, ID, IN, KY, LA, MA, MD, MT, NH, NM, NV, OH, PA, RI, SC, TN, UT

Support	AL, AZ, DC, GA, IN, MA, MD, NH, RI, SC, TN
Administrator	AL, AZ, GA, IN, MA, MD, NH, NM, RI, SC, TN
Vocational	AZ, DC, GA, MD, NH, RI, SC, TN